Food • Fun • Relaxing • Sleeping

A TOUCH of GEORGIA

WELCOME! WE'RE GLAD GEORGIA'S on YOUR MIND

Shopping • Historic Sites & Much More

OLIVER NELSON

THOMAS NELSON PUBLISHERS
Nashville • Atlanta • London • Vancouver

Published in Nashville, Tennessee, by Thomas Nelson, Inc., Publishers, and distributed in Canada by Word Communications, Ltd., Richmond, British Columbia.

All maps, drawings, and photographs in this book are the property of Judy Rogers and are used by permission.

NOTICE: Telephone area codes for the surrounding areas of Atlanta have been subject to change during the writing of this book, due to a massive reorganization of the expanding Georgia area code system. Every attempt has been made to provide correct area codes, but if you encounter difficulties, please check with the operator.

Library of Congress Cataloging-in-Publication Data

Murphey, Cecil B.
   A touch of Georgia : where to go and what to do in the Peach State.
      p.   cm.
   Compiled by Cecil Murphey and Judy Rogers.
   ISBN 0-7852-7500-2
   1. Georgia—Guidebooks. I. Rogers, Judy, 1939– . II. Title.
F284.3.M87   1996
917.5804'43—dc20   96–5194
                                                                                   CIP

Printed in the United States of America.

1 2 3 4 5 6 — 01 00 99 98 97 96

This book is dedicated to the gracious state of Georgia, one of the thirteen original colonies, whose history is both heroic and colorful. It is dedicated also to the people of Georgia, both those native born and those for whom Georgia is their adopted home, whose hospitality and welcome to all continue to ensure for Georgia a fond place in the memory of all who visit.

CONTENTS

CONTENTS

FOREWORD

Poet Robert Frost once said that the first requisite for a great place is "a good piece of geography." And that is what we have in Georgia—a good piece of geography. By land area, Georgia is the largest state east of the Mississippi River.

We are a geographically diverse state. Georgia's broad lakes region offers a wide range of water recreation and scenic golf courses, like the National in Augusta where the world-renowned Masters Tournament is played.

The North Georgia mountains, among the oldest in the world, contain rock formations more than 600 million years old and more kinds of flowering plants than the entire continent of Europe.

No description of Georgia is complete without mention of our beautiful coast, with its rich colonial history, white sand beaches, and live oaks draped with Spanish moss. Trailing along our coast like jewels on a necklace is a string of semitropical islands, some with first-class resorts and convention facilities, others protected as natural preserves where wild ponies roam and rare sea turtles lay their eggs in the sand.

Inland is the famous Okefenokee Swamp, and past the South Georgia swamp, some of the most fabulous farmland in the world.

Right in the middle of all this natural beauty, Georgia has a man-made gem—the city of Atlanta—capital city of a region that will surpass the Northeast in population within the next five years.

All this and more are highlighted in *A Touch of Georgia,* and I hope you find it a valuable guide to the great state of Georgia.

Zell Miller
Governor of Georgia

Acknowledgments

We can't begin to list all the individuals, magazines, and books we used for research, but we particularly want to say thanks to

- all those in Georgia who took time to answer a stranger's questions and assist with information.
- AAA for their tourbook.
- the Atlanta Committee for the Olympic Games (ACOG).
- the Information Line of the Atlanta-Fulton Public Library.
- C–C Hege and Rachel Hodges for the artwork.
- Jim Berardinelli and Southeastern Reprographics for their assistance with the maps.
- Marty Sik of Georgia's Office of Planning and Budget.

A Note from the Publisher

This book was compiled for Thomas Nelson, Inc., by Cecil Murphey and Judy Rogers, two happily adopted children of Georgia. A few explanatory notes here will make the book even more helpful.

Throughout the book, CC is used as an abbreviation for "country club" and GC is used for "golf club/course."

Restaurant listings are coded:

    ★ below $20   ★★ $21–$35   ★★★ above $35

The codes are intended only as a general indication because prices fluctuate.

The maps at the beginning of each geographic section are keyed to the *At a Glance* pages accompanying them. Only cities mentioned on the *At a Glance* pages are indicated on the maps.

INTRODUCTION

Welcome to Georgia, the Peach State.

But first, an explanation of why it's the Peach State.

Just like the camellias and silkworms, peaches came to Georgia from China during the early 1800s.

In the 1870s, Samuel H. Rumph, a Macon County planter, invented the wood packing crate and used a refrigerated carrier to ship peaches across the country. The invention brought national fame to the state.

By the 1930s, the state boasted of 16 million peach trees. That's when it picked up the nickname. (California does produce more peaches, but don't tell Californians.)

In 1940, the symbol of the peach first appeared on Georgia license plates. (Georgia produces more peanuts than peaches, but we'll stick with the fruit as our symbol.)

KUDZU

A visitor from Rhode Island drove through Georgia and commented on the beautiful greenery. "How do things grow in such artistic shapes?" he asked.

That was his first time to witness the work of kudzu. From a distance, the leafy green vine looks beautiful as it covers and reshapes trees, telephone poles, highway signs, and anything else that doesn't move.

Although kudzu was known in the U.S. in the latter part of the 19th century, most Americans in the Southland knew little about it until the 1930s. The U.S.

Soil Conservation Service imported kudzu, a product of Japan, in the 1930s because of its ability to stop soil erosion. Within months, the Conservation Service had planted kudzu across the South.

Kudzu did stop erosion.

Kudzu

But the experts didn't realize that kudzu constantly seeks more space for growth. People used the attractive multileaved plant to cover unsightly things such as tree stumps. But then they discovered the truth about kudzu. The plant grows—fast. One landscape expert in North Georgia said, "Under ideal conditions of heavy rain and warmth, I have known it to grow 25 inches in a single day." Generally, however, during the summer months, it grows a foot a day.

Kudzu grows by crawling across the ground, trees, bushes, or anything else. As it touches the ground, it sends down roots and continues to spread. It's not unusual to have unchecked kudzu creep 100 feet during the summer.

The vine is spreading. It has moved into Florida and headed west. It has also been moving slowly northward. Farmers and gardeners slow down the growth only by cutting the vine. The only effective way to get rid of kudzu is to get to the roots and dig them up or to poison the roots.

Farmers say their cattle like the taste of kudzu. People who are into crafts make decorative wreaths out of the dried vines. A few brave souls say that they cut the tender tendrils and cook them as a vegetable. Most people in Georgia see kudzu as an ongoing curse. In Japan, however, they grind the plant into powder for cooking and flavoring. They also claim it has medicinal power to combat upset stomach, fight influenza, and increase sexual desire.

In the meantime, the kudzu grows.

And grows.

You can't fool me—nothing grows that fast.

You'll find a lot to see and do in this wonderful state, and we hope our book will help. Most visitors to Georgia are interested in *Gone with the Wind*. We've included a special section on the fascinating subject.

And we didn't want to overlook the opportunity to let you know about some of the famous folk who claim Georgia as their birthplace, so check out **Georgia's Famous Sons and Daughters**. You might be surprised at some of the names you'll find there.

The 1996 Centennial Olympic Games have had Georgians buzzing ever since the day of the announcement that Atlanta was chosen as the host city for the games. **Georgia Hosts the 1996 Olympics** tells you what's going on and where.

Georgia's Gorgeous Outdoors describes areas that are a pleasure to visit and camp in. Contact the Georgia Department of Natural Resources, State Parks, and Historic Sites, 205 Butler St. SE, Atlanta, GA 30334, for information and pamphlets. Or call the Public Information Office, 404-656-3530, Mon.–Fri. 8 a.m.–4:30 p.m. Toll-free numbers for making reservations at state parks are 770-389-PARK for callers in the Atlanta area and 800-864-PARK for everyone else.

Georgians love **Festivals**, so we've included an alphabetical list of them. (You'll also find a *Festival* section in each geographic division.) This gives you a taste of the variety of festivals going on in Georgia. If you know the name of a festival you're particularly interested in, you can locate some information about it in this section. Although we have made the festival list as complete as possible, because of the number of festivals (and the number of new ones added each year), it's quite possible we've missed a few.

A section on the *Outdoors* is included in each geographic division, and has information specific to that area. The following general information is not repeated in each geographic division.

GEORGIA OUTDOORS

Fishing. Contact the state's Department of Natural Resources, Fish and Game Division, for brochures on fishing areas and regulations. Contact the division's Fisheries section: 404-918-6418. *Fishing in Georgia Lakes* is published by the state's Department of Industry, Trade, and Tourism: 404-656-3590.

Golfing. Golf courses are available at some state parks, and they are listed in the appropriate sections. Call 404-656-3590 to ask for Georgia's Official Golf Guide, published by *GolfWeek* in cooperation with the

Georgia Department of Industry, Trade, and Tourism. Information regarding some of the more popular golf courses has been listed according to area, but it is not meant to be all-inclusive.

Hunting. You can get a copy of the annual *Hunting Seasons and Regulations Guide* with information on hunting seasons, restrictions, limits, licenses, and fees, as well as maps of wildlife management areas. Write Georgia Department of Natural Resources, Fish and Game Division, 2123 US 278 SE, Social Circle, GA 30279; or call 770-918-6418.

Interstate Highway System in Georgia

Don't Miss. Occasionally, you'll find an attraction noted this way. We believe it's one of those places all visitors want to see (or at least we think they ought to see) in the Peach State.

Deciding Where You Want to Go. In today's world, most people identify locations of cities and attractions in terms of the interstates. Here is a list of interstate highways in Georgia:

I-75 and **I-85** (north and south): I-75 enters at the northwest Georgia border near Chattanooga, Tennessee. It goes through Atlanta, continues south through the middle of the state, and exits Georgia at the Florida border south of Valdosta. I-85 enters Georgia from South Carolina on the northeast border near Hartwell Lake. It goes through Atlanta and exits Georgia near West Point on the west border at Atlanta.

I-20 (east-west) enters Georgia from the South Carolina border at Augusta, goes west across the state through Atlanta, and exits Georgia at the Alabama border west of Atlanta.

I-16 (east-west) goes from Savannah on the Georgia coast to Macon in the middle of the state.

I-95 (north-south along the coastal area) enters Georgia from South Carolina at Savannah on the coast and follows the coastline into Florida on the south border of Georgia.

I-59 (north-south) briefly crosses the northwest corner of the state.

I-185 branches off **I-85** S near LaGrange and ends in the Columbus area.

I-285 circles the Metro Atlanta area. Many Atlantans refer to it as the perimeter.

I-475 is the Macon bypass on **I-75** S.

I-575 branches off **I-75** north of Atlanta

and runs into the northwest portion of the state.

I-516 edges Savannah and **I-520** edges Augusta.

I-675 off **I-285** provides quick access to **I-75** S.

I-985 branches off **I-85** northeast of the Metro Atlanta area and ends north of Gainesville.

Becoming familiar with the interstate system will prove helpful in visiting sites.

■■

We have divided the state into six geographic sections:

1. Metropolitan Atlanta includes the city of Atlanta and surrounding areas inside the I-285 perimeter. Other towns and cities included in Metro Atlanta are Chamblee, Doraville, Decatur, East Point, College Park, Hapeville, and Brookhaven.

2. North Georgia includes the top one-third of the state, from the northern border to I-20 as the southern border. It does not include Metro Atlanta or Haralson and Carroll Counties. Some of the best-known cities in this section include Athens, Rome, Dahlonega, and Helen.

3. Middle Georgia is the area between I-20 on the north and I-16/GA 96/US 80 on the south. Major cities are Macon and Augusta.

4. West Georgia consists of seven counties on the western border below I-20: Haralson, Carroll, Coweta, Heard, Troup, Meriwether, and Harris. Although there are

other areas farther south on the western border of the state, these seven counties have come to be known popularly as West Georgia. Three well-known cities are Newnan, LaGrange, and Warm Springs.

5. South Georgia takes in the portion of the state below I-16/GA 96/US 80 to the Florida state line, but it does not include the coastal area. Plains, Columbus, and Perry are three well-known locations.

6. Coastal Georgia means everything east of I-95 from Savannah to the Florida state line. Well-known names include Savannah, St. Simons, Jekyll Island, Cumberland Island, and Brunswick.

■■

Geographic Divisions

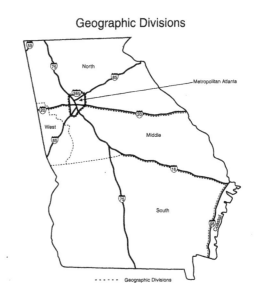

.... Geographic Divisions

In each of the geographic divisions, you will find the following information:

At a Glance. As the title indicates, it

summarizes information to help you decide where to visit. (There is no *At a Glance* section for Metropolitan Atlanta.)

Where to Go and What to See. This listing includes historic sites, museums, restored or historic communities, and other popular places for Georgians and tourists.

Eating. Grits and sausage? Hush puppies, field peas, and black bottom pie? Corn bread and greens? You can get traditional American food anywhere in Georgia, but southern cookin' teases your taste buds and introduces you to a new culinary world. You'll find recipes at the beginning of each of these sections for southern cooking dishes.

As you move out into some of the counties away from Metro Atlanta, you will discover that many of the restaurants don't serve wine, beer, or alcoholic beverages on Sunday.

Many restaurants outside Metro Atlanta aren't open on Sunday, so bear this in mind when planning your travels. (This caution does not apply to most national chains.)

Sleeping. If you want to stay at one of the bed-and-breakfast establishments (B&B), you need to call ahead for reservations. Also, it is helpful to ask in advance whether children are accepted as guests, and whether smoking is allowed. Many B&Bs include breakfast in the price of the room. (We have not listed hotel and motel chains.)

Shopping. Wherever you travel, you're sure to find out-of-the-way shops (where everyone hopes to find a special treasure no one else has spotted) in addition to outlet malls and major shopping centers. Yard sales

and flea markets are popular in Georgia. So you'll find plenty of places to catch your attention in addition to those listed in the book.

Antiques and Crafts. You'll find antiques and crafts on display, testifying to the skills of the people in Georgia. Quilting, weaving, and pottery making have enjoyed a revival in the past decade, and quality craft items are available.

Outdoors. General information on hunting, fishing, and golfing is given earlier in this introduction. Specific items of interest in different areas, such as canoeing, hiking, and horseback riding, are listed in the *Outdoors* section.

Entertainment. This section includes theme parks, zoos, botanical gardens, theaters, and boat expeditions. In addition, you'll find some special events that aren't noted with the *Festivals*.

Festivals. A listing of festivals in the area is given by month. Circumstances change. So do phone numbers, hours, and prices. This is the most accurate information we have at the time of publication.

RAILROADS

Railroads have figured prominently in Georgia's history and development. By 1833, the state had charted the Central Railroad & Canal Company from Savannah to Macon. The Georgia Railroad moved west from Augusta to Athens, while the Monroe Railroad made plans for a line between Macon and Forsyth.

In 1836, the state legislature created the first state-owned rail line, the Western & Atlantic, to prevent Charleston from drawing Piedmont commerce away from Savannah markets. During the Civil War (1861–65), most of the state's 1,200 miles of railroad tracks were destroyed. By the turn of the 20th century, expanding railroads once again connected Georgia's population centers for both commerce and travel. Mergers and consolidations later resulted in two major systems serving the state: the Norfolk Southern and Seaboard System railroads.

A FINAL WORD ABOUT LANGUAGE

Georgians speak English. If you're a stranger to the South, however, you may hear a few odd-sounding terms or words used in a different way from what you're used to. If you don't know what poke sallit is, just ask. Or maybe someone will pick it from a patch of weeds in the yard. If you listen carefully, you'll usually get the meaning. But to be at home in Georgia, you need to know about two important rules of real southern English.

Rule 1. The word *you* is singular. The plural form is *y'all.* You say the plural form as one syllable. (Rather clever to distinguish this way, isn't it?)

Rule 2. Real Georgians have two special verbs. The first is *fix.* This is a multiple-use word that we use to mean (this is an abbreviated list):

get ready	repair	make
attach	stabilize	assign
set right	intend	make ready
stop	spay or castrate	

Just remember that we're always fixing to do something. Which leads us to the second verb: *start.* We don't *do* anything, but we start to do things:

I'm starting to go to work.

I'm starting to catch a cold.

I'm starting to feel bad about this.

If the speaker is a real-real Georgian, you may hear, "I'm fixing to start to go."

CHAPTER ONE

A TOUCH OF GEORGIA'S HISTORY

IMPORTANT DATES

1540 De Soto's expedition enters Georgia.

1732 King George II grants a charter for the colony of Georgia.

1733 James Edward Oglethorpe and a group of settlers arrive at Savannah.

1742 Battle of Bloody Marsh ends Spanish influence in Georgia.

1754 Georgia becomes a royal province of England.

1776 Georgia adopts its first constitution and ratifies it a year later.

1785 University of Georgia (Athens) begins.

1786 Proclamation of 1786 makes Louisville the capital.

1788 Georgia ratifies the U.S. Constitution on January 2 and becomes the fourth state.

1804 Milledgeville becomes the state capital with the Act of 1804.

1828 Gold is discovered in northern Georgia.

1838 The Trail of Tears begins.

1845 Georgia Railway is completed.

1861 Georgia secedes from the Union.

1864 General Sherman's troops invade Georgia and begin their march to the sea.

1865 Civil War ends.

1868 Atlanta becomes the state capital during Reconstruction.

1870 Georgia is readmitted to the Union.

1922 Rebecca Felton is the first woman to serve in the U.S. Senate.

1962 General Assembly passes a law allowing the governor to be elected by popular vote rather than by the county-unit system.

1974 Atlanta's first African-American

mayor, Maynard Jackson, takes office.

1976 Former governor Jimmy Carter wins election to become the nation's 39th president.

1983 Martin Luther King, Jr.'s birthday becomes a national holiday.

1996 Atlanta hosts the Centennial Games.

Colonial History. People have lived in what is now Georgia for thousands of years. Long before the discovery of North America by Europeans, Native American hunters lived and roamed throughout the countryside. The first to settle and plant crops, they built flat-topped pyramids or mounds around a plaza. Farmlands lay beyond the settlements in the fertile river valleys.

The first Europeans who came to Georgia found two large groups of Native Americans: The Cherokee lived in the mountains to the north; the Creek occupied the rest of the area. A smaller tribe, the Guale Indians, lived along the coast.

Hernando de Soto came from Spain with a large expedition and landed at present-day Tampa in 1539. After a year of difficult travel, they entered Georgia—making them the first Europeans to set foot in the area. The Native Americans of Georgia were friendlier than those of Florida. After a short stay, de Soto left Georgia for the long march to the Mississippi River.

Beginning in 1566, the Spaniards built missions on the Sea Islands along the coast of Georgia. From there, missionaries and explorers moved into the interior. By 1681, Spain had outposts near Columbus and at the junction of the Chattahoochee and Flint Rivers.

During the same period, English traders from South Carolina began to stir up trouble for the Spanish missions. By 1686, the Spaniards had abandoned all their missions north of the St. Marys River. For more than 50 years, neither nation tried to settle the land.

In 1729, James Edward Oglethorpe, a member of Parliament, chaired a committee appointed to investigate conditions in the English penal system. Appalled by the conditions of imprisoned debtors of good character, Oglethorpe and a group of humanitarian reformers sought alternatives to jail for financially distressed people.

Oglethorpe suggested that the more respectable inmates of debtors' prisons would be excellent settlers of a new colony in America. He widely promoted the idea and others agreed with him. English Protestants wanted a refuge for Protestants in other countries as well. Philanthropists hoped

Georgia would offer poor people a new start with free land, Christian fellowship, and protection from such moral evils as liquor and slavery.

A more practical matter, however, was that having settlers in Georgia would be a buffer against the encroachment of the Spanish from Florida and would make settlers in South Carolina rest easier. British merchants also saw possibilities for profit. Georgia's rich coastal areas could produce silk, olives, wine, and tropical fruit, and the British would no longer have to import them from foreigners in distant lands.

Three motives (true charity, national defense, and profit) provided an unbeatable incentive to form the colony. The endeavor received financial support from the government and from individuals. Parliament contributed more money to the colonization of Georgia than to any other place in America.

In 1733, James Edward Oglethorpe led a group of 125 carefully screened settlers. They arrived on February 12, 1733, and founded the Georgia colony for England.

War broke out between the British and Spanish in 1739. Oglethorpe made several unsuccessful advances against the Spanish. In 1742, Oglethorpe fought and defeated the Spanish at the battle of Bloody Marsh on St. Simons Island. This battle ended Spanish influence in Georgia.

Even though Oglethorpe wanted Georgia to be a haven for those in debtors' prison, that did not happen. No more than a dozen people ever came from English prisons. Few African-Americans reached the colony because slavery was illegal until 1750. Once the prohibition was lifted, the slave population grew rapidly.

In 1754, Georgia became a royal province of England. Largely because of slave labor, the colony prospered. The silk industry, however, proved unprofitable. Cotton and other agricultural products became increasingly prominent.

Scotch-Irish people arrived in increasing numbers after 1768. By 1775, between 40,000 and 50,000 people lived in the colony—nearly half of whom were slaves.

The Revolutionary War. In the 1760s, few Georgians owned large plantations, and most of the holdings were less than 250 acres. Radical northern colonists began to polarize into anti- and pro-British groups. Eventually, they began to stir Georgians over matters such as taxation and the rights of the governing assembly.

Riots and occasional violence and raids on the British arms at Savannah marked the first six months of 1775. The leaders voted to end diplomatic and trade relations with Britain and to support all the measures of the Continental Congress of the 13 colonies. By the following year, although most Georgians favored complete independence, many loyalists opposed the Revolution.

The Revolutionary War began in 1776. The Georgians suffered several military setbacks, but with the help of troops under Continental commander Anthony Wayne, they began to rout the British. The British, however, continued to occupy Savannah at the coast until six months after the surrender of Lord Cornwallis at Yorktown, when the war had virtually ended.

Georgia, one of the original 13 English colonies, fought in the Revolutionary War to gain independence from England. It became the fourth state to ratify the United States Constitution, and one of only three states to do so unanimously.

The Cherokee Nation. The Cherokee in northern Georgia were a highly civilized people. In 1827, they organized a government with a written constitution, with headquarters for the Cherokee Nation at New Echota. The federal government, but not the state, recognized them as a legitimate government. The state declared that state laws should prevail throughout the Cherokee territory.

New Echota Building

It is unfortunate that President Andrew Jackson sided with Georgia against the Cherokee. In 1835, the federal government made a treaty with the Cherokee at New Echota. The Native Americans gave up their claim to all lands east of the Mississippi River. In return, they received a sum of money and lands west of the Mississippi. Their forced migration in 1838 has gone down in history as the Trail of Tears because of the hardships, deprivation, and death suffered along the way. Of the 17,000 who began the 800-mile trip, 4,000 perished because of disease and inadequate food and clothing.

The Civil War. Slavery became the burning issue during the 1850s. The Southern states had developed an agricultural economy based on slavery. In January 1861, Georgia and other Southern states seceded from the Union and formed the Confederate States of America. In May 1864, the Union Army under General William T. Sherman invaded Georgia. His troops cut a 60-mile-wide swath and burned houses, crops, and sometimes whole towns. He and his troops occupied Atlanta in September and burned it on November 14. By the end of the year, Sherman had completed his march to the sea and captured Savannah. The Civil War ended in 1865.

After the war, Georgia, like the rest of the South, was in economic and political shambles. Yankee troops imposed a mandatory "reconstructed" system of society, government, and labor. Georgia was not readmitted to the Union until 1870. Federal troops stayed on until 1876. Many Southerners considered Reconstruction the worst of evils, with opportunists exploiting them. Northerners arrived by trainloads with tapestry duffels and were immediately called carpetbaggers.

For African-Americans, Reconstruction transformed slaves into free citizens, guaranteeing them the right to move, hold office, and engage in an interracial society. But it didn't last long. Southern white supremacy returned in 1871. Racial liberties didn't resurface significantly until the modern civil rights movement.

Modern Georgia. Modern Georgia properly begins with the end of Reconstruction. Large plantations became a series of small holdings. People moved away from the farms and toward the cities. Georgians increasingly spoke of their being part of the "New South," a phrase coined by Henry Grady.

Grady, an Atlanta newspaperman, was the strongest spokesperson for modernization. During the late 1800s, he and others pleaded for industrial development. They urged farmers to use the land to grow crops other than cotton.

By 1900, industries began to grow. But the important changes to agriculture didn't come until the late 1930s when farmers began to enjoy the prosperity already seen in other parts of the country.

World War II (1941–45) brought economic opportunity with military bases established throughout the state. Southerners of all races enlisted in the armed forces. After the war, southern soldiers returned home

with broadened visions of a more equal society.

Civil Rights. Explosive strife and violence characterized the civil rights era of the 1960s in the South. Atlanta, long a leader as the racially progressive capital of the New South, provided a platform for enlightened voices. Atlanta-born Martin Luther King, Jr., followed the nonviolent resistance principles of India's Mohandas Gandhi. In 1963, Atlanta's mayor Ivan Allen, Jr., Coca-Cola president Robert Woodruff, *Atlanta Constitution* editor Ralph McGill, and others aligned with African-American leaders and brought about a relatively progressive slate of city leaders who also affected statewide politics.

Education reform became the most difficult battle, but with the backing of the federal government, schools opened their once-segregated doors to African-Americans. In 1961, the first African-American student enrolled at the University of Georgia in Athens.

Voting laws also brought about changes. The former voting system, called the county-unit system, gave nearly equal electoral weight to all counties regardless of population, which offset the votes of liberals, African-Americans, and urbanites in favor of rural conservatives. This system was dissolved in 1962 in favor of "one person, one vote."

In 1974, Maynard Jackson became the first African-American mayor of a major southern city. He set and enforced strict quotas for minority contracts and representation.

In 1964, Jimmy Carter became governor and took a strong stand for human rights reform. (In 1976, Carter was elected to become the 39th president of the United States.)

Beginning in the 1960s, Atlanta continued to expand. A line of magnificently tall buildings rose toward the sky. The city became host to professional baseball (Braves), football (Falcons), and basketball (Hawks). The first trains of the city's rapid-rail line (MARTA) began to operate in 1979. Hartsfield International Airport has grown into the world's second busiest airport.

In 1980, Sweet Auburn, a revitalized African-American neighborhood of about 10 blocks, became a National Historic District. Ted Turner's CNN aired the same year. The decade of the 1980s witnessed the opening of the High Museum of Art and

Atlanta Skyline

the reopening of the renovated Cyclorama. And Underground Atlanta, a group of stores and restaurants located underneath the city, got its start.

When the International Olympic Committee chose to hold the 1996 Summer Games in Georgia, it marked the global affirmation of the state's goal of racial harmony and economic growth.

LITTLE-KNOWN FACTS ABOUT GEORGIA

State Name: Named for Britain's King George II, who granted the charter to James Edward Oglethorpe and a board of trustees to found the colony.

Statehood: January 2, 1788. One of the original 13 colonies, it was the fourth state admitted into the United States.

State Flower: Cherokee rose

State Bird: Brown thrasher

State Tree: Live oak

State Motto: "Wisdom, justice, and moderation"

State Capital: Atlanta

Size and Location: Georgia has 58,876 square miles. It is 300 miles long and 241 miles wide. It is bordered by Tennessee and South Carolina on the north, the Atlantic Ocean on the southeast, Florida on the south, and Alabama on the west.

Climate: The average temperature throughout the state is about 78° in summer and 45° in winter. Georgia gets about 50 inches of precipitation a year. Snow is rare, except in the mountains. The growing season is approximately 180 days in the Blue Ridge area to 270 days along the Atlantic coast.

Elevation: Georgia's lowest point is sea level, along the Atlantic Ocean. The highest point in the state is at Brasstown Bald (or Mount Etowah), which is 4,784 feet above sea level.

Population: Based on the 1990 census, the population was 6,478,216. (The estimated 1995 figure is 7,055,336.) The two most numerous age groups are these:

ages 5–17	1,231,768
ages 25–44	2,190,594

Georgia reports 208,975 people ages 75 to 84, and 57,244 who are over age 85.

According to the 1990 census, of the 6,478,216 people in Georgia, 3,333,713 were female and 3,144,503 were male.

By the way, there are 195,689 telephone units in the state.

(Note: These figures released in 1995 by the state of Georgia are based on a sample and are subject to variability.)

HOUSING

Where Do Georgians Live? In urban settings, you'll find 4,096,216 or 63.2 percent of the population. Those who live in rural areas account for 36.8 percent with 80,083 of them being farm population.

Total Housing Units: There are 2,638,416, of which 2,366,615 are occupied. Among these units are 72,938 condominium hous-ing units. Of the housing units, 1,158,826 have three bedrooms, 24,923 have one bedroom, and 63,960 have five bedrooms.

Value of Housing: From a sample of 1,138,775 (1990), the specific owner-occupied units are as follows:

Less than $50,000	314,490
$50,000–$99,999	531,167
$100,000–$149,999	163,205
$150,000–$199,999	66,878
$200,000–$299,999	39,499
$300,000 or more	23,086

Median: $71,300

Contract Rent for specific renter-occupied units for a sampling of 759,499 units:

Monthly Payments	Units
Less than $250	251,826
$250–$499	361,984
$500–$749	127,415
$750–$999	13,143
$1,000 or more	5,131

Median: $344

Water: Those who use a public or private company for water are 2,144,049, and 970,686 houses use septic tanks or cesspools.

Heating:

Utility gas	1,262,087
Bottled or LP gas	327,065
Electricity	643,877
Fuel oil, kerosene, etc.	35,493
Coal or coke	435
Wood	90,918
Solar energy	495

Other fuel	2,052
No fuel used	4,193

Owner Costs: There are 1,153,109 owner-owned mortgaged houses. The *median* (not average) cost is $737 a month. For houses with mortgage payments, these are the monthly owner costs:

Less than $300	47,122
$300–$499	147,042
$500–$699	177,631
$700–$999	236,400
$1,000–$1,499	138,880
$1,500–$1,999	38,097
$2,000 or more	25,431

Of houses without a mortgage, the median monthly cost is $182.

What About the Percentage of Rent They Pay by Household Incomes? These are from 1989, the last available figures, for a sampling of 808,365 units:

Less than 20 percent	246,059
20–24 percent	115,860
25–29 percent	92,610
30–34 percent	65,638
35 or more percent	233,360
Not computed	54,838

Households by type:

Total units	2,366,615
Families	1,713,072
Married-couple families	1,306,756
Other family, male householder	76,675
Other family, female householder	329,641
Nonfamily households	653,543
Householder living alone	557,702
Householder 65 years and over	185,027

Average persons per household: 2.66

RACE AND ORIGIN

The predominant race is Caucasian with 4,600,148 people. African-Americans make up 27 percent of the population with 1,746,565; Native Americans (including Eskimos or Aleuts) are 0.2 percent; Asians and Pacific Islanders are 1.2 percent; and those of Hispanic origin are 1.7 percent.

Of the residents of the state, 66.3 percent were born here.

In 1990, Georgia had a foreign-born population of 173,126, of which 90,063 entered the U.S. between 1980 and 1990.

EDUCATION

Of those age three or older, 1,643,859 are enrolled in some kind of school, with 7.2 percent in private schools.

High school graduates	1,192,935
Some college, no degree	684,109
Associate degree	199,403
Undergraduate degree	519,613
Graduate/professional	257,545

LABOR FORCE STATUS

Of those over age 16, 4,938,381 were working in 1990; 73,135 were in the armed forces, of which 7,571 were female. The percentage of working adults was 67.9.

Of males (16 and over), 76.6 percent were employed, and the figure for females was 59.9 percent.

What About Getting to Work?

	Percent
Drive alone	76.6
Ride in car pools	15.1
Use public transportation	2.8
Use other means	1.2
Walk or work at home	4.4

Mean travel time to work: 22.7 minutes

Atlanta Traffic

What Kind of Work Do Georgians Do?

From the figure of 3,090,276 (some people list themselves as having two primary occupations), Georgians work in the following areas:

Agriculture, forestry, fisheries	73,647
Mining	8,890
Construction	214,359
Manufacturing, nondurable goods	329,711
Manufacturing, durable goods	255,712
Transportation	159,217
Communications, other public utilities	104,202
Wholesale trade	156,836
Retail trade	508,861
Finance, insurance, real estate	301,422
Business, repair services	151,096
Personal services	97,466
Entertainment and recreation services	31,911
Health services	227,489
Educational services	233,818
Other professional services	168,587
Public administration	167,050

INCOME

The latest available figures (1989) from a sampling of 2,366,575 list household incomes:

Less than $5,000	187,826
$5,000–$9,999	210,252
$10,000–$14,999	204,142
$15,000–$24,999	418,568
$25,000–$34,999	383,733
$35,000–$49,999	420,917
$50,000–$74,999	341,667

$75,000–$99,999	109,354
$100,000–149,999	56,974
$150,000 or more	33,142

Median: $29,021

How Does Georgia Compare with Other States in Housing?

State	Median Housing Value
Alabama	$53,700
Alaska	$94,400
Arizona	$80,100
Arkansas	$46,300
California	$195,500
Colorado	$82,700
Connecticut	$177,800
Delaware	$100,100
District of Columbia	$123,900
Florida	$77,100
GEORGIA	**$71,300**
Hawaii	$245,300
Idaho	$58,200
Illinois	$80,900
Indiana	$53,900
Iowa	$45,900
Kansas	$52,200
Kentucky	$50,500
Louisiana	$58,500
Maine	$87,400
Maryland	$116,500
Massachusetts	$162,800
Michigan	$60,600
Minnesota	$74,000
Mississippi	$45,600
Missouri	$59,800
Montana	$56,600
Nebraska	$50,400
Nevada	$95,700
New Hampshire	$129,400
New Jersey	$162,300
New Mexico	$70,100
New York	$131,600
North Carolina	$65,800
North Dakota	$50,800
Ohio	$63,500
Oklahoma	$48,100
Oregon	$67,100
Pennsylvania	$69,700
Rhode Island	$133,500
South Carolina	$61,100
South Dakota	$45,200
Tennessee	$58,400
Texas	$59,600
Utah	$68,900
Vermont	$95,500
Virginia	$65,042
Washington	$93,400
West Virginia	$47,900
Wisconsin	$62,500
Wyoming	$61,600
United States	*$79,100*

FESTIVALS OF GEORGIA

Crowd at Lewis Grizzard Storytelling, Barbecue, and Southern Celebration Festival

The people of Georgia, from those who live in the smallest town to those who live in the largest city, love festivals. Twelve months of the year, a festival is going on somewhere in Georgia. The festivals usually celebrate something special or unique to the town or area in which they are held. They're times for fun and provide the opportunity to learn everything from local history to local opinion on the world at large.

Festivals are also listed in the geographic sections in which they occur. Check the local newspapers for exact dates. At most Welcome Centers, you can usually find copies of the bimonthly *Southern Festivals*. Pick a festival and have a wonderful time.

A

Alpenfest, Stone Mountain. October. Stone Mountain Park. 770-498-5702.

Alpenlights, Helen. November–February. Christmas lights. 706-878-2181.

American Indian Festival, Lawrenceville. May. Native American foods, crafts, music, and demonstrations. Covered arena. 770-795-5743.

Andersonville Historic Fair, Andersonville. Memorial Day and first weekend in October. Craft makers, blacksmiths, potters, glassblowers, quilters, basket makers, square dancers, and cloggers. Flea market. 912-924-2558.

Apple Annie Christmas Craft Festival, Marietta. December. Catholic Church of St. Ann, 4905 Roswell Rd. 770-993-5640.

Arrowhead Arts and Crafts Festival, Macon. October. Native American authentic encampment, storytelling, and crafts. Lake Tobesofkee at Arrowhead Park. 912-474-8770.

Art in the Park, Marietta. September. Glover Park. 770-429-1115.

Arts Festival of Atlanta, Atlanta. September. Paintings, sculptures, photographs, ceramics, jewelry, crafts, puppets, workshops for children, and performances in dance, music, and theater. Piedmont Park. 404-885-1125.

Arts in the Heart of Augusta, Augusta. September. The Riverwalk. 706-826-4702.

Arts on the Courthouse Square, Duluth. September. 770-822-5450.

Arts on the River Weekend, Savannah. May. 912-651-6417.

Atlanta Greek Festival, Atlanta. September. Greek Orthodox Cathedral. 404-633-6988.

Atlanta Jazz Festival, Atlanta. June. Performances by international and local artists. Admission: free. Weekends in Grant Park. Weekday lunchtime concerts in Woodruff Park. 404-653-7160.

Atlanta Jewish Festival, Dunwoody. September. Zaban Park, 5342 Tilly Mill Rd. 770-875-7881.

Atlanta Storytelling Festival, Atlanta. February. Multicultural event with folktales, myths, and legends. Atlanta History Center. 404-814-4000.

Azalea Festival, Pine Mountain. March or April (depending on blooming). Callaway Gardens. 800-282-8181; 706-663-2281.

B

Banks County Festival, Homer. September. Family fun downtown on the square. 706-677-2108.

Banks County Halloween Festival, Homer. October. Hayride, contests, candy, and fun. The Recreation Complex. 706-677-2108.

Barnesville Buggy Days, Barnesville. September. Arts, crafts, parade, fireworks, and antique car display. 404-358-2732.

Bartow County Fair, Cartersville. September. Fairgrounds. 770-382-4207.

Beach Music Festival, Jekyll Island. August, usually third Sat. 800-841-6586; 912-635-3636.

Big Cedar Arts and Crafts Show, Cave Spring. September. Big Cedar Campgrounds. 706-777-8555.

Big Pig Jig, Vienna. October. Barbecue cooking championship contest, parade, arts, crafts, and entertainment. 912-268-8275.

Big Shanty Festival, Kennesaw. Celebrates April 12, 1864, locomotive chase. 770-427-2117.

Blessing of the Fleet, Darien. April or May (depends on tides). 912-437-4192.

Blind Willie Blues Festival, Thomson. September. Celebration of legend of blues great Blind Willie McTell; live performances by blues singers. 706-595-5584.

Blueberry Festival, Alma. June. Arts, crafts, blueberry products, singing, cloggers, and archery. 912-632-5859.

Bluegrass Festival, Adairsville. May. Barnsley Gardens. 770-773-7480.

A Blue Ribbon Affair, Marietta. September. More than 250 artists displaying their works. Jim R. Miller Park. 770-423-1330.

Bonfire and Marshmallow Roast, Decatur. December. Downtown. 404-371-8386.

Brooklet Peanut Festival, Statesboro. August. 800-LOVE-301.

Brown's Crossing Fair, Milledgeville. Third weekend in October. Major regional exhibition of handmade arts and crafts. Held at an extinct cotton-ginning town. Nine miles west of town at 400 Browns Crossing Rd. NW. 912-452-9327.

Burwell Arts and Crafts Festival, Carrollton. October. 770-258-2469.

C

Calico Harvest Arts and Crafts Festival, Stone Mountain. October. Juried fine arts and crafts festival. 770-921-9440.

Cannons Across the Marsh, Fort King George, Darien. July 4. 912-437-4770.

Carnesville Fall Festival, Carnesville. October. 706-384-4849.

Cat Face Turpentine Festival, Statesboro. September. 800-LOVE-301.

Catfish Festival, Kingsland. September (Labor Day weekend). Food (steaming catfish stew, spicy Cajun-style catfish, southern fried catfish), parade, beauty pageant, Catfish 5K Fun Run, bicycle races, arts and crafts, big-name entertainment, a catfishing tournament, and Catfish Classic Golf Tournament. I-95 at exit 2. Kingsland Tourism Authority: 912-729-5999; 800-433-0225.

Cave Spring Arts Festival, Cave Spring.

Second weekend in June. Contact City of Cave Spring, Box 365, Cave Spring, GA 30124. 706-777-3382.

Chamblee Fall Antique Festival, Chamblee. September. Off Peachtree Industrial Blvd. exit off I-285 E. 770-458-1614.

Chattahoochee Mountain Fair, Clarkesville. September. The fairgrounds. GA 17 N. 706-778-4654.

Chehaw National Indian Festival, Albany. May. Native American dances and ceremonies along with demonstrations of skills, games, and weaponry. 912-436-1625.

Cherokee Capital Fair, Calhoun. September. Cherokee Capital Fairgrounds. 706-629-2238.

Cherry Blossom Festival, Conyers. March. International crafts, arts, exhibits, and games. 770-918-2169.

Cherry Blossom Festival, Macon. For 10 days in March, you can enjoy one of the most scenic festivals as 170,000 cherry trees bloom with their light pink blossoms. Bed races, hog-calling contests, storytelling, floats, parades, hot-air balloons, and cultural art performances. 912-743-3401.

Cherry Log Festival, Cherry Log. October. Ten miles north of Ellijay. 706-276-2200.

Chiaha Festival, Rome. October. 706-295-5576.

Christ Church Tour of Homes, St. Simons Island. March. 912-638-8683.

Christmas at Callanwolde, Atlanta. Late November–December. Callanwolde on Briarcliff Rd. 404-872-5338.

Christmas at the Wren's Nest, Atlanta. 1050 R. D. Abernathy Rd. SW. December. 404-753-7735.

Christmas Candelight Tour of Homes, St. Marys. December. Admission: $10 in advance; $12 at the door. 912-882-4000.

Christmas House, Mableton. December. Gift items and crafts. The Historic Mable House. 770-739-0189.

Christmas in Dixie! Crawfordville. November–December. Approximately 170,000 lights on Christmas display and Christmas music. Bennett Family Compound, six miles off I-20 at exit 55. 706-456-2265.

Christmas on Main Street, Lilburn. December. Old Town Lilburn. 770-921-2353.

Christmas on the Square, Blakely. December. Arts, crafts, parade, and car show. 912-723-3741.

Christmas Parade, Toccoa. December. 706-886-8451, ext. 269.

Christmas Tour of Homes, Savannah. December. 912-234-4088.

Coosa River Lighted Boat Parade, Rome.

October. Downtown levee. 706-295-5576.

Cotton Jamboree, Adairsville. September. Barnsley Gardens. 770-773-7480.

Cotton Pickin' Country Fair, Gay. October. 706-538-6814.

Country by the Sea Music Festival, Jekyll Island. June. 800-841-6586; 912-635-3636.

Coweta County Fair and Art Festival, Newnan. Sepember (Labor Day weekend). Ranked as one of the top 100 events in North America. Art, handiwork, flowers, poultry, livestock, midway rides, and live entertainment. 770-253-2413.

Creative Arts Guild's Festival, Dalton. September. Fine arts and crafts festival, and entertainment. 706-278-0168.

D

Daffodil Festival, Adairsville. March. 770-773-7480.

Dawson County Mountain Moonshine Festival, Dawsonville. October. 706-216-4089.

Decatur Arts Festival, Decatur. May. 404-371-8386.

Dogwood Festival, Atlanta. April. Parade, driving tours, and hot-air balloon race. 404-892-0538.

Dogwood Festival, Jesup. March. Arts, crafts, antiques, and collectibles. 912-427-2080 or 427-7833.

Dogwood Festival, Leslie. April. 912-924-2646.

Dogwood Festival, Perry. First week in April. Arts, crafts, parades, and 5K run. 912-987-1234.

Down by the Riverside Arts and Crafts Festival, West Point. September. Entertainment, rides, crafts, and arts. 770-429-0239.

Downtown Vidalia Christmas Festival, Vidalia. December. Parade, entertainment, arts, and crafts. 912-538-8687.

Dulcimer Festival, Westville (Lumpkin Co.). March. Musical events and workshop with live performances. 912-838-6310.

Duluth Fall Festival and Parade, Duluth. September. 770-476-3434.

E

Egleston Christmas Parade, Atlanta. December. Peachtree St. 404-264-9348.

Emancipation Proclamation Celebration, Midway. January. Dorchester Academy. 912-884-2347.

F

Fair of 1850, Westville. October–November. Lumpkin Co. 912-838-6310.

Fall Encampment and Reenactment, Fort

King George, Darien. November. 912-437-4770.

Fall Sugar Creek Bluegrass Festival, Blue Ridge. October. Sugar Creek Music Park. 706-632-2560.

Fantasy in Lights, Pine Mountain. November–January 1. Purchase tickets in advance. Callaway Gardens. 800-282-8181; 706-663-2281.

Farm City Week Festival, Calhoun. October. Cherokee Capital Fairgrounds. 706-625-3200.

Festival of Cultures, Atlanta. October. Downtown. 404-817-0800.

Festival of Life, Roswell. October. Roswell Municipal Auditorium. 770-594-6232.

Festival of Trees, Atlanta. Starts first Sat. in December. Beautifully decorated trees and holiday activities. World Congress Center. 404-264-9348.

Festival of Trees, Rome. December. The Forum. 706-295-5576.

First Night Athens, Athens. December 31. 706-546-1805.

First Night Atlanta, Atlanta. The family-oriented, nonalcoholic events begin at 3 p.m. New Year's Eve and end at 12:30 a.m. Admission: $10 in advance or $12 at the event. 404-881-0400.

First Saturday Festival(s), Savannah. First Sat. February–December. Historic Waterfront. 912-234-0295.

Flatlanders Fall Frolic, Lakeland. September. Country music, beauty pageant, arts, and crafts. 912-482-3100.

Folk Festival for Preservation, Sautee-Nacoochee. September. Folk music outdoors, arts, crafts, and history museum. Sautee-Nacoochee Arts and Community Center. 706-878-3300.

Folklife Festival, Atlanta. October. Tours of house and gardens; demonstrations of 19th-century crafts, pottery making, and dulcimer music. The Tullie Smith House. 404-814-4000.

Forsythia Festival, Forsyth. April. Arts, crafts, 5K run, fishing, golf, games, entertainment, and parade. 912-994-9239.

Fort Morris Revolutionary War Encampment, Midway. Second Sat. in September. 912-884-5999.

Fourth of July Barbeque and Craft Show, Fort McAllister, Richmond Hill. July 4. 912-727-2339.

Fourth of July Festival, Fort Benning, Columbus. July 4. A military pageant of skydiving paratroopers, gleaming bands, single-step parades in full battle dress uniform, and fireworks. 706-545-2238.

Fourth of July Festival, St. Marys. July 4. Downtown/waterfront. 800-868-8687.

Fourth of July Fireworks, Savannah. July 4. Tybee Beach. 912-786-5444.

Fourth of July Fireworks Extravaganza, Jekyll Island. July 4. 800-841-6586; 912-635-3636.

G

Georgia Apple Festival, Ellijay. Two weekends in October. 706-635-7400.

Georgia Marble Festival, Jasper. October. Pickens Co. 706-692-5600.

Georgia Mountain Fair, Hiawassee. Twelve days in August. Bluegrass fiddlers, gospel singers, clog dancers, craft makers in woodworking, pottery, painting, leatherwork, furniture, jewelry, basket weaving, needlework, quilting, macramé, and dolls. 706-896-4191.

Georgia Music Festival, Atlanta. September. Underground Atlanta. 404-523-2311.

Georgia National Fair, Perry. Early October. Only state-sponsored fair held at the Fairgrounds and Agricenter. 912-988-6483; 800-987-3247.

Georgia Peach Festival, Byron and Fort Valley. Mid-June. Weeklong event: parades, street dances, peach pie cook-off, peach-eating contests, and a king and queen coronation. 912-825-4002.

Georgia-Sea Island Festival, St. Simons Island. Third weekend in August. 912-265-9545 or 264-5373.

Georgia Shakespeare Festival, Atlanta. June. Shakespearean classics performed in open-air tent. Oglethorpe University. 404-688-8008.

Georgia State Fair, Macon. Third week in October. Carnival games, livestock shows, arts, and crafts. 912-746-7184.

Ghostly Gatherings, Sandy Springs. October. The Williams-Payne House. 404-851-9111.

Gnat Days, Camilla. Second and third weeks of June. Boat cruises, professional tennis tournament, arts, and crafts. Especially visit the Gnat Market. 706-336-5255. (Note: the Gnat Line is an imaginary boundary that separates the folk traditions of South Georgia from the more urbanized northern section.)

Golden Isles Arts Festival, St. Simons Island. Second weekend in October. Fine arts and crafts. 912-638-8770.

Gold Rush Festival, Dahlonega. October. 706-864-3711.

Gold Rush Festival, Villa Rica. September. 770-459-3885.

Granite City Arts and Crafts Festival, Elberton. April. Children's events, parade, 5K race/walk, barbecue, and vendors. 706-283-7499.

Great Halloween Caper, Atlanta. October. Zoo Atlanta. 404-624-5000.

Great Locomotive Chase Festival, Adairsville. September–October. 770-773-3451.

Great Miller Lite Chili Cook-off, Stone Mountain Park. October. 404-872-4731.

Great Pumpkin Arts and Crafts Festival, Lake Lanier Islands. October. 770-932-7200.

Green Grass Fair, Warm Springs. First weekend in April and in November. Antiques, collectibles, arts, and crafts. Two miles north of Warm Springs on GA 41 and US 27 Alt. 706-655-2468.

Gwinnett County Fair, Lawrenceville. September. Gwinnett Fairgrounds. 770-822-8000.

H

Habitat for Humanity Birdhouse Artfest, Atlanta. October. Lenox Square. 404-264-3999.

Hahira Honeybee Festival, Hahira. October. Tribute to the honeybee, food, and music in a weeklong event. 912-794-3617.

Halloween Festival, Villa Rica. October. Gold Dust Park. 770-459-7011.

Halloween Happenings, Marietta. October. Glover Park. 770-528-0616.

Halloween in the Alley, Atlanta. October. Underground Atlanta. 404-523-2311.

Happy Acres Resort Arts and Crafts Festival, Screven. October. Two-day event. Antiques and original arts and crafts. Happy Acres Resort and RV Park. 912-586-6767.

Harvest Festival, Thomasville. October. 912-225-3920.

Harvest Festival, Toccoa. November. Includes Civil War reenactment. 706-886-8451, ext. 269.

Hawkinsville Harness Festival, Hawkinsville. April. Trotters and pacers. 912-783-1717.

Heritage Festival, Decatur. October. 404-371-8386.

Heritage Holidays, Rome. October. 706-295-5576.

Hillside Bluegrass Festival, Cochran. May and September. Music, arts, and crafts. 912-934-6694.

Hispanic Festival of the Arts, Atlanta. February or March. Multimedia festival held at Georgia Tech Center for the Arts. 770-938-8611.

Historic Courthouse Tree Lighting Ceremony, Homer. December. Walking tour of Homer. 706-677-2108.

Historic Marietta Antiques Street Festival, Marietta. September–October. Marietta Square. 770-429-1115.

Holiday Candlelight Tour of Homes, Decatur. December. 404-371-8386.

Holiday Celebration, Stone Mountain Park. November–December. 770-498-5702.

Homespun Festival, Rockmart. July. Arts, crafts, parade, road race, fireworks, and entertainment. Polk Co. 770-684-8774.

Howard Finster Arts Festival, Summerville. May. Chattooga Co. 706-857-4033. (See *Howard Finster* feature in **North Georgia**.)

Hunt's Meadow Country Fair, Hiram. October. Arts, crafts, antiques, and music. 770-445-7166.

I

Indian Cultural Festival, Columbus. October. Authentic Native American storytelling, flute music, hoop dances, stickball games, and basket weaving of the region's Native Americans. Columbus College campus. 706-568-2049.

Inman Park Festival, Atlanta. April. Tour of Victorian homes, music, and crafts. 404-242-4895.

J

Jonesboro Fall Festival and Battle Reenactment, Jonesboro. October. Stately Oaks Plantation. 770-473-0197.

Jones County Wildlife Cook-off and Crafts Festival, Gray. April. 912-986-1433.

July Fest Shark Tournament, Yellow Bluff Fishing Camp. July. 912-876-3457.

K

Kolomoki Festival, Blakely. October. Fine arts and crafts; Native American skills demonstrations and artifacts. 912-723-3079 or 723-5296.

Kwanzaa, Atlanta. December 26–January 1. African-American celebration based on African tradition and culture. Created in 1966, it is now celebrated in more than 100 major cities. 404-730-4001, ext. 110, or 404-521-9014.

L

Labor Day County Fair of 1896, Tifton. September. Georgia Agrirama. 912-386-3344.

Lewis Memorial Fall Arts and Crafts Festival, Appling. October. 706-541-0156.

Lighting of the Chateau, Braselton. November. Chateau Elan. 770-932-0900.

Lighting of the Rich's Great Tree, Atlanta. November. Underground Atlanta. 404-523-2311.

Lilburn Daze, Lilburn. October. Old Town Lilburn. 770-921-2210.

Little Five Points Halloween Festival, Atlanta. October. 404-681-2831.

M

Madison County Agriculture Fair, Comer. September. Madison Co. Fairgrounds. 706-795-2096.

Magical Nights of Lights, Lake Lanier Islands. November–January 1. 770-932-7200.

Magnolia Blossom Festival, Newnan. June. Local artisans and craft makers. 770-254-3703.

Marietta Pilgrimage: A Christmas Home Tour, Marietta. December. Tour of six homes decorated for the season. 770-429-1115.

Marigold Festival, Winterville. June. Arts, crafts, antiques, antique cars, and barbecue. 706-742-8600.

Martin Luther King, Jr., Street Festival, Atlanta. October. 404-522-3249.

Mayhaw Festival, Colquitt. May. One-day event celebrates mayhaw berry, famous for the jelly it makes. Arts, crafts, games, contests, and parade. Spring Creek Park. 912-758-2400.

McIntosh Reserve Fall Festival, Whitesburg. October. 770-830-5879.

Memorial Day Celebration: Confederate Reenactment, Fort McAllister, Richmond Hill. May. 912-727-2339.

A Merry Olde Marietta Christmas, Marietta. December. The square. 770-429-1115.

Mideastern Festival, Atlanta. November. St. Elias Antiochian Orthodox Church. 404-687-9266.

Mistletoe Market, Albany. November. Albany Civic Center. 912-435-1897.

Monroe Crepe Myrtle Festival, Monroe. September. 770-267-4613.

Montreaux/Atlanta International Music Festival, Atlanta. September (Labor Day weekend). European guest artists perform with other known artists; variety of styles. Piedmont Park. 404-953-3278, ext. 225.

Mossy Creek Barnyard Arts and Crafts Festival, Perry. Third weekend in April and in October. Showcase for nationally recognized artists and craft makers, clogging, hayrides, and a petting zoo. 912-922-8265.

Mule Camp Market Festival, Gainesville. October. Folk art festival and entertainment. 770-531-0385.

Mule Day, Washington. October. Callaway Plantation. 706-678-2013.

Mule Roundup, Guysie. October. Pioneer farm demonstrations, arts, crafts, parade, and mule rodeo. Five miles west of Alma and 19 miles east of Douglas on GA 32. 912-632-5570.

Music Midtown Festival, Atlanta. May. Live performances by big-name performers. Sponsored by Midtown Alliance. Admission: $11–$17. 404-892-4782.

N

National Black Arts Festival, Atlanta. July;

only in even-numbered years. African-American culture, dance, music, and folklore. 404-224-1142.

Native American Festival, Indian Springs. September. 770-775-6735.

Native American Festival, Lithia Springs. June. Sweetwater Creek State Park. 770-732-5876.

New Manchester Days, Lithia Springs. September. Sweetwater Creek State Park. 770-732-5876.

New Salem Mountain Festival, Rising Fawn. May and October. 706-398-1988.

North Georgia Folk Festival, Athens. October. Sandy Creek Park. 706-613-3620.

North Georgia State Fair, Marietta. September. Live entertainment by top country music stars. Jim R. Miller Park. 770-423-1330.

O

Oconee Riverfest, Lake Oconee. September. Children's activities, boat rides, arts, crafts, barbecue, and entertainment. Parks Ferry Recreational Area. 706-453-7592.

Okefenokee Festival, Folkston. October. Celebrate life on the edge of the great swamp. 912-496-2536.

Okefenokee Pogofest—A Swamp Celebration, Waycross. October. Exchange Club Fairgrounds. 912-285-4400.

Oktoberfest, Helen. September–October. Parade, music, and dances. 800-858-8027; Welcome Center 706-878-3677.

Olde Christmas Storytelling Festival, Atlanta. December 25–January 6. Callanwolde mansion. 404-872-5338.

Olde English Festival, Atlanta. October. St. Bartholomew's Episcopal Church. 404-634-3336.

Olde Gristmill Festival, Juliette. October. 912-994-5189.

Olde Towne Fall Festival, Conyers. October. Games, arts, and crafts. 770-483-8615 or 929-0572.

Old Madison Days, Madison. October. Cotton Patch Craft Fair and Madison Agricultural Exposition. 706-342-4454.

An Old South Christmas Festival, Macon. December. Dressed-up historic homes with period decorations and costumed guides. 912-743-3401.

Old-Timers' Day, Blairsville. September. Vogel State Park. 706-745-2628.

Old Town Sharpsburg, Sharpsburg. Spring Festival third weekend in April. Fall Festival third weekend in September. Christmas Open House first full weekend in November. Exit 10 off I-85 S, then east on GA 154 to sign. 770-251-8440.

Old Tyme Country Fest, Murrayville. September. Eight miles north of Gainesville on GA 60. 770-536-6828.

Ormewood Park Fall Festival and Tour of Homes, Atlanta. October. 404-622-9323.

P

Paulding Meadows Arts and Crafts Festival, Dallas. September. 770-943-6793.

Peach Drop and New Year's Eve Party, Atlanta. December 31. Underground Atlanta. World's Largest Tailgate Party on eve of Peach Bowl game. 404-523-2311.

Peach State Marching Festival, Rome. October. 706-236-5082.

Peachtree Crossings Country Fair, Fairburn. September. 770-434-3661.

Pelham Wildlife Festival, Pelham. October. Arts, crafts, wildflower exhibit, entertainment, and street dance. 912-294-4924.

Pine Log Arts and Crafts Festival, Rydal. September. Pine Log United Methodist Church. 770-386-3324.

Pine Mountain Heritage Festival, Pine Mountain. October. Arts, crafts, and entertainment. Pine Mountain Heritage Festival, P.O. Box 177, Pine Mountain, GA 31822.

Pioneer Days Arts and Crafts Festival, Acworth. September. Acworth Beach. 770-775-6859.

Plains Country Days, Plains. Third weekend in May. Parade, street dance, homespun fun. 912-824-7477.

Possum Hollow Arts and Crafts Fair and Country Music Show, Dexter. September. 912-875-3104.

Powder Springs Day, Powder Springs. September. Arts, crafts, games, road race, entertainment, and parade. 770-943-3912.

Powers Crossroads Country Fair and Art Festival, Newnan. September (Labor Day weekend). Opportunities to learn about southern traditions and visit a country store; artists and craft makers. 770-253-2270.

Prater's Mill Country Fair, Dalton. Second weekend in May and in October. Event centers on Benjamin Prater's 1859 gristmill. 706-275-6455.

Puckett Station Arts and Crafts Fair, Moreland. July 4 weekend. Exhibits, entertainment, and food. 770-253-0567.

R

Raccoon Creek Bluegrass Festival, Dallas. September. 770-445-3574.

Resaca Festival/Civil War Battle of Resaca Reenactment, Calhoun. May. Gordon Co. 706-625-3200.

Rhododendron Festival, Hiawassee. Last weekend in April and first weekend in

May. Arts and crafts show. 706-896-4966.

Riverfest Arts and Crafts Festival, Canton. September. Boling Park. 770-479-3017.

Rock Shrimp Festival, St. Marys. First Sat. in October. 800-868-8687; 912-882-6200.

Rose Festival and Parade, Thomasville. April. Crafts, arts, and parade. 800-704-2350.

Roselawn Arts Festival, Cartersville. September. Roselawn Museum. 770-382-8277.

Roswell Antebellum Spring Festival and Colors Cultural Arts Festival, Roswell. March. Fine arts, crafts, and a barbecue. 800-776-7935.

Roswell Arts Festival, Roswell. September. Historic town square. 770-640-3523.

S

St. Patrick's Day, Savannah. March 17. 912-233-4804.

St. Patrick's Festival, Dublin. March (monthlong festival). World's largest pot of Irish stew, parade, and music. 912-272-5546.

St. Simons by the Sea Art Festival, St. Simons. First weekend in October. 912-634-0404.

Savannah Jazz Festival, Savannah. September. 912-944-0456.

Scottish Festival and Highland Games, Stone Mountain. October. Three days of Scottish pageantry, folk dancing, and clan meetings. 770-498-5702.

Sea Island Festival, St. Simons. August. A celebration of the folklore, crafts, stories, games, and rituals of former slaves who settled on the islands. 912-638-9014.

Sharpsburg Old Town Festival, Sharpsburg. See listing for *Old Town Sharpsburg.*

Smyrna Jonquil Fall Festival, Smyrna. October. Village Green. 770-434-3661.

Snellville Arts in the Park, Snellville. October. 770-985-3535.

Snellville Days Festival, Snellville. May. Arts, crafts, concerts, and parade. 770-985-3500.

Soberfest, St. Marys. April. 800-868-8687.

Sorghum Festival, Blairsville. October. 706-745-4745.

Southeastern Flower Show, Atlanta. February. Ponce Square in midtown. 404-876-5859.

Southern Appalachian Sampler Festival, Blue Ridge. September. Sugar Creek Music Park. 706-492-3819.

Southern Crescent Celebration, Morrow. September. Artistic demonstrations, business exhibits, and children's activities. Clayton State College. 770-961-3580.

Southern Heartland Arts Festival, near Conyers. September. Entertainment, arts, and crafts. Salem Campground, exit 43 off I-20. 770-760-8846.

Southern Jubilee, Macon. Two-week-long event in September. Home tours, a folk art festival, and a music weekend outdoors. 912-741-8000.

Spring Encampment and Reenactment, Fort King George, Darien. March. 912-437-4770.

Springfest, Stone Mountain Park. May. Barbecue competition, live entertainment, arts, and crafts. 770-498-5702.

Spring Fling, Juliette. May. Arts, crafts, and entertainment. Juliette River Club, P.O. Box 84, Juliette, GA 31046.

Spring Music Festival, Hiawassee. May. 706-896-4191.

Stand Up for America Day, Port Wentworth. May. 800-218-3554; 912-748-8080.

Sunshine Festival, St. Simons Island. July 4th weekend. 912-638-9400.

Sweet Auburn Festival, Atlanta. April. Tours, parades, ethnic foods, and music. African-American historical neighborhood. 404-577-0625.

Sweetwater Fever Fine Arts and Crafts Festival, Mableton. May. Arts, crafts, Native American art, children's events, and live music. 770-739-0189.

Swine Time Festival, Climax. November. Arts, crafts, exhibits, and pork in many forms, including barbecue. Climax Community Club, P.O. Box 131, Climax, GA 31734.

Sylvania Air Show and Fly-In, Sylvania. September. Wing walkers, crop dusters, helicopters, flying shows, arts, and crafts. Plantation Air Park. 800-972-7887.

T

Taliaferro County's Labor Day Fair, Crawfordville. September. Arts, crafts, rides, amusements, and music. Alexander H. Stephens State Park. 706-456-2536 or 456-2140.

Tannery Row Festival of the Arts, Buford. November. 770-271-0436.

Taste of Thomaston, Thomaston. September. Courthouse square. 706-647-8311.

Theater Festival, Madison. Mid-August. Tour of antebellum homes. 706-342-4454.

Tour of Southern Ghosts, Stone Mountain Park. October. Antebellum Plantation. 770-498-5702.

Town and Country Arts and Crafts Festival, Lincolnton. October. 706-359-4300.

Tunis Campbell Festival on the Waterfront, Darien. Fourth Saturday in June. 912-437-3900.

U

An Underground Christmas, Atlanta. November–December. Underground Atlanta. 404-523-2311.

V

Vinings Jubilee Fall Festival, Vinings. October. 770-438-8080.

W

Watermelon Days Festival, Cordele. July. Continues for a week or 10 days. 912-273-3526 C/C.

Wildflower Festival of the Arts, Dahlonega. May. Fine art. 706-864-7449.

Winefest, Helen. May. Free wine tasting from Georgia wineries and live entertainment. 800-858-8027.

Y

Yellow Daisy Festival, Stone Mountain Park. September. Arts, crafts, concerts, and entertainment. 770-498-5702.

COVERED BRIDGES AND GRISTMILLS OF GEORGIA

COVERED BRIDGES

More than ever, covered bridges have captured the interest of the American people. Since the publication of the book *The Bridges of Madison County* (1992) and the production of the film version (1995), these reminders of the past have taken on a new romanticism. Even though the Madison Co. ones are in Iowa, Georgia has its share of covered bridges.

Covered bridges remind us of the craft and lifestyle of our past. In the past century of rapid road building, the hooded structures spanned rivers, creeks, and streams across the United States. Before the modern use of concrete and steel, people built bridges from wood. To prevent quick decay, they enclosed the bridges in a shell of clapboard siding and roofing shingles. The material was cheap and easily replaced.

Today, only 15 of Georgia's one-time total of 250 covered bridges remain. During the Civil War (1861–65), many of them disappeared. Federal troops destroyed bridges to prevent the Southerners from using them for moving troops and shipping supplies. Not one of the bridges that Sherman and his troops crossed on the 1864 march through Georgia to the Atlantic survives today. When Confederates fled the Northern troops, they burned many bridges behind them.

Of those that remain, most are on back roads where they have deteriorated. One has been moved, and a few have been restored.

In early 1995, the U.S. government awarded $1.1 million in federal funds to restore the state's covered bridges.

HORACE KING

Horace King—sometimes called Georgia's master builder of covered bridges—built 125 such structures in Georgia, Alabama, and Mississippi. Fifteen of those bridges spanned the Chattahoochee River. Unfortunately for us, only two remain in Georgia: one over Red Oak Creek and one that has been moved to Callaway Gardens.

What many don't know is that King was born a slave in 1807 in South Carolina. After John Godwin, a builder and architect, bought King, he recognized the slave's outstanding mechanical abilities.

In 1832, King and his master moved to what is now Phenix City, Alabama. Together they designed and built an elaborate covered bridge over the wild Chattahoochee River. (It was the first bridge in that part of the country to use a Town lattice truss assembly—crisscrossed planks fastened together with wood pins.) They were soon building bridges everywhere.

Godwin freed King in 1846, and the former slave began his own construction business in LaGrange, Georgia. After that, King and his sons built bridges all over the Southeast, especially over hazardous crossings that others refused to attempt.

King's eldest son, Washington, also built a number of fine bridges, including what is now Georgia's longest covered span, Watson Mill Bridge.

Auchumpkee Creek Covered Bridge, Upson Co. (Middle Georgia). This 120-foot-long bridge stretched across a shallow creek and was built around the turn of the century. In 1985, the bridge was beautifully restored. The devastating floods of 1994 partially destroyed two-thirds of the bridge. Through federal funds and money raised by real estate agent Bobby Smith, the bridge is to be restored, with a projected completion date of April 1996. It's on US 19, 12 miles south of Thomaston.

Big Clouds Creek Bridge, Madison and Oglethorpe Cos. (North Georgia). It's 110 feet long and was built in 1905, but it has been abandoned and is in danger of falling.

Callaway Gardens Bridge, Harris Co. (West Georgia). Built in 1870, it spans 79 feet and was originally called the Neely Bridge. It is going to be restored.

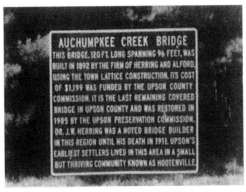

Auchumpkee Creek Bridge Sign

Auchumpkee Creek Bridge Pieces Covered with Tarps

Coheelee Creek Covered Bridge, Early Co. (South Georgia). This bridge spans 96 feet across the Coheelee Creek. (*Coheelee* is a Creek Indian word that may mean "Standing Cane" or "Good Cane Place," or it can be a short form of *Cochecalechee,* "broken arrow.") In 1883, the county board appointed a committee to decide if the community needed a bridge across the creek at McDonald's Ford. They agreed on the need for a bridge but recommended Sowatchee Creek, which is where they built the bridge. However, years later, local residents still wanted a bridge at McDonald's Ford. In 1891, the county agreed. Within four months, three dozen workers completed the bridge for a cost of $490.41. The bridge at Sowatchee has long since disappeared, but the Coheelee Creek Bridge has been preserved and is in fine condition today. It is the southernmost covered bridge in the U.S. and is maintained as a county park. It's on Old River Rd., two miles north of Hilton, off GA 62.

Coheelee Creek Bridge Sign

Concord Bridge, Cobb Co. (North Georgia). Built in 1872, it spans 133 feet and handles 9,500 vehicles a day. It's between Smyrna and Mableton.

Cromer's Mill Bridge, Franklin Co. (North Georgia). Built in 1906, this 111-foot-long bridge is no longer considered safe for foot traffic and has been closed.

Coheelee Creek Bridge

Elder's Mill Bridge, Oconee Co. (North Georgia). This 1897 bridge is 75 feet long. The nearby mill ruins are picturesque.

Euharlee Creek Bridge, Bartow Co. (North Georgia). This 116-foot-span dates back to 1886. Thanks to a nearby fire station, it survived an arsonist's attempts in 1990.

Lowry Covered Bridge, Bartow Co., near Cartersville (North Georgia). This 116-foot-long weatherboarded structure is now closed to vehicles, but you can stop to admire it. The bridge was made from heartwood pine for strength and durability on stone piers 13 feet high. Except for a modern tin roof, it looks much as it did when a miller named Daniel Lowry supervised its construction.

Lowry operated a gristmill only feet from the bridge. When a violent storm washed away the first bridge, he insisted on a new one. The mill disappeared long ago, but the beautifully designed bridge remains. It's off GA 113, west of Cartersville.

Lula Bridge, Banks Co. (North Georgia). Depending on how it's measured, some say this is 31 feet long, which makes it the state's shortest surviving covered bridge. (See *Sautee Bridge.*) Built in 1915, it was restored in 1976 on a private golf course.

Pool's Mill Covered Bridge, Forsyth Co. (North Georgia). This 95-foot-long bridge has an interesting history. In the early 1820s, Chief George Welch, a mixed-blood Cherokee, built a gristmill. Because of the U.S. government's Cherokee gold lottery and the evacuation of Native Americans, he lost the land. (He was later reimbursed $12,500.) The land had several owners, and then it came into the possession of Dr. Marcus Lafayette Pool in 1870. Although Pool died 25 years later, the bridge that carries his name still exists. A three-storied combination of sawmill and gristmill adjacent to the bridge has disappeared. If you look, you'll see a few iron rods where the wooden dam once stood. The bridge still exists, and bicyclists and pedestrians can use it.

As a footnote to the bridge, spring rains destroyed a previous bridge in 1900, but mill owner John Wafford decided to replace it. He took poplar planks from Pool's mill for the bridge, planed, cut, drilled, and piled everything next to the creek. But somehow Wafford miscalculated: The timber didn't fit together properly, and he had drilled the holes for the interconnecting wooden pegs in the wrong places. A discouraged Wafford abandoned the project. Someone else rebored the holes and completed the project. It's the only covered bridge in Georgia with two sets of holes in each of its Town lattice trusses. (See *Watson Mill Bridge.*) It's about 10 miles northwest of Cumming.

Red Oak Creek Covered Bridge, Meriwether Co. (West Georgia). This is a 400-foot-long bridge, of which only 116 feet is covered. It was one of the first covered bridges built in Georgia, and it was built by master bridge builder Horace King. The bridge still survives. If not the oldest surviving bridge in the state, it is certainly one of them. It's on an unpaved road east of GA 85, midway between Gay and Woodbury.

Sautee Bridge

Sautee Bridge, White Co. (North Georgia).

This bridge dates to 1905. A leaky roof has been causing the bridge to deteriorate. Some measure it at 34 feet long. Others make it less so that it becomes Georgia's shortest bridge. (See *Lula Bridge*).

Stone Mountain Covered Bridge, DeKalb Co., Stone Mountain Park (North Georgia). This now-famous 151-foot bridge was moved in 1964 from Athens, about 60 miles away. Built by Washington King, the eldest son of famous bridge builder and former slave, Horace King, in 1892, it stretched across the north fork of the Oconee River. It was called the College Avenue Bridge, but was popularly known as Effie's Bridge after a nearby bordello. Built in 1892 for $2,500, the move cost $18,000. You can see it today inside Stone Mountain Park, 16 miles east of Atlanta on US 78, off I-285.

Watson Mill Bridge, Madison and Oglethorpe Cos. (North Georgia). Spanning 229 feet, it is Georgia's longest remaining covered bridge, and it's located on its original site over the S. Fork Broad River as the centerpiece of the Watson Mill State Park. Many think this is the most beautiful of Georgia's covered bridges.

The bridge was named for the owner of a gristmill, Gabriel Watson, in the 1800s. It is made of three wooden spans supported by a lattice truss called the Ithiel Town truss. It's a web of plain planks held together by wood pins and looks like an oversized trellis. Most of the timbers are the original ones.

This bridge was designed and built in 1885 by Washington King. You can see it six miles south of Comer on GA 22.

For more specific directions, call the Georgia Department of Industry, Trade, and Tourism: 404-656-3590.

GRISTMILLS

If you had traveled across Georgia in the mid-19th century, you would have seen gristmills everywhere. The small, privately owned mills ground wheat and corn. Few mills remain to remind you of this bygone period of history.

Cochran Mills, Fulton Co. (Middle Georgia). In the early 1800s, Cheadle Cochran began to farm near the growing town of Palmetto, and he built an 80-foot-long mill on his land at Little Bear Creek. After Cochran's death, his son Owen successfully operated the mill for many years. In 1870, Owen's brother Berry built a 48-foot mill on the main branch of Bear Creek.

The property changed owners over the years. In the 1940s, Dr. Hiram Evans, head of the Ku Klux Klan, owned the land. He put up an electric fence. To provide power for the fence and other facilities, Evans built a concrete-reinforced dam downstream from Berry Cochran's mill. No one knows exactly what Evans did with the mills during his ownership.

Both mills remained unused for years. In 1967, vandals burned Owen Cochran's mill and dynamited the dam. In 1972, someone destroyed Berry's gristmill, but the dam itself remains intact. Fulton County Parks System now owns the property. The ruins are located on Cochran Mill Rd. To see the ruins, you have to walk over a steel-and-wood-truss bridge that dates back to the mid-19th century.

Hamburg Mill, Hamburg State Park, Washington Co. (Middle Georgia). In 1850, Robert Warthen from North Carolina built the gristmill, about 100 feet above the present site. He used a conventional waterwheel. In 1921, the Gilmores from Agricola, Georgia, built the present one. Located inside Hamburg State Park, the water-powered gristmill still operates.

Hamburg Mill

Old Mill, Rome, the campus of Berry College (North Georgia). Originally, the 42-foot-diameter wooden waterwheel was located at Hermitage in northwestern Georgia. The Republic Mining and Manufacturing Company donated the mill to Berry College, and Henry Ford had it transported to its present site in 1930. Berry students rebuilt the wheel and constructed the mill complex. Gravity-fed water powers the working mill. It's 75 minutes from Atlanta. Take I-75 N and US 41 to intersection US 411 north of Cartersville, and then on US 411 to Rome.

Prater's Mill, Whitfield Co., near Dalton (North Georgia). Benjamin Prater and Tilmond Pitner jointly purchased 80 acres of land. A sawmill had already been built near the Coahulla Creek. They built quite an industry. At one time they had not only the sawmill, but also a gristmill, cotton gin, wood corder, blacksmith shop, general store, and hotel.

The mill closed in the 1950s, but it's still functional. During the spring and fall arts and crafts festival held on the site (see **Festivals of Georgia**), the old mill operates. It's 10 miles north of Dalton on GA 2.

Watson Mill, Madison and Oglethorpe Cos. (North Georgia). The mill was built around 1880. You can see a covered bridge and a gristmill under the single roof. Although named Watson Mill, it did not belong to Hubert Watson until he bought it in 1943. For the next 32 years he successfully operated the mill. In 1975, the state of Georgia bought the mill and preserved it as part of the Watson Mill Bridge State Park. It's six miles south of Comer on GA 22.

CHAPTER
FIVE

GEORGIA'S FAMOUS SONS AND DAUGHTERS

Georgians are proud of their many famous sons and daughters, those who were born in Georgia, sometimes going into other parts of the world to become famous. We've tried to make this list as comprehensive as possible. Of course, it's impossible to include everyone. Right up until the last minute, we were still adding names.

We have also included a few adopted sons and daughters. Although they didn't have the good fortune to be born here, they did spend a significant part of their life working in Georgia, so we feel they deserve to be included.

We've had a few notorious people who probably belong on this list, but you won't find them here. For instance, Alice Riley arrived in the colony of Georgia in 1734. One year later, she was hanged for murdering her employer. As far as we know, she was the first woman hanged in Georgia.

Some of the people listed are so well known that we give only the briefest description. For those who are lesser known (but who in our opinion deserve recognition), we have added a few details.

AN EXTRA TOUCH OF GEORGIA: QUEEN OF COFACHIQUI

When de Soto and his Spanish army came to the Savannah River (where Augusta is today) in the spring of 1540, they met the queen, who was the leader of the tribe. Because they were unfamiliar with the tribal language, they called her queen.

One of the soldiers compared her to Cleopatra on her famous barge because she came to them in a decorated and roofed canoe. A second canoe, filled with her warriors, drew hers from across the river.

They exchanged gifts. De Soto gave her a ruby and gold ring, and she gave him a rope of river pearls "as thick as hazelnuts" (so the story goes). The necklace was long enough to circle her neck three times, and it still fell almost to her knees.

The river pearls appeared to the Spaniards as great wealth for which they had been searching. Instead of showing them more pearls, the queen of Cofachiqui showed them mica and copper her tribe had gotten by trading shells with other tribes from the North—the only metals they had that were silver and gold colored.

Afraid of the Spaniards, the queen encouraged them to take the hundreds of pounds of river pearls that lay in the tribe's burial mounds. They took all they could find.

When the ungrateful soldiers left, they forced the queen to go with them as their guide, convinced she would lead them to treasures. She went, but after a few days of travel, she stole the trunk that contained the most flawless pearls and escaped.

■■

Aaron, Henry (Hank). b. 1934. Mobile, AL. An outfielder for the Milwaukee (later Atlanta) Braves, he held 21 major-league records, including the most home runs, when he shattered Babe Ruth's record of 714 home runs in 1974. He retired in 1976 with 755 homers. He is a member of the Baseball Hall of Fame.

Allman Brothers Band. Georgia-born Duane and Gregg Allman and various others who have been part of the group worked to produce the "Macon, Georgia, sound" as one of the top rock music groups of the 1970s. Although one critic referred to them as the "southern-fried boogie band," in 1971 their album *Eat a Peach* went to platinum with three singles that hit the top of the charts. After the death of Duane in 1971, Gregg carried on the group. Recent albums include *Shades of Two Worlds* (1991), *An Evening with the Allman Brothers* (1992), and *Where It All Begins* (1994).

Anderson, Bill. b. 1937. Columbia, SC. He is ranked among the all-time great country music songwriters with more than 500 songs to his credit. His "City Lights" in 1955 and "Still" in 1963 both became the number one songs. One of his best-known songs is "Po' Folks" that gave the name to his band and the chain of restaurants with which his name is associated.

Anderson, Paul. 1932–94. Toccoa. When he won the Olympic gold in 1956 for weight lifting, he was called the world's strongest man. He founded the Paul Anderson Youth Home in Vidalia, where the courts sent youth.

Atlanta Rhythm Section. Based in Doraville, it is made up of six talented musicians, of which three are from Georgia.

Some have called them a southern boogie band with class, but their album title *Champagne Jam* has become the name applied to the group.

B-52s. Taking their name from the sixties slang for a beehive hairstyle (a la Marge on *The Simpsons*), they began in 1976 in Athens, Georgia. Their sound consisted of a brisk top-heavy drumbeat and deep synthesized bass, over which they played an electric guitar and added bongos, wireless receivers, toy percussion, and vocals. In 1979, they released their first album, *The B-52s.* Their "Rock Lobster" hit the Top 10 in 1979. Following the death of one of their members from cancer, the group recorded albums in 1989 and 1993.

Baldwin, Abraham. 1754–1807. Guilford, CT. This scholar, minister, and lawyer was a chaplain in the Continental Army. He was also a member of the Georgia House of Representatives and the Continental Congress. He is a signer of the Constitution of the United States, and he was a member of the first five Congresses as a U.S. senator.

Basinger, Kim. b. 1953. Athens. Film actress.

Berry, Martha McChesney. 1866–1942. Rome. Educator, founder of Berry College. She devoted most of her lifetime to providing educational opportunities for some of the country's poorest children—mostly "highlanders" from the southern Appalachians. The original Berry School was a day

school in a cabin, and it has since grown to a college campus of 33,000 acres. Berry developed a system of vocational education that served as a model for other school systems. She had a program that consisted of hard work, on-the-job training, and students' commitment to their own education.

Birney, Alice McLellan. 1858–1907. Marietta. She is the founder of the PTA (Parent-Teacher Association) that began with the National Congress of Mothers in 1897. In 1925, the organization was renamed the National Congress of Parents and Teachers, and eventually, it became the PTA. (See *Selena Sloan Butler.*)

Bowie, James. 1796?–1836. Burke Co. Legends have sprung up about Bowie, but apparently he didn't invent the famous knife bearing his last name—that was the work of his brother Rezin. The bowie knife was a heavy foot-long hunting knife with a guarded handle that was so well balanced, men could throw it with great accuracy. Bowie died at the Alamo (San Antonio, TX) in the fight for independence from Mexico.

Brown, James. Born either in 1928 in Pulaski, TN, or (as Brown himself has said) in 1933 in Macon. Despite his up-and-down personal life, including a time in prison, he is the "Godfather of Soul," although he has sold best in the rhythm and blues field.

Burns, Olive Ann. 1924–90. Banks Co. Longtime newspaper columnist for the

Atlanta Journal under the name of Amy Larkin; best known for her 1984 novel *Cold Sassy Tree.*

Butler, Selena Sloan. 1867–1964. Thomasville. Born of mixed parentage (her mother was white, her father African-American and Native American), she organized the first night school for African-Americans in Atlanta. Eventually, she organized the Parent-Teacher Association for Negroes and later called it the National Congress of Colored Parents and Teachers. Although she was a contemporary of Alice McLellan Birney (see above), they probably never met. (Note: In 1976, the governor of Georgia declared Founders Day and unveiled portraits of Birney and Butler to hang in the State Education Building in Atlanta.)

Caldwell, Erskine. 1903–87. White Oak. Popular author of 1930s and 1940s, whose novels include *Tobacco Road* and *God's Little Acre.*

Candler, Asa Griggs. 1851–1929. Villa Rica. He bought the formula for a revolutionary drink in 1886 from J. S. Pemberton for $2,300. In 1890, he began to manufacture something called Coca-Cola.

Carter, Jimmy (James Earl). b. 1924. Plains. A nuclear physicist and farmer, he was governor of Georgia and then president of the U.S. (1977–81). Since leaving public office, Carter has become known as an ambassador of peace through the work of the Carter Presidential Center in Atlanta. He and his wife, Rosalynn, have been active in Habitat for Humanity—a volunteer organization that builds quality houses for low-income people.

Charles, Ray (born Ray Charles Robinson). b. 1930. Albany. This singer, pianist, and composer was blinded by glaucoma at age six. In 1951, his "Baby, Let Me Hold Your Hand" was one of the top rhythm and blues numbers for the year. Three of his biggest hits ("You Don't Know Me," "You Are My Sunshine," and "I Can't Stop Loving You") came out in 1962. In 1967, he popularized the song "Georgia on My Mind." (In 1979, it became the official state song of Georgia.)

Coachman, Alice. b. 1926. Albany. Called the "black pearl of the 1948 Olympiad," she was the first African-American woman to win an Olympic gold. She won the gold for the high jump and set a world record that held until 1960. Inducted into Georgia Hall of Fame and Black Hall of Fame, 1974.

Cobb, Ty. 1886–1961. Narrows, Banks Co. This baseball player was known as the "Georgia Peach."

Coburn, Charles. 1877–1961. Macon. Actor. He won the best supporting Oscar for his role in *The More the Merrier* (1943). Among his other better-known films are *The Devil and Miss Jones* (1941) and *Gentlemen Prefer Blondes* (1953).

Conroy, Pat. b. 1945. Atlanta. His novels have been made into movies such as *The*

Prince of Tides, The Water Is Wide (filmed as *Conrack*), and *The Great Santini* (film version has also been released as *Mr. Ace*). He wrote the 1995 best-seller *Beach Music*.

Davis, Mac. b. 1941. Lubbock, TX. This songwriter-singer hit the top of the charts in 1961 when Lou Rawls recorded his "You're Good to Me" and Glen Campbell did his "Within My Memory." In 1968, Elvis Presley recorded his "A Little Less Conversation." For Presley, he also wrote "In the Ghetto," "Memories," and "Don't Cry, Darling." His best-known song, which he and more than 50 artists recorded, is "I Believe in Music."

Dickey, James. b. 1923. Atlanta. Poet and writer of *Deliverance*.

Dorsey, Thomas Andrew. 1899–1993. Villa Rica. He has been called the father of gospel music. He wrote more than a thousand songs, but he is most identified with "Precious Lord, Take My Hand." In 1979, he was the first African-American elected to the Nashville Songwriters Association's International Hall of Fame. He was the subject of the film *Say Amen, Somebody* (1982).

DuBois, William Edward Burghardt. 1868–1963. Great Barrington, MA. He lived in Atlanta 23 years and taught at Atlanta University. This civil rights leader was the first African-American to receive a Ph.D. at Harvard (1895). In 1910, he helped found the National Association for the Advancement of Colored People (NAACP).

Felton, Rebecca Ann Latimer. 1835–1930. DeKalb Co. This columnist and author became an important factor in Georgia politics when society discouraged feminine participation. The Democrats of Georgia called her a thorn in the flesh because of her outspoken advocacy of political and social reform. By interim appointment, in 1922, she became the first female U.S. senator.

Foxworthy, Jeff. b. 1958. Hapeville. Comedian. His TV sitcom *The Jeff Foxworthy Show* debuted in 1995 on ABC. His album *You Might Be a Redneck if . . .* has sold more than two million copies.

Fraser, Alexa Stirley. 1897–1977. Atlanta. Top female golfer. When she won the Women's National at age 18, she was the youngest ever to win the coveted prize. (Note: Fraser grew up with golf great Bobby Jones. She claimed she once beat Jones in a game—in childhood.)

Georgia Satellites. This Atlanta-based rock group began in 1982 and broke up two years later. But because their former road manager took one of their rejected demo tapes to London, they reunited and became an instant hit there. In 1987, they released their first big seller, "Keep Your Hands to Yourself."

Gingrich, Newt (Newton Leroy). b. 1943. Harrisburg, PA. The Georgia Republican was first elected to the House of Representatives in 1975. After the 1994 elections, he became the first Republican Speaker of the House in 40 years. A former history professor, he and other Republican House members wrote *Contract with America* (1994). He is the author of *To Renew America* (1995) and a World War II novel with William R. Fortschen called *1945*.

Grady, Henry Woodfin. 1850–99. Athens. Spokesman for the "New South," he was the managing editor of the *Atlanta Constitution*. He worked passionately to draw northern capital; he urged diversification and helped move Georgia from an agrarian to an industrialized state.

Grant, Amy. b. 1961. Augusta. At age 22, she was named Gospel Artist of the Year by the Gospel Music Association and won the Dove Award for her "Age to Age." By the early 1990s, she had moved into pop music with her album *Baby, Baby*.

Grizzard, Lewis. 1946–94. Moreland. Columnist and author of volumes of humor such as *Kathy Sue Loudermilk, I Love You* and *Won't You Come Home, Billy Bob Bailey?*

Hardy, Oliver. 1892–1957. Harlem. The comedian with the expressive eyes, cherubic face, and bulky figure began his career at age eight, but he won enduring fame after he teamed with Stan Laurel in 1926. They started in silent one-reel comedies and endured until the early 1950s.

Harris, Corra. 1869–1935. Born somewhere in Georgia. The *Saturday Evening Post* sent her to Europe during World War I as a war correspondent. She holds the distinction of being the first American female war correspondent.

Harris, Joel Chandler. 1848–1908. Eatonton. This short-story writer was sometimes called Georgia's Aescp. His creations such as Uncle Remus and Brer Rabbit are better known than the writer. Yet both Mark Twain and James Whitcomb Riley called him "a writer of originality and talent." His Uncle Remus stories began with "Tar-Baby Story" in 1879.

Hart, Nancy Morgan. Unknown dates and places of birth and death, although probably born in North Carolina. She was called the scourge of the Tories and British on the Georgia frontier during the American Revolution. The Native Americans called her War Woman. This six-foot-tall woman fought beside General Clark and his men, and one time she was in charge of a fort when it was attacked by the British. Almost single-handedly, she drove away the enemy. Congress appropriated money in Hart Co. for a monument to her in 1931. (Note: LaGrange is the home of the only female militia to serve in the Civil War. They were called the Nancy Harts and fought on April 17, 1865. The Civil War had already ended, although they didn't know it. Supposedly, enemy soldiers allowed themselves to be captured and promised not to burn the town's business district.)

Hartsfield, William Berry. 1890–1971. Atlanta. He was a lawyer-politician, and longtime Atlanta mayor. The Atlanta airport is named after him.

Heisman, John William. 1869–1936. Cleveland, OH. He is considered one of the top football coaches in the history of the sport. He never had a losing season at Georgia Tech in 16 years. He also wrote *Principles of Football* (1922). The Heisman Trophy was named after him. This is awarded annually to the nation's top college football player as elected by sports writers.

Henderson, Fletcher Hamilton, Jr. 1897–1952. Cuthbert. Musician, pianist, and orchestra leader.

Hunter, Holly. b. 1958. Atlanta. Stage and Oscar-winning actress (*The Piano,* 1993).

Indigo Girls. Based in Decatur, one of the duo, Amy Ray, is a native, while Emily Saliers grew up in New Haven, CT. They began to play together in 1983 in local clubs. The platinum debut album *Indigo Girls* was released in 1989. They appeared with Whoopi Goldberg in the 1995 film *Boys on the Side.*

Jackson, Alan. b. 1958. Newnan. Currently one of the top country singers.

James, Harry. 1916–83. Albany. He was one of the most famous orchestra leaders and trumpeters of the big band era of the 1930s and 1940s. He and his orchestra also appeared in a number of films, most notably *Springtime in the Rockies* (1942) in which he starred with his future wife, Betty Grable.

John, Elton. b. 1947. Pinner, Middlesex, England. He began to play when he was four years old. He writes most of his own music with lyricist Bernie Taupin. This famous resident of Atlanta has had a long string of hits such as his albums *Friends* (1971), *Goodbye, Yellow Brick Road* (1973), and *Too Low for Zero* (1983). Among his singles are "Don't Let the Sun Go Down on Me" (1974) and "I'm Still Standing" (1983). He composed the music for the Disney film *Lion King.*

Johnson, Nunnally. 1897–1977. Columbus. Movie producer and director, but best known as screenwriter for *Grapes of Wrath* and *Tobacco Road.*

Jones, Bobby (Robert Tyre, Jr.). 1902–71. Atlanta. He is still referred to as the world's greatest golfer. He founded the Masters Tournament. He is the only person ever to win the Grand Slam (the four major golf championships in one year: U.S. Open, British Open, Masters, and PGA championship). He retired in 1930, but his record remains unsurpassed.

Jordan, Clarence. 1912–69. Talbotton. Clergyman. Founder of Koinonia Farm in 1942. Openly opposed Ku Klux Klan (KKK).

Kemble, Frances Ann. 1809–93. England. This British actress never lived in Georgia, but she visited a Georgia plantation and wrote her observations in her journal. It was published at the height of the Civil War as

Journal of a Residence on a Georgian Plantation in 1838–1839. It became extremely popular in the North and in England. Many believe it persuaded English leaders to side with the Union. Had they supported the South, the Confederacy might have won. (Note: A portrait of her by Thomas Sully hangs in the White House!)

King, Coretta Scott. b. 1927. Marion, AL. Since the death of her husband, Martin Luther King, Jr., in 1968, she has been the president of the Martin Luther King, Jr., Center for Social Change, headquartered in Atlanta.

King, Martin Luther, Jr. 1929–68. Atlanta. Preacher and civil rights leader. Advocate of nonviolent social change. In 1963, he led the most momentous march of his career in Washington, D.C., with a crowd of nearly 250,000—at least a third of them whites. Winner of 1964 Nobel Peace Prize.

Knight, Gladys. b. 1944. Atlanta. Singer. With her group, the Pips, she made her first hit in 1961 with "Every Beat of My Heart." It was a rhythm and blues hit as well as pop success. Their recording of "I Heard It on the Grapevine" (1967) put them at the top of the music field. "Midnight Train to Georgia" is one of her more popular songs.

Lanier, Sidney. 1842–81. Macon. Musician (flutist) and poet. Best-known poems are "The Marshes of Glynn" and "Song of the Chattahoochee."

Lee, Brenda (born Brenda Mae Tarpley). b. 1944. Lithonia. Nominated twice for a Grammy, "Little Miss Dynamite" has never won, although she has won every other major music award. She has sold about 100 million records, including 12 gold singles.

Little Richard (born Richard Wayne Penniman). b. 1935. Macon. His recording of "Tutti Frutti" (1956) sold a million copies and became the official rock song of Georgia in 1989. His other best-known recording is "Good Golly, Miss Molly." In 1986, he was inducted into the Rock 'n' Roll Hall of Fame.

Long, Crawford Williamson. 1815–78. Danielsville. Physician believed to have been the first to use ether for surgical anesthesia.

Low, Juliette Magill Kinzie Gordon. 1860–1927. Savannah. She is the founder of Girl Scouts of America. She was later honored by having her picture on an official U.S. postage stamp.

Lowery, Joseph E. b. 1924. Huntsville, AL. A Methodist pastor in Birmingham and Atlanta, and a one-time instructor at Emory University, Lowery was an early civil rights activist. He has been president of the Southern Christian Leadership Conference (SCLC) since 1977.

Lundquist, Steve. b. 1961. Jonesboro. He won two Olympic gold medals in 1984 for the 100-meter breaststroke and the 400-meter medley relay.

Lynyrd Skynyrd. This group was founded by Ronnie Van Zant, who died in a plane crash in 1977. It took its name in 1965 by respelling the name of a high school gym teacher, Leonard Skinerd, who made them get haircuts. Van Zant's lyrics spoke of the rage of working-class southern youths finding it impossible to achieve the good life. Many young people resonated with the songs.

McCullers, Carson (Lula Carson Smith). 1917–67. Columbus. She is the author of *A Member of the Wedding* and *The Heart Is a Lonely Hunter*. Longtime editor of the *Atlanta Constitution,* Ralph McGill, wrote at the time of her death, "I think Carson was one of the two or three best Southern writers."

McIntosh, William (Tustunugee Hutkee). 1778–1825. Coweta Town. This Coweta chieftain was a Creek political leader.

McLendon, Mary Latimer. 1840–1921. DeKalb Co. Temperance and women's suffrage leader, sometimes called Mother of Suffrage in Georgia.

Mason, Lowell. 1792–1872. Medfield, MA. He was a musician, composer, and educator, best known for his arrangement of "When I Survey the Wondrous Cross." We claim him in Georgia because he was the organizer-director of Savannah's Independent Presbyterian Church.

Melton, James. 1904–61. Moultrie. He was unquestionably one of the most versatile singers of his day. He was equally good with folk songs or operatic roles. The United Press International said at the time of his death that he was "one of the most popular music personalities ever produced by the United States." He did concerts with George Gershwin, and he made several musical films in the 1930s. For 10 years, beginning in 1942, he sang with the Metropolitan Opera. His success was credited with ending a prejudice of the Met against singers from the popular music field.

Mercer, Johnny. 1909–76. Savannah. One of the great lyricist composers of popular music, he wrote "Laura," "That Old Black Magic," "Autumn Leaves," and "Ac-Cent-Tchu-Ate the Positive" with a total of 701 published songs, 90 film credits, six Broadway musicals, and 37 hit parade songs. He won four Oscars (out of 15 nominations) for lyrics he wrote for songs for the screen, "On the Atchison, Topeka, and Santa Fe" from *The Harvey Girls* (1946); "In the Cool, Cool, Cool of the Evening" from *Here Comes the Groom* (1951); "Moon River" from *Breakfast at Tiffany's* (1961); and the title song from *Days of Wine and Roses* (1962). He also appeared in several films.

Miller, Zell Bryan. b. 1932. Young Harris. Gov. of Georgia since 1990. Lt. gov. 1975–90. He is a former professor of political science and history at the University of Georgia and the author of *The Mountains Within Men, Great Georgians,* and *They Heard Georgia Singing.*

Milsap, Ronnie. b. 1944. Robbinsville, NC. Born blind from congenital glaucoma, Milsap graduated from Young Harris College in North Georgia. He has won three Grammys (out of five nominations) for Best Male Country Vocal Performance. In 1977, he swept the Country Music Association Awards when he received the awards for Entertainer, Male Vocalist, and Album of the Year. He holds virtually every other country music award for which he has been eligible. He has six gold albums, one platinum album, and the only gold braille album ever awarded to an artist. His 1980s single hits include "She Keeps the Home Fires Burning," "I Wouldn't Have Missed It for the World," and "Any Day Now." In 1987, he had a hit with Kenny Rogers singing "Make No Mistake, She's Mine."

Mitchell, Margaret (Peggy). 1900–1949. Atlanta. Author who received the Pulitzer Prize in fiction for *Gone with the Wind* in 1937.

Mother's Finest. The Atlanta-based group is a southern band with "neo-soul," and in 1976, they debuted with their first album. They achieved success with *Another Mother Further* in 1977.

Musgrove, Mary (born: Cousaponakeesa). 1700?–1763. Coweta Town. She and her husband, John Musgrove, established a trading post in 1732 near the Yamacraw Indians and settlers. Because the Native Americans trusted her and so did the English, she spoke both languages, became a mediator, and helped to make the settlement of Georgia peaceful. Because of her, Chief Tomochichi and General Oglethorpe were friendly. (Note: The English treated Cousaponakeesa badly and didn't pay her as they had promised. At one point she and a band of Native Americans marched on Savannah. The British gave her a cash settlement and title to St. Catherine's Island.)

Norman, Jessye. b. 1945. Augusta. This opera singer has a three-octave range (she can sing from contralto to mezzo to lyric or dramatic soprano), and she was recognized for her unique talent in Europe long before she joined the New York Metropolitan Opera in 1983.

Nunn, Sam (Samuel). b. 1938. Perry. A conservative Democrat, Nunn was elected to the U.S. Senate in 1972. Since 1985, he has been chairman or the ranking member of the Armed Services Committee and the dominant presence on the panel. He was so popular that in 1990, the Republicans did not run anyone against him. In 1995, he announced he would not run for reelection after his current term expires.

O'Connor, (Mary) Flannery. 1925–64. Milledgeville. Author best known for her short stories, such as "A Good Man Is Hard to Find." Her novel *Wise Blood* was made into a successful film.

Pemberton, John Smith. 1831–88. Knoxville. He invented the formula for Coca-Cola and sold it to Candler.

Piano Red (born William or Willie Lee Perryman). b. 1906. Hampton. In 1951, he made a record "Rockin' with Red"—which was the first rock 'n' roll record. His record, released by RCA Victor, went gold.

Queen of Cofachiqui. (See feature.)

Rainey, "Ma" (Gertrude). 1886–1939. Columbus. Famous blues singer with well-known bands and band leaders such as Louis Armstrong.

Redding, Otis. 1941–67. Dawson. Although he died in a plane crash in 1967, he is known as the writer and singer of sentimental soul ballads that built a bridge between black and white music. "(Sittin' on) the Dock of the Bay" was his only gold single.

Reed, Jerry (born Jerry Reid Hubbard). b. 1937. Atlanta. He has written more than 400 songs, won two Grammys and a number of other music awards, and acted in several films.

R.E.M. Athens. This rock group was formed in the early 1980s. They claim their name comes from a random sequence of letters, though matched with rapid eye movement—the state of sleep when dreaming takes place. "Talk About the Passion" became one of the critics' early favorites.

Roberts, Julia. b. 1967. Smyrna. Screen actress, best known for her roles in *Steel Magnolias, Pretty Woman,* and *Something to Talk About.*

Robinson, Jackie (Jack Roosevelt). 1919–72. Cairo. In 1946, Robinson became the first African-American to play in organized professional baseball. In 1947, he joined the Dodgers in Brooklyn. In 1949, he won the National League's batting championship and was also named its most valuable player. In 1962, he was the first African-American elected to the National Baseball Hall of Fame.

Rusk, David Dean. 1909–94. Cherokee Co. First Georgian to hold the office of the secretary of state since John Forsyth under Andrew Jackson. He served in that position longer than anyone else except Cordell Hull (under Franklin Roosevelt). Except for the eight years of the Eisenhower administration, when he was president of the Rockefeller Foundation, he was involved in the formulation or execution of every major foreign policy decision of the U.S. from World War II until the end of the Johnson administration in 1969.

Sequoyah, or George Guess. 1770?–1843. Taskgi, TN. Silversmith, artist, and spokesperson for the Cherokee, he is best known as the inventor of the Cherokee syllabary (written language using phonetic approach of 86 basic sounds). In 1827, he published *Missionary Herald* in Georgia and beginning in 1828, *Cherokee Phoenix,* a national bilingual newspaper, for six years.

Smith, Lillian. 1897–1966. Jasper, FL. Writer and human rights advocate. Her controversial novel *Strange Fruit* (1944) was censored or banned in many cities, but it still became a best-seller and was translated into 14 languages. Her novel, an indictment against southern culture, especially segregation, was a love story about a white man who loved and married a black woman. In her book *Killers of the Dream,* she wrote that southern women of both races, working through their churches, were trying to fight the system and find better ways to live together.

South, Joe. b. 1943. Atlanta. This songwriter-singer is best known for "Games People Play" (1969), which has been recorded by 125 other major artists, and Lynn Anderson's recording in 1971 of his "(I Never Promised You a) Rose Garden."

Stevens, Ray (born Harold R. Ragsdale). b. 1939. Clarksdale. This versatile performer once played in a combo with Jerry Reed and Joe South. He has recorded both humorous and serious music, and he is a keyboard artist. He wrote the lyrics to a French tune and called it "Everything Is Beautiful."

Stuckey, Williamson Sylvester. 1909–77. Eastman. He is associated with Stuckey's pecans and pralines. He became so successful that Pet Milk bought the name and the product.

Tomochichi, chief of the Yamacraws. 1640?– 1737. Born somewhere in the South. He is remembered for aiding in the founding of the Georgia colony. He was a benefactor of Sir James Edward Oglethorpe (who founded the Georgia colony).

Tritt, Travis. b. 1953. Marietta. His first three albums went platinum: *Country Club* (1990), *It's All About Change* (1991), and *T-R-O-U-B-L-E* (1992). Two hit singles from 1994 are "Here's a Quarter, Call Someone Who Cares" and "Can I Trust You with My Heart?" Among his many awards, he was *Billboard* magazine's top new vocalist in 1990; he received the Country Music Horizon Award (1991); he was named CMA Vocal Event of the Year (1992); and he was inducted into the Grand Ole Opry in 1992.

Troutman, Joanna E. 1820–79. Baldwin Co. In 1835, she presented a volunteer company of soldiers from Macon with a flag she had made. They carried the flag through their battles in Texas on behalf of independence from Mexico. It was made of white silk with a blue star in the center. It later became the official flag of Texas, the Lone Star State.

Turner, Ted (Robert Edward III). b. 1938. Cincinnati, OH. This entertainment mogul took over the family business of Turner Advertising. Today he owns TV channels TBS, CNN, CNN International, and CNN Headline News, and more recently, he launched a TV channel for romance classics. He owns a portion of the MGM/RKO film library that contains the best films of the past, including *Gone with the Wind.* (In 1995, Turner announced the sale of TBS to Time-

Warner to create the world's largest media company. He will remain as vice chairman.) Turner also owns the Atlanta Hawks basketball team and the 1995 World Series winners, the Atlanta Braves.

Tyus, Wyomia (later Tyus-Simberg). b. 1945. Griffin. Olympic runner. In 1964, she won the gold medal for the 100-meter dash. In 1968, she set the world record in 100 meters, and she won three gold medals and one silver.

Vann, Joseph. 1800–1844. Cherokee Nation (Murray Co.). Cherokee leader.

Vinson, Carl. 1883–1981. Baldwin Co. He served an unequaled record of more than 50 years in the U.S. House of Representatives.

Walker, Alice. b. 1944. Eatonton. Author and Pulitzer Prize winner for *The Color Purple.*

Wesley, Charles. 1707–88. Epworth, England. One of the founders of Methodism and younger brother of John Wesley, he is best known as a writer of 6,500 hymns. His two best known are "Jesus, Lover of My Soul" and "Love Divine, All Loves Excelling." He was once secretary to James Edward Oglethorpe, the founder of Georgia.

Wesley, John. 1703–91. Epworth, England. One-time missionary to the Colony of Georgia. He bears the name most associated with the founding of the Methodist Church.

Wet Willie. Now based in Atlanta, the original five members of this "Dixie rock" group played together in high school in Mobile, AL. In the 1970s, their big hit was "Keep on Smiling," and they followed it with two other biggies, "Street Corner Serenade" and "Weekends."

Whitney, Eli. 1765–1825. Westboro, MA. He adapted the roller-style cotton gin in Georgia and received a patent for it.

Woodruff, Robert W. 1889–1985. Columbus. He became president of Coca-Cola at age 33 and proved himself to be a genius of industrial concepts and merchandising techniques. For more than half a century, he was a philanthropist and leading Atlantan. He not only saw to it that the soft drink reached the rest of the world, but he promoted civil rights and gave away more than $400 million to Atlanta educational, artistic, civil, and medical projects such as the High Museum, the Woodruff Arts Center, and Emory University.

Woodward, Joanne. b. 1930. Thomasville. She won an Oscar for best actress for her film role in *The Three Faces of Eve* (1957), based on a true study of a mental patient in Augusta. She also won the Cannes Film Festival award for best actress for *The Effect of Gamma Rays on Man-in-the-Moon Marigolds* (1972), and an Emmy for best actress for her role in the TV movie *See How She Runs* (1978).

Wylie, Lollie Belle. 1858–1923. She was the first woman in Georgia to hold a regular job as a reporter with a daily newspaper. She also composed the music for Robert Loveman's poem "Georgia," which became the official state song in 1922. (In 1979, the Hoagy Carmichael–Charles Gorell tune "Georgia on My Mind" became the new official state song.)

Yearwood, Trisha. b. 1964. Monticello. Before bursting into the spotlight on her own, this country singer was the opening act for Garth Brooks. Her first album, *Trisha Yearwood* (1991), went platinum (sold more than a million copies). She's the first female in country music to have a debut single reach the number one spot on the charts. The song was "She's in Love with Love." In 1992, Yearwood's album *Hearts in Armor* was nominated for a Grammy, as was *Walk Away, Joe* in 1994. The Academy of Country Music named her the top new female vocalist in 1992.

Young, Andrew. b. 1932. New Orleans, LA. He was an early figure in the civil rights movement, along with Martin Luther King, Jr., and others. From 1962 to 1970, he held positions with the Southern Christian Leadership Conference (SCLC). He served in the U.S. House of Representatives (1972–76), was the U.S. ambassador to the United Nations (1977–79), and was mayor of Atlanta (1982–90).

MUSIC! MUSIC!

Here are a few of the individuals and groups that come from Georgia originally or have strong associations with our state.

Peabo Bryson, who calls himself a romantic ballad singer, continues to bring out top recordings and concerts. He has sung with top female vocalists such as Natalie Cole, Roberta Flack, and Melissa Manchester. **Fiddlin' John Carson** (1868–1949; Fannin Co.) was the first to record country music and broadcast in the days of those media's infancy in the early 1920s. **The Tams**, five young men with the desire to break out of the Atlanta ghetto, developed a unique dancing and singing style. They wore T-shirts and jeans with matching multicolored tam-o'-shanters that go back to the 1950s. Since the 1960s, they have been favorites with rhythm and blues music fans. **Hedy West**, born in 1938 in Cartersville, is a classic folk singer, better known in Europe than America. **Atlanta** country music group has done well since being nominated by the Country Music Association in 1984 for Group of the Year. **Carole Joyner** of Decatur composed "Young Love" with Ric Carty that sold more than 15 million copies and was a hit for Lesley Gore, Tab Hunter, Sonny James, and Donny Osmond. **Anita Sorralls Wheeler Mathis** was the only woman to win the Georgia Fiddler Championship (1934).

Singer **Jim Nabors,** long before his TV work on *Gomer Pyle,* worked for a TV station in Augusta. Atlanta-born **Bert Parks** was the singing master of ceremonies for years for the Miss America Pageant. Before he played in the TV series *The Dukes of Hazzard,* Atlanta-born singer and actor

John Schneider became a teenage sensation at the Crystal Pistol Revue at Six Flags Over Georgia. One of the finest rock groups to come out of the South has been **.38 Special**. One of its founders, Jeff Carlisle, is from Atlanta, although most of the group grew up in Jacksonville, Florida. You've probably never heard of **Roba Stanley,** but in 1924, she was country music's first sweetheart—long before Loretta Lynn and Dolly Parton came along. She was the first female to sing solo on radio and record.

GEORGIA MUSIC HALL OF FAME INDUCTEES

1979 Bill Lowery (nonperformer)
Ray Charles (performer)

1980 Zenas "Daddy" Sears (nonperformer)
Ray Stevens (performer)
Johnny Mercer (posthumous)

1981 Thomas A. Dorsey (nonperformer)
Joe South (performer)
Otis Redding (posthumous)

1982 Boudleaux Bryant (nonperformer)
Brenda Lee (performer)
Duane Allman (posthumous)

1983 Albert Coleman (nonperformer)
James Brown (performer)
Harry James (posthumous)
Piano Red Perryman
   (pioneer award)

1984 Buddy Buie (nonperformer)
Little Richard Penniman
   (performer)
James Melton (posthumous)
Fiddlin' John Carson
   (pioneer award)

1985 Zell Miller (nonperformer)
Bill Anderson (performer)
Graham Jackson (posthumous)
Eva Mae LeFevre (pioneer award)

1986 Phil Walden (nonperformer)
Tommy Roe (performer)
George Riley Puckett (posthumous)
Hovie Lister (pioneer award)

1987 Alex Cooley (nonperformer)
Jerry Reed (performer)
Felton Jarvis (posthumous)
Bob Richardson (pioneer award)

1988 Robert L. Shaw (nonperformer)
Billy Joe Royal (performer)
Gid Tanner (posthumous)
Joe Williams (pioneer award)

1989 Harold Shedd (nonperformer)
Gladys Knight (performer)
Fletcher Henderson (posthumous)
Lee Roy Abernathy (pioneer award)

1990 Chips Moman (nonperformer)
Ronnie Milsap (performer)
Willie Samuel McTell (posthumous)
Wendy Bagwell (pioneer award)

1991 Ray Whitley (nonperformer)
Lena Horne (performer)
Roland Hayes (posthumous)

Cotton Carrier (pioneer award)

1992 Emory Gordy, Jr. (nonperformer)
Connie Haines (performer)
Gertrude "Ma" Rainey
(posthumous)
The Tams (pioneer award)
The Lewis Family (group)

1993 J. R. Cobb (nonperformer)
Curtis Mayfield (performer)
Sam Wallace (posthumous)
Dennis Yost & Classics IV
(group)

1994 Gwen Kessler (nonperformer)
Isaac Hayes (performer)
Chuck Willis (posthumous)

1995 Joel Katz (nonperformer)
Chet Atkins (performer)
Ray Eberle (posthumous)

RACING

Georgians have also represented themselves well on the NASCAR circuit. The best known is Dawsonville's **Bill Elliott,** but other top Georgia drivers include **Lloyd Seay** and **Roy Hall** from Dawson Co.

Elliott, Bill. b. 1955. Dawsonville. Known as Awesome Bill from Dawsonville, this NASCAR–Winston Cup champion was voted eight times as the most popular NASCAR driver. Today he is considered one of the top ten drivers.

Mundy, Franklin. b. 1917. Atlanta. This two-time national NASCAR champion and three-time Winston Cup Event winner retired in 1956. However, he set numerous stock car records that still stand.

GEORGIA'S GORGEOUS OUTDOORS

We think Georgia is the best place to visit in the United States. For us, this state has just about everything. Think about the varied—and beautiful—mountains, coast, woods, rivers, and swamplands. Although Georgia gets a few nippy days of winter and some snow, its mild climate makes the state a fantastic place for every type of outdoor recreation at least 10 months a year.

THREE NATIONAL PARKS IN GEORGIA

1. Chattahoochee–Oconee National Forest. This national forest covers 859,000 acres of prime woodland. The Chattahoochee portion encircles most of North Georgia, and the Oconee offers a piedmont forest north of Macon (Middle Georgia). The many campgrounds provided by the

Forest Service (FS) range from primitive isolated sites to developed recreation area camps. Three hundred miles of trails for hikers and backpackers include three outstanding long-distance trails through the Blue Ridge Mountains.

The world's most famous trail, the Appalachian Trail (AT), begins in North Georgia and runs 78 miles within the state. From there it runs 2,036 miles through 14 states and seven national parks and ends in Maine. The 50-mile Benton MacKaye Trail, named for the founder of the AT, runs laterally across Georgia from the Tennessee line to its junction with the AT. Traditionally, May is the month for "thru-hikers"— those who want to hike all the way to Maine.

If you're a hiker, you might want to try the 30-mile William Bartram Trail, named for the 18th-century naturalist who pioneered the route. This trail runs through the most dense and remote corner of Georgia's Blue Ridge. Among the trails in the national forest, you'll find a variety to accommodate mountain bikes, horses, off-road vehicles, or persons with disabilities. In the forest you'll find places to swim as well as lakeshore beaches, rock-climbing routes, and thousands of acres of boating lakes and streams for fishing.

Visit any ranger station for recreation area directories and trail maps, or write to the central office for more information: U.S. Forest Service, 508 Oak St. NW, Gainesville, GA 30501. Or call 706-536-0541 (reach the "leaf watch" newsline at 706-536-1310).

2. Cumberland Island National Seashore. Cumberland Island National Seashore at Georgia's southern coast preserves the natural environment of the lovely subtropical island. This 16-mile-long barrier island is the place to watch native wild horses, bobcats, and wild turkeys. It is also the breeding ground for the loggerhead sea turtle and the rare right whale. Like most of Georgia's undeveloped barrier islands, Cumberland has a fine beach. Make reservations early, especially if you plan to visit in the summer. The FS allows only 300 visitors a day. A daily ferry operated by the National Park Service from St. Marys is the only access to the island. Admission: adults $7.50 round-trip; discounts for seniors and children. Reservations: 912-882-4335.

3. Okefenokee Swamp. The name means "Land of the Trembling Earth." This term describes the principal feature of most of the land in the swamp. New vegetation grows faster than the old can decompose and produces deep layers of peat on top of the sand that was once the ocean floor. The decomposing layers of peat produce methane gas, which causes great masses of peat to break away from the bottom of the swamp and float to the surface. Grasses, shrubs, and eventually trees grow on the masses, and it then forms a new island. The island is anchored somewhat by roots, but it shakes when you step on it, hence the name trembling earth.

The swamp encompasses 423,721 acres of southeastern Georgia with a few acres in the northeastern corner of Florida. Up to 90 percent of the water that enters the swamp comes from rainfall. The water not lost to evaporation goes into the Suwanee River and the St. Marys River. The Okefenokee itself is the sluggish headwaters for those two rivers.

The Okefenokee is one of the largest and most ecologically intact swamps in North America. All over the swamp grow the tangled forests of holly, bay, cypress, and black gum. The black waters mirror majestic scenery with a mosaic of vegetation such as open prairies, scrub forests, towering bald cypress, and tupelo stands. A profusion of wildflowers blooms from early spring until late fall.

Everywhere you go, you'll see the famous shallow "black water"—stained by the tannic acid of decaying vegetation. It flows quietly into the swamp's outlets at the Suwanee and St. Marys Rivers. Along the watery lowland you can glimpse about 70 islands filled with southern pines that leave a lingering visual impression.

Okefenokee Swamp

The Okefenokee Swamp National Wildlife Refuge provides a sanctuary for alligators, softshell turtles, black bears, and many other animal species, which can best be seen by boat (rentals available). Canoeists can explore the exotic deep swamp wilderness on day or overnight trips (up to five days). The U.S. Fish and Wildlife Service, 912-496-3331, administers the refuge, which covers most of the swamp. (A state park administers another swamp entrance, and a private attraction occupies the third major access point.)

STATE PARKS

The 59 state parks and historic sites cover more than 60,000 acres of scenic variety and highlight many aspects of Georgia's natural and cultural heritage. Although available all year, most historic sites and all swimming and golf facilities are closed on Mondays, except on legal holidays.

Information about each of the state-operated historic sites is listed with the region in which it is found. Many of them (but not all) offer picnic facilities, museums, and nature or hiking trails. (Historic sites do not offer campsites, lodges, or cottages.) These sites include the following:

Dahlonega Gold Museum (see **North Georgia**)

Etowah Indian Mounds (see **North Georgia**)

Fort King George (see **Coastal Georgia**)

Fort Morris (see **Coastal Georgia**)

Hofwyl-Broadfield Plantation (see **Coastal Georgia**)

Jarrell Plantation (see **Middle Georgia**)

Lapham-Patterson House (see **South Georgia**)

Little White House (see **West Georgia**)

New Echota Cherokee Capital (see **North Georgia**)

Pickett's Mill Battlefield (see **North Georgia**)

Robert Toombs House (see **North Georgia**)

Traveler's Rest (see **North Georgia**)

Chief Vann House (see **North Georgia**)

Wormsloe (see **Coastal Georgia**)

Special Programs. Throughout the year you can take advantage of special programs that will help you experience and understand the rich natural and historic resources at Georgia's state parks and historic sites. Canoe excursions, backpacking clinics, hikes, wildflower displays, folk skills, living history demonstrations, music festivals, and special family-oriented holiday programs provide great getaway experiences. Call the nearest park or historic site or the division's Public Information Office at 404-656-3530 for up-to-date program information. Each March the Public Information Office issues a free guide to special events.

Georgia ParkPass. You'll have to buy a Georgia ParkPass to park in state parks. It is valid at all state parks visited the same day and is transferable among vehicles registered to the same household. It costs $2 for the daily parking fee, or you may purchase an annual parking pass for $25. For those 62 and older, the cost is $12.50. Wednesdays are free for day-use visitors. If you stay in lodges, cottages, or campgrounds, you pay one fee for the duration of your stay. Or-

ganized school groups visiting in buses are exempt.

Reservations. Toll-free numbers for making reservations at state parks: 770-389-PARK for callers in the Atlanta area; 800-864-PARK for everyone else.

For More Information. Contact the Georgia Department of Natural Resources, State Parks, and Historic Sites, 205 Butler St. SE, Atlanta, GA 30334. (Enclose a business-size SASE for speedy reply.) Or call the division's Public Information Office, Mon.–Fri. 8 a.m.–4:30 p.m. (EST): 404-656-3530.

Park Hours: Daily 7 a.m.–10 p.m., except for Panola Mountain, Providence Canyon, and Stephen C. Foster, which operate special seasonal schedules.

Historic Site Hours: Tue.–Sat. 9 a.m.–5 p.m.; Sun. 2–5:30 p.m. Closed Mon. and major holidays. Hours vary at the *Little White House:* Daily 9 a.m.–5 p.m. Closed major holidays. *Dahlonega Gold Museum:* Mon.–Sat. 9 a.m.–5 p.m.; Sun. 10 a.m.–5 p.m. Closed major holidays.

There is a small admission charge at historic sites; registered lodge and cottage guests are admitted free or at discounted rates.

Here's an alphabetical list of state parks with addresses and phone numbers, a brief note on location, and the overnight facilities available.

A. H. Stephens Historic Park, P.O. Box 283, Crawfordville, 30631. 706-456-2602. Two miles north of I-20 in Crawfordville.

North Georgia. Tent and trailer sites. Near I-20.

You can always tell the first-time campers...

Yeah. They forget to check for spiders **before** they get in the shower.

Amicalola Falls Park and Lodge, Star Rt., Box 215, Dawsonville, 30534. 706-265-8888. Sixteen miles northwest of Dawsonville via GA 183 and 52. North Georgia. Tent and trailer sites; lodge.

Black Rock Mountain Park, P.O. Drawer A, Mountain City, 30562. 706-746-2141. Three miles north of Clayton via US 441. North Georgia. Tent and trailer sites; cottages.

Bobby Brown Park, 2509 Bobby Brown State Park Rd., Elberton, 30635. 706-213-2046. Twenty-one miles southeast of Elberton off GA 72. North Georgia. Tent and trailer sites.

Cloudland Canyon Park, Rt. 2, Box 150, Rising Fawn, 30738. 706-657-4050. Twenty-five miles northwest of La Fayette off GA 136. North Georgia. Tent and trailer sites; cottages. Near I-59.

Crooked River Park, 3092 Spur 40, St. Marys, 31558. 912-882-5256. Seven miles north of St. Marys on GA Spur 40. Coastal Georgia. Tent and trailer sites; cottages. Near I-95.

Elijah Clark Park, 2959 McCormick Hwy., Lincolnton, 30817. 706-359-3458. Seven miles east of Lincolnton off US 378. North Georgia. Tent and trailer sites; cottages.

F. D. Roosevelt Park, 2970 GA Hwy. 190, Pine Mountain, 31822. 706-663-4858. Five miles southeast of Pine Mountain on GA 190. West Georgia. Tent and trailer sites; cottages. Near I-185.

Florence Marina Park, Rt. 1, Box 36, Omaha, 31821. 912-838-6870. Sixteen miles west of Lumpkin at end of GA 39 C. South Georgia. Tent and trailer sites; cottages.

Fort McAllister Historic Park, Rt. 2, Box 394-A, Richmond Hill, 31324. 912-727-2339. Ten miles east of I-95 and US 17 on Spur 144. Coastal Georgia. Tent and trailer sites. Near I-95.

Fort Mountain Park, 181 Fort Mountain Park Rd., Chatsworth, 30705. 706-695-2621. Eight miles east of Chatsworth via GA 52. North Georgia. Tent and trailer sites; cottages.

Fort Yargo Park and Wile-A-Way Recreation Area, P.O. Box 764, Winder, 30680. 770-867-3489 or 867-5313. One mile south of Winder on GA 81. North Georgia. Tent and trailer sites; cottages. Facilities for persons with disabilities.

General Coffee Park, Rt. 2, Box 83, Nicholls, 31554. 912-384-7082. Six miles east of Douglas on GA 32. South Georgia. Tent and trailer sites.

George L. Smith Park, P.O. Box 57, Twin City, 30471. 912-763-2759. Four miles southeast of Twin City off GA 23. Middle Georgia. Tent and trailer sites.

George T. Bagby Park and Lodge, Rt. 1, Box 201, Fort Gaines, 31751. 912-768-2571. Four miles north of Fort Gaines off GA 39. South Georgia. Lodge; cottages.

Georgia Veterans Park, 2459-A US Hwy. 280 W, Cordele, 31015. 912-276-2371. Nine miles west of Cordele via US 280. South Georgia. Tent and trailer sites; cottages. Near I-75.

Gordonia-Alatamaha Park, P.O. Box 1047, Reidsville, 30453. 912-557-6444. City limits of Reidsville off US 280. South Georgia. Tent and trailer sites.

Hamburg Park, Rt. 1, Box 233, Mitchell, 30820. 912-552-2393. Sixteen miles northeast of Sandersville on Hamburg Rd. Middle Georgia. Tent and trailer sites.

Hard Labor Creek Park, P.O. Box 247, Rutledge, 30663. 706-557-3001. Two

miles north of Rutledge off US 278. North Georgia. Tent and trailer sites; cottages. Near I-20.

Hamburg State Park

Hart Park, 1515 Hart Park Rd., Hartwell, 30643. 706-376-8756. Three miles north of Hartwell off US 29. North Georgia. Tent and trailer sites; cottages.

High Falls Park, Rt. 5, Box 202-A, Jackson, 30233. 912-994-5080. Ten miles north of Forsyth off I-75 (exit 65). Middle Georgia. Tent and trailer sites. Near I-75.

Indian Springs Park, 678 Lake Clark Rd., Flovilla, 30216. 770-775-7241. Five miles south of Jackson on GA 42. Middle Georgia. Tent and trailer sites; cottages.

James H. "Sloppy" Floyd Park, Rt. 1, Box 291, Summerville, 30747. 706-857-5211. Three miles southeast of Summerville off US 27. North Georgia. Tent and trailer sites.

John Tanner Park, 354 Tanner's Beach Rd., Carrollton, 30117. 770-830-2222. Six miles west of Carrollton on GA 16. West Georgia. Tent and trailer sites; cottages. Near I-20.

Kolomoki Mounds Historic Park, Rt. 1, Box 114, Blakely, 31723. 912-723-5296. Six miles north of Blakely off US 27. South Georgia. Tent and trailer sites.

Laura S. Walker Park, 5653 Laura Walker Rd., Waycross, 31503. 912-287-4900. Ten miles southeast of Waycross on GA 177. South Georgia. Tent and trailer sites.

Little Ocmulgee Park and Lodge, P.O. Box 149, McRae, 31055. 912-868-7474. Two miles north of McRae off US 441. South Georgia. Tent and trailer sites; lodge; cottages.

Magnolia Springs Park, Rt. 5, Box 488, Millen, 30442. 912-982-1660. Five miles north of Millen on US 25. Middle Georgia. Tent and trailer sites; cottages.

Mistletoe Park, 3723 Mistletoe Rd., Appling, 30802. 706-541-0321. Eight miles north of I-20 (exit 60). North Georgia. Tent and trailer sites; cottages.

Moccasin Creek Park, Rt. 1, Box 1634, Clarkesville, 30523. 706-947-3194. Twenty miles north of Clarkesville on GA 197. North Georgia. Tent and trailer sites.

Panola Mountain Conservation Park, 2600 Hwy. 155 SW, Stockbridge, 30281. 770-389-7801. Eighteen miles southeast of Atlanta on GA 155. Middle Georgia. No overnight facilities. Near I-20.

Providence Canyon Conservation Park, Rt. 1, Box 158, Lumpkin, 31815. 912-838-6202. Seven miles west of Lumpkin on GA 39 C. South Georgia. No overnight facilities.

Red Top Mountain Park and Lodge, 653 Red Top Mountain Rd. SE, Cartersville, 30120. 770-975-0055. One and one-half miles east of I-75 (exit 123). North Georgia. Tent and trailer sites; lodge; cottages. Near I-75.

Reed Bingham Park, Rt. 2, Box 394 B-1, Adel, 31620. 912-896-3551. Six miles west of Adel on GA 37 via I-75 (exit 10). South Georgia. Tent and trailer sites. Near I-75.

Richard B. Russell Park, 2650 Russell State Park Rd., Elberton, 30635. 706-213-2045. Ten miles north of Elberton off GA 77 on Ruckersville Rd. North Georgia. No overnight facilities.

Seminole Park, Rt. 2, Donalsonville, 31745. 912-861-3137. Sixteen miles south of Donalsonville via GA 39. South Georgia. Tent and trailer sites; cottages.

Skidaway Island Park, 52 Diamond Causeway, Savannah, 31411-1102. 912-598-2300. Six miles southeast of Savannah off Diamond Causeway. Coastal Georgia. Tent and trailer sites.

Stephen C. Foster Park, Rt. 1, Box 131, Fargo, 31631. 912-637-5274. Eighteen miles northeast of Fargo via GA 177. South Georgia. Tent and trailer sites; cottages.

Sweetwater Creek Conservation Park, P.O. Box 816, Lithia Springs, 30057. 770-732-5871. Fifteen miles west of Atlanta off I-20 (exit 12). Middle Georgia. No overnight facilities. Near I-20.

Tallulah Gorge Park, Terrora Park and Campground, P.O. Box 248, Tallulah Falls, 30573. 706-754-8257 or 754-6036. City limits of Tallulah Falls on US 441. North Georgia. Tent and trailer sites.

Tugaloo Park, 1763 Tugaloo State Park Rd., Lavonia, 30553. 706-356-4362. Six miles north of Lavonia off GA 328. North Georgia. Tent and trailer sites; cottages. Near I-85.

Unicoi Park and Lodge, P.O. Box 849, Helen, 30545. 706-878-2201. Two miles north of Helen on GA 356. North Georgia. Tent and trailer sites; lodge; cottages.

Victoria Bryant Park, 1105 Bryant Park Rd., Royston, 30662. 706-245-6270. Four miles west of Royston off US 29. North Georgia. Tent and trailer sites. Near I-85.

Vogel Park, 7485 Vogel State Park Rd., Blairsville, 30512. 706-745-2628. Eleven miles south of Blairsville via US 19/129. North Georgia. Tent and trailer sites; cottages.

Watson Mill Bridge Park, Rt. 2, Box 190, Comer, 30629. 706-783-5349. Six miles south of Comer on GA 22. North Georgia. Tent and trailer sites.

GEORGIA HOSTS THE 1996 OLYMPICS

Olympic Countdown Sign in Midtown Atlanta

Atlanta, the youngest city ever to host the Olympic Games, has prepared for the 1996 event (July 19–August 4) with new hotels, tour packages, the 70,500-seat Georgia Dome (which cost $214 million), the 10,000-seat open-air Olympic Velodrome at Stone Mountain Park, and an Olympic Village on the campus of the Georgia Institute of Technology.

The sites for most of the 1996 Summer Games lie within the Olympic Ring (an imaginary circle with a 1.5-mile radius extending from the center of Atlanta) and Stone Mountain Park, 16 miles east of Atlanta. Within the Ring are venues for 20 sports competitions, the Main Press Center, and the International Broadcast Center.

Some events will take place outside Atlanta such as archery and cycling (track) in the Stone Mountain Park, whitewater canoeing on the Ocoee River in Tennessee near the Georgia border, and yachting competitions off the coast of Savannah, 250 miles southeast of Atlanta. Some soccer events will take place at locations outside the state of Georgia: Birmingham, Alabama; Miami, Florida; Orlando, Florida; and Washington, DC.

INFORMATION SOURCES

For the latest information, the best source is the Atlanta Committee for the Olympic Games (ACOG): 404-224-1996. The ACOG operates a public information gallery and gift shop called the Olympic Experience (404-658-1996) in Underground Atlanta at the corner of Upper Alabama and Peachtree Streets, Mon.–Sat. 10 a.m.–9:30 p.m.; Sun. noon–6 p.m. Or call the Atlanta Convention and Visitors Bureau: 404-222-6688.

The Georgia Council for International Visitors provides a language bank of about 45 languages: 404-873-6170, Mon.–Fri. 9 a.m.–5 p.m. for assistance with translators, interpreters, or tour guides. Travelers Aid numbers: Airport: 404-766-4511, daily 10 a.m.–6 p.m. Greyhound Bus Terminal on International Blvd.: 404-527-7411, Mon.–Fri. noon–8 p.m.; Sat. 10 a.m.–6 p.m. Greyhound Bus Terminal on Pryor Street: 404-527-7400, Mon.–Fri. 8 a.m.–5 p.m.; 24-hour phone. Visitors might also contact the Atlanta Convention and Visitors Bureau (ACVB): 404-222-6688.

TICKETS

The International Olympic Committee set ticket prices for the 1996 games so that most of them would not exceed $75. The most expensive tickets—for the opening and closing ceremonies—cost $200 to $600. For other events, ticket prices range from $6 (for preliminary baseball) to $250; the average seat will cost $39.72. Every sport will have at least one session with tickets available at or below $25. Only nine sports have tickets priced more than $75. Prices include transportation to and from the event.

The all-but-impossible tickets to buy are for the opening and closing ceremonies and finals in basketball, gymnastics, track and field, boxing, and volleyball.

All the Olympic Games don't sell out. The Atlanta Games will be the largest in history, with more tickets than those sold at Los Angeles and Barcelona combined. The ACOG will have 11 million tickets available. The committee is pioneering a new ticket sales system that allows the public to buy tickets for any event at any location, and regular updates about tickets will be available on site.

THE OLYMPIC EVENTS

Olympic events include preliminary, intermediate, and final rounds, a total of 560 events. Here are the areas of competition:

Archery	Basketball
Athletics	Boxing
(Track and Field)	Canoe/Kayak
Badminton	(Slalom)
Baseball	

Canoe/Kayak (Sprint)
Cycling (Mountain Bike)
Cycling (Road)
Cycling (Track)
Diving
Equestrian
Fencing
Gymnastics (Artistic)
Gymnastics (Rhythmic)
Handball
Hockey (Field)
Judo
Modern Pentathlon
Rowing
Shooting
Soccer (Football)
Softball
Swimming
Synchronized Swimming
Table Tennis
Tennis
Volleyball
Volleyball (Beach)
Water Polo
Weight Lifting
Wrestling (Freestyle)
Wrestling (Greco-Roman)
Yachting

TRANSPORTATION

For the first time, ticket prices include bus and rail transportation to and from Olympic sites. Atlanta's public transit system, Metropolitan Atlanta Rapid Transit Authority (MARTA), will be the backbone of the Olympic transportation system, with most events in the Olympic Ring located at or near rapid rail systems. During the 17 days of the Games, you can board free satellite buses from outer areas. The ACOG has designed most Olympic venues and transportation vehicles to be accessible to persons with disabilities.

The Olympic transportation system is an interconnected system of shuttle buses, rapid rail, pedestrian corridors, and park-and-ride lots to accommodate all spectators to sites inside the Olympic Ring. A supplemental fleet of more than 1,000 transit buses, provided by cities from across the United States, will move spectators from areawide park-and-ride lots to Olympic venues or nearby MARTA stations.

Newly designed and lighted pedestrian walkways, easy-to-understand signs, and interactive information kiosks will add to the efficiency of the transportation network.

There will be no spectator parking facilities at Olympic venues (with the exception of the shooting and beach volleyball) in the Metro Atlanta area.

Some streets will be closed. They include all streets in the Olympic Village (Georgia Tech Campus and surrounding streets), International Boulevard between the Georgia Dome and Spring Street, Luckie and Marietta Streets between Alexander Street and Techwood Drive, and Capitol Avenue at the I-20 ramp to Little Street.

Part-time closures (7:30 a.m. to midnight) include the southbound exit ramps of I-75 and I-85 at Williams and Courtland Streets, the northbound exit ramp at Central Avenue, the westbound exit ramp at Capitol Avenue, and portions of Alexander Street and Techwood Drive.

A BRIEF LOOK AT THE MODERN OLYMPICS

Begun in ancient Greece, the Olympic Games continued for about 1,200 years and ceased by A.D. 400. Baron Pierre de Coubertin of France originated the idea of reviving the event. His dream came true with the event in 1896 held at the rebuilt Athens stadium. The event in Atlanta marks 100 years since this revival.

The modern Olympic Games are a series of competitive sports events for amateur athletes of all nations, without consideration of their race, creed, or political beliefs. Although most events are for amateur athletes only, some events (such as tennis and basketball) allow professional athletes to compete. Held every four years, they are conducted under special rules by an international governing body that acts cooperatively with international sports federations and national committees.

In the U.S., men and women receive places in the competition by tryouts. Each Games committee determines the time, place, and method of holding tryouts in its own sport. The athletes chosen receive their places solely on the basis of performance in the tryouts. Team members must be U.S. citizens, be certified as amateurs (if required) by the governing body of their sport, and pass medical examinations.

In many countries, the governments defray all expenses of competitors. The U.S. Olympic Committee, believing the American public prefers to finance the team free from government control, raises funds through donations.

From Athens, Greece, to Atlanta, Georgia, from 1896 to 1996, winners in the Olympic Games flourish on the strength of individual excellence. Their names are as legendary as the Olympic Games themselves.

Here are a few highlights of the past one hundred years:

- **1896:** James Connolly won the first gold medal for the U.S. in the first modern Olympic Games. He won for the triple jump.
- **1912:** Jim Thorpe won the decathlon gold in Stockholm. King Gustav dubbed him "the greatest living athlete."
- **1932:** Babe Didrikson is still the only athlete in the world to win medals in the high jump, hurdles, and javelin.
- **1936:** African-American Jesse Owens's four gold medals humiliated Adolf Hitler and his doctrine of racial superiority. But the German people wildly applauded Owens.
- **1948:** Georgia's Alice Coachman became the first African-American woman to win the gold. (She won for the high jump.)
- **1960:** American boxer Cassius Clay won the gold in the light heavyweight division. The young Louisville boxer floated "like a butterfly" and stung "like a bee." Years later, the world knew him as Muhammad Ali.
- **1968:** George Foreman, Bob Beamon, Dick Fosbury, Mark Spitz, Jan Henne, and Debbie Meyer led one of the most-medaled U.S. Olympic teams in history.

- **1972:** Mark Spitz went to Munich and beat Olympic records by winning seven gold medals—more than any athlete in any sport in any Olympic Games.
- **1976:** Nadia Comaneci scored seven perfect 10s—the most ever. American Olympian winners were Edwin Moses, Bruce Jenner, Michael and Leon Spinks, and Sugar Ray Leonard.
- **1984:** Carl Lewis was the first to repeat Jesse Owens's medal sweep by taking the gold in four events in track and field. Mary Lou Retton, Evander Holyfield, and Greg Louganis joined the list of Olympic heroes.
- **1988:** Sisters-in-law Florence Griffith-Joyner and Jackie Joyner-Kersee, Janet Evans, Matt Biondi, Ray Mercer, and Lennox Lewis triumphed at Seoul.
- **1992:** America's Dream Team played basketball and won the gold.

EVENTS OF THE 1996 OLYMPICS

Opening and Closing Ceremonies

Location: Olympic Stadium.
Ticket prices starting from $212.

Many who have seen the parade of athletes and the lighting of the Olympic cauldron agree that the Olympic Games ceremony is the single most emotional presentation of any athletic event. More than 3.5 billion people are expected to watch the spectacle of the world's most time-honored celebration on TV. Distinction of nationality isn't part of the closing ceremony. The athletes march in, united by the bond of the Olympic sport.

As the Olympic flame is extinguished, young athletes of the world prepare to come together for the Games in Sydney, Australia, in the year 2000.

Archery

Location: Stone Mountain Park.
Ticket prices starting from $11.

Changed for modern times, the ancient sport of archery will use composite bows and electronic scoring in 1996, and will feature the new format of single-elimination, head-to-head competition for the gold. Arrows travel at speeds of up to 150 miles an hour toward the target 80 yards away. (The bull's-eye is smaller than the size of an apple.) The U.S. has won 12 gold medals in archery, including four of the last six men's individual titles.

Athletics (Track and Field)

Location: Olympic Stadium.
Ticket prices starting from $22.

This 44-medal event promises to produce world-record excitement. Sprinter Carl Lewis and heptathlete Jackie Joyner-Kersee are expected to compete in their fourth Olympic Games.

Badminton

Location: Georgia State University.
Ticket prices starting from $16.

The shuttlecock travels at more than 200

miles per hour in the world's fastest racket sport. During the early rounds, there will be simultaneous action on three courts. Events include singles, doubles, and (for the first time) mixed doubles.

Baseball

Location: Atlanta-Fulton Co. Stadium.
Ticket prices starting from $7.

Team USA, made up of future professional stars, hopes to follow in the footsteps of earlier Olympic gold-medalists-turned-major-leaguers that include Will Clark (1984 Olympian, Texas Rangers), Mark McGwire (1984 Olympian, Oakland A's), Jim Abbott (1988 Olympian, New York Yankees), and Ed Sprague (1988 Olympian, Toronto Blue Jays). A round-robin tournament of the world's eight best teams decides who will advance to the semifinal and medal round games at the 52,000-seat Atlanta-Fulton Co. Stadium, home of the Atlanta Braves and site of the 1991 and 1992 World Series.

Basketball

Locations: Georgia Dome; Morehouse College.
Ticket prices starting from $11.

The U.S. hopes to bring home another gold with NBA greats Shaquille O'Neal, Alonzo Mourning, and Reggie Miller as the team faces challengers such as Russia, Spain, and Greece.

For the women's games, experts predict the American team will face the fiercest competition ever encountered. Three-time

Olympian Teresa Edwards will probably lead the team, along with six-foot-five-inch Lisa Leslie. Although most sessions will take place at the Georgia Dome, for a closer look, attend preliminary sessions at the 6,000-seat Morehouse College facility.

Boxing

Location: Alexander Memorial Coliseum, Georgia Tech.
Ticket prices starting from $27.

In the past, the U.S. has dominated Olympic boxing by winning twice as many golds as any other country. The Cubans, who won seven of the 12 gold medals awarded at the 1992 Olympic Games, should provide an exciting challenge. The world's top amateurs fight as many as six bouts during the competition.

Canoe/Kayak (Slalom)

Location: Ocoee Whitewater Center.
Ticket prices starting from $26 (includes transportation from Ocoee spectator parking lots to venue).

This summer Olympic sport is a battle with nature. The slalom canoe/kayak competition (or whitewater slalom) will be held on the Ocoee River in the Cherokee National Forest in Tennessee. Competitors must use their skill, strategy, and strength as they race against the clock and battle the whitewater currents as they negotiate 25 upstream and downstream gates.

Canoe/Kayak (Sprint)

Location: Lake Lanier.
Ticket prices starting from $11.

Native Americans invented canoes and kayaks. One-, two-, and four-person boats compete for the gold. In this exciting event, sometimes the difference between the gold and silver can be only a fraction of a second. Competition takes place at Lake Lanier, located in the foothills of Georgia's Blue Ridge Mountains.

Cycling (Mountain Bike)

Location: Georgia International Horse Park.

Ticket prices starting from $16.

For a sport that's only 10 years old, mountain bike racing has stirred a lot of interest by being added to the 1996 Games. Bikers do several loops over the hilly course at the Georgia International Horse Park.

Cycling (Road)

Location: City of Atlanta.

Tickets not needed.

You don't need a ticket to watch the road cycling events that will take place on a 15-kilometer course through Atlanta neighborhoods. Someone has dubbed it the South's Tour d'Atlanta. Set up a chair along the course and watch as the cyclers fly past. This features two events for both men and women: (1) a mass start road race and (2) an individual time trial, known as the Race of Truth. In this, athletes race only against the clock. Among the favorites, the U.S. sends world champion Lance Armstrong.

Cycling (Track)

Location: Stone Mountain Park.

Ticket prices starting from $27.

Track cycling involves the combination of human and machine as athletes race around a banked track (a velodrome) at high speeds on bicycles without brakes. Competition will be held at the newly built Olympic Velodrome.

Diving

Location: Georgia Tech Aquatic Center.

Ticket prices starting from $22.

Of all gold medals ever awarded in Olympic diving, the U.S. has won almost two-thirds of them. The sport's aerial beauty, combined with America's past success, makes this one of the major attractions of the Games.

Equestrian

Location: Georgia International Horse Park.

Ticket prices starting from $11.

Horse and human compete as one in three equestrian disciplines:

1. Dressage emphasizes beautiful movements.
2. Show jumping focuses on speed and grace (usually the most popular event).
3. Three-day event is an equestrian triathlon that involves dressage, jumping, and a cross-country run. You'll see women and men in both individual and team competition.

Fencing

Location: Georgia World Congress Center.

Ticket prices starting from $11.

Fencing is one of the oldest forms of

individual competition. It has evolved into a sport that is so fast moving, it is now electronically scored. Just a touch of the opponent's weapon causes a light to flash. Each touch indicates a point in the three events of épée, foil, and saber. In the 100-year history of Olympic fencing, America has won 18 golds.

Gymnastics (Artistic)

Location: Georgia Dome.
Ticket prices starting from $27.

The power, flexibility, and creativity of competitors have made this into one of the world's favorite Olympic events—which means it's hard to buy tickets. Participants seek to win a total of 14 gold medals (team and individual). As many as six events take place at the same time.

Gymnastics (Rhythmic)

Location: University of Georgia, Athens.
Ticket prices starting from $32.

You can expect tickets to rhythmic gymnastics to be among the most sought after in 1996. Athletes compete in four events: ball, rope, ribbon, and clubs. Although the individual events have been part of the Games for 12 years, for 1996 officials have added group competition—five women competing together for the team gold. Their routines are done to music.

Handball

Locations: Georgia World Congress Center; Georgia Dome.
Ticket prices starting from $16.

To many Americans, team handball with its dribbling, passing, and structured offense may seem more like basketball than the handball game they know. To score, competitors must throw the ball through a soccer-style goal. Worldwide, this fast-paced game now numbers more than four million players.

Hockey (Field)

Locations: Morris Brown College; Clark Atlanta University.
Ticket prices starting from $11.

Described by someone as "soccer with sticks," field hockey originated in ancient Egypt, and it may well be the oldest of the Olympic events. It has been part of the modern Games since 1908 in London. Teams play 35-minute halves; there is no time-out.

Judo

Location: Georgia World Congress Center.
Ticket prices starting from $22.

Judokas (as the competitors are called) are all blackbelts. They compete in seven weight categories. To get an ippon (similar to a knockout in boxing), judokas use armlocks, strangling techniques, throws, and mat holds. The popularity of this sport—invented in Japan—brought about the women's judo as a full-medal sport in 1992.

Modern Pentathlon

Locations: Wolf Creek Shooting Complex (shooting); Georgia World Congress Center (fencing); Georgia Tech Aquatic Center (swimming); Georgia International Horse Park (riding/running).

Ticket prices starting from $27.

As the name implies, athletes compete in five events: shooting (10-meter air pistol), fencing (épée), swimming (300-meter freestyle), riding, and a 4-kilometer run. All five events take place the same day (a first for Olympics), and one ticket is good for all events.

Rowing

Location: Lake Lanier.
Ticket prices starting from $11.

Among the best-conditioned competitors of the Games are the rowers. In 1996, there will be 600 of them. Boats carry from one to nine athletes who race across a 2,000-meter course. Their speed and power are such that they make as many as 40 strokes a minute.

Shooting

Location: Wolf Creek Shooting Complex.
Ticket prices starting from $22.

The shooting competition has four disciplines: rifle, pistol, running target, and clay target with a total of 15 events. The bull's-eyes are 50 meters away, and the clay targets fly through the air at 65 miles per hour. On an electronic monitor, competitors and spectators instantly see the location and score of every shot. With the purchase of a ticket, you have access to all four ranges at the Wolf Creek Shooting Complex.

Soccer (Football)

Locations: Legion Field, Birmingham, Alabama; Orange Bowl Stadium, Miami, Florida; Florida Citrus Bowl, Orlando, Florida; RFK Stadium, Washington, D.C.; Sanford Stadium, Athens, Georgia. Ticket prices starting from $20.

Soccer became a medal sport at the 1908 Olympic Games, and it consistently has drawn some of the largest crowds. This is the first year that women's soccer has been an Olympic event. This game, known elsewhere as football, is the world's most popular sport—and it's gaining popularity in the U.S.

Four of America's most famous stadiums play host to first-round and quarterfinal Olympic soccer matches. Each community will conduct its own opening ceremony prior to its first match. The final game takes place at Sanford Stadium on the campus of the University of Georgia in Athens.

Softball

Location: Golden Park Stadium, Columbus.
Ticket prices starting from $16.

The U.S. women's team will play for the first time in an Olympic league. They are also the favorite in fast-pitch softball.

Swimming

Location: Georgia Tech Aquatic Center.
Ticket prices starting from $27.

The always-popular swimming competition, with 32 medals at stake, has been dominated by American swimmers. Experts predict that records will fall as times drop because of tougher competition from Russia, Hungary, Australia, and China.

Synchronized Swimming

Location: Georgia Tech Aquatic Center.

Ticket prices starting from $11.

The athletes use their ability and creativity in the events. They are judged on artistic impression and technical merit during a five-minute free routine done to music. These scores and scores from an earlier technical program determine the winners. For 1996, eight-women teams have replaced solo and duet events.

Table Tennis

Location: Georgia World Congress Center.
Ticket prices starting from $11.

This isn't Ping-Pong! In Olympic table tennis, players send a ball across the table at speeds up to 100 miles an hour. This sport takes place on several tables at once with singles and doubles competitions for men and women.

Tennis

Location: Stone Mountain Park.
Ticket prices starting from $21.

More than 100 of the world's top professionals compete in this popular event. Games take place in early rounds on 10 or more courts. As competitors are eliminated, it finally comes down to the final matches on a center court.

Volleyball

Locations: Omni Coliseum; University of Georgia, Athens.
Ticket prices starting from $16.

Volleyball, following soccer, is the world's second most popular team participation sport. In this fast-paced game, you can expect dramatic finishes.

Volleyball (Beach)

Location: Atlanta Beach, Jonesboro.
Ticket prices starting from $25.

Beach volleyball will be played for the first time in the 1996 Games. Two-player teams cover the same court area that requires six players indoors.

Water Polo

Location: Georgia Tech Aquatic Center.
Ticket prices starting from $20.

This sport appears simple and precise as players pass the ball and shoot at the goal. But the game is one of physical strength and determination. Players must battle for position in soccerlike fashion as they tread water and swim nonstop for four periods.

Weight Lifting

Location: Georgia World Congress Center.
Ticket prices starting from $20.

Men try to win the title of the "World's Strongest Man," which involves far more than strength, as they compete in 10 weight categories. Athletes combine their best weights lifted in two events (the snatch and the clean and jerk).

Wrestling

Location: Georgia World Congress Center.
Ticket prices starting from $20.

You can see 10 weight classes in both freestyle and Greco-Roman competition. Freestyle wrestling, popular with Americans, is similar to high school and college competitions. Popular in Europe is the

Greco-Roman style, where athletes are forbidden to use holds below the waist.

Yachting

Location: Wassaw Sound, Savannah.
Ticket prices TBD.

The sport is extremely demanding. Skill and judgment combine as the leaders guide their boats over buoyed courses. Four hundred men and women compete separately in six events, including windsurfing.

OTHER EVENTS

The Olympic Arts Festival

The 1996 Olympic Arts Festival tries to feature something for everyone. There will be hundreds of free and ticketed concerts, exhibitions, and performances, all scheduled to complement sports competitions. Most of the events will be located within the Olympic Ring to allow festival ticketholders to enjoy the convenience of the Olympic transportation system. Dates are June 1 to August 3; for information, call 404-224-1835.

Music

Nightly concerts in Centennial Olympic Park's new amphitheater will feature Willie Nelson, James Brown, Chinese superstar Wei Wei, African sensation Anglique Kidjo, Lynyrd Skynyrd, Travis Tritt, and Trisha Yearwood.

For classical music, performances in the Woodruff Arts Center include the Atlanta Symphony, the Montreal Symphony, the Australian Youth Orchestra, and Georgia-born, world-renowned opera diva, Jessye Norman.

Theater and Dance

Performances by world-class international and regional theater ensembles will include premieres by Pulitzer Prize–winner Sam Shepard; Alfred Uhry, creator of *Driving Miss Daisy;* and Pearl Cleage.

Dance troupes such as Alvin Ailey and Pilobolus will perform.

Festival of the American South

Located in the heart of Centennial Olympic Park will be the Festival of the American South. It will feature thousands of artists and craft makers from the mountains and urban centers of a nine-state region. Admission: free.

Exhibitions

Atlanta's galleries and museums will offer an array of exhibitions:

- Rings: Five Passions in World Art, a one-time-only collection of 100 masterpieces of painting and sculpture from all over the world
- The Olympic Woman, a first-ever multimedia exhibition tracing the evolution of women athletes in the modern Olympic Games through interactive technology
- Olympic collectibles, a large exhibi-

tion of Olympic Games stamps, coins, and memorabilia in Olympic history

- A series of remarkable exhibitions showcasing the unique vision of southern artists, and a rare opportunity to see major public artworks, including the 132-foot-high Centennial Olympic Cauldron by renowned public artist Siah Armajani

CENTENNIAL OLYMPIC PARK

For a $35 tax-deductible contribution per brick, you can help build the beautiful Centennial Olympic Park in downtown Atlanta. This 72-acre park will be a major gathering place for the 1996 Olympic Games as well as the focal point for the Olympic Arts Festival. Alongside fountains, trees, and a natural amphitheater will be commemorative brick-paved paths bearing the names of thousands of Olympic supporters. Once the Games are over, an Olympic museum and signature plaza are planned for the park, ensuring that your bricks are a lasting legacy to your participation and pride in the 1996 Olympic Games.

OLYMPIC QUILTS

You won't have to look hard to see the Quilt of Leaves. It will be everywhere you turn in Atlanta during the Olympics—on street banners, signs, buses, venue fences, concession stands, volunteer uniforms, the tickets, medals, and hundreds of Olympics publications.

The six-foot-square quilt that imparts the look of the 1996 Centennial Olympics features rough-edged laurel and olive leaves overlaid on a pattern of irregular-shaped squares. It portrays Atlanta's abundance of natural greenery, the ancient traditions of the Olympic Games, and the South's cultural heritage.

The warm and cozy look is intended as an antidote to the high-tech tension of the modern city. As it points back to a simpler time, the quilt offers a tangible representation of the past alongside Atlanta's corporate image. The quilt is made of hot pink, turquoise, gold, and green on a purple background. It was pieced and sewn by Barbara Abrelat of Decatur. Sammie Simpson of Alpharetta provided the decorative hand sewing in the trapunto style that features padded designs in high relief outlined by single stitches. The two women put more than 200 hours of work into the project.

Simpson is a member of the Georgia Quilt Project, which is bringing together 400 quilts, two of which will be given to each country represented at the 1996 Games.

CENTENNIAL LEGACY

Among the many legacies of the 1996 Centennial Olympic Games, perhaps the most evident will be the history-making efforts of women athletes.

Women made their Olympic debut at the 1900 Olympic Games in Paris, where 11 of them competed in the "ladylike" sports of tennis and golf. In the same Games, more than 1,300 men competed in a dozen sports.

How far have the Games come since lawn tennis player Charlotte Cooper became the first woman to win an Olympic gold medal at the turn of the century?

Of the 10,700 athletes expected to compete in 1996, more than 3,700 will be women. This number represents the largest group of women ever to compete in the Olympic Games, and 700 more than the number of women who competed in the 1992 Olympic Games in Barcelona.

In 1996, two new sports for women will debut: soccer and softball. Both men and women will compete in the new Olympic sports of mountain bike racing and beach volleyball.

In addition, events for women have been added in athletics (track and field), swimming, cycling, fencing, and shooting; four women's teams have been added in basketball and volleyball.

GONE WITH THE WIND:
MARGARET MITCHELL, THE BOOK,
AND THE FILM

THE SIGHTS AND SOUNDS

Georgia is *Gone with the Wind* country. There is no such literal plantation as Tara because Margaret Mitchell wrote her Pulitzer Prize–winning novel after doing meticulous research, and Tara is probably a composite of places. But in the minds of many people, Tara has its own reality.

Gone with the Wind remains as significant to Georgia today as it did with the release of the book (1936) and the film (1939). Here are the places to visit if you want the best of Tara and the Atlanta history.

Gone with the Wind Theme Park, Villa Rica, Douglas Co. At the time of this writing, the park has not opened. The original schedule was to be ready by the time of the 1996 summer Olympics. Projected to cost $50 million, the theme park will open on a less grand scale in 1996 and be completed by 1998. West of Atlanta on I-20.

Inn Scarlett's Footsteps, Pike Co., south of Atlanta. K. C. and Vern Bassham converted the former Magnolia Farms into a southern plantation B&B in the style of *Gone with the Wind*. The five bedrooms are named in memory of the characters of the movie: Scarlett, Rhett, Melanie, Ashley, and Mr. Gerald (Scarlett's father). The museum room is filled with *GWTW* memorabilia. If you stay there, you can tour the museum free. 706-495-9012; 800-886-7355. Group tours by appointment Tue.–Sun. 11 a.m.–3 p.m. 138 Hill St., Concord, midway between I-75 and I-85 south of Atlanta. Drive south from Griffin on US 19, and follow US 19 to Zebulon. At Zebulon, turn right at the traffic light onto GA 18. Follow GA 18 through Concord half a mile past the R. F. Strickland Building. Sign is on the right.

Mitchell Home, Atlanta. Daimler-Benz, makers of the Mercedes-Benz, donated $5 million to renovate the former home of the *GWTW* writer. Renovations should be completed by June 1996.

News releases say the corporation has made a one-time donation to create a museum in the apartment house where Mitchell lived while writing her novel. She referred to it as the Dump. After its renovation, Mercedes-Benz will turn the house over to the Margaret Mitchell Foundation, which will own and run the museum at 979 Crescent Ave. (near 10th and Peachtree Rd. NE).

Inn Scarlett's Footsteps

Road to Tara Museum, Atlanta. Housed in the Georgian Terrace, this 6,000-square-foot museum is on the concourse level. Memorabilia collected from all over the world that relate to *GWTW* are on display. The name comes from one of the earlier titles Mitchell considered for the novel.

The Georgian Terrace, once a hotel, is now a condo-apartment complex. Harold Latham, a representative of Macmillan Publishing Company, was a guest at the hotel in 1935 when he received the bulky manuscript from Mitchell. Four years later, when the film premiered in Atlanta, cast members Clark Gable, Vivien Leigh, and Olivia de Havilland stayed at the Georgian Terrace. You'll see everything from original posters and photos from the film, as well as a hundred different *GWTW* dolls and an exhibit of the battle of Atlanta. The David O. Selznick's Screening Room—a mini-35-seat theater—has clips of the film and the life of Margaret Mitchell. Mon.–Sat. 10 a.m.–6 p.m.; Sun. 1–6 p.m. Tours by appointment. 659 Peachtree St. (across from the Fox Theater). 404-897-1939.

THE BOOK AND THE AUTHOR

Margaret Mitchell (Margaret Munnerlyn "Peggy" Mitchell Marsh)

Born in Atlanta, November 8, 1900; died August 16, 1949

Reporter, writer, winner of 1937 Pulitzer Prize for fiction for *Gone with the Wind*

Atlantan Margaret Mitchell was a blue-eyed brunette with an oval-shaped face. She

HERB BRIDGES

Herb Bridges, who lives in Sharpsburg in Coweta Co., owns what is most likely the largest privately held collection of *GWTW* memorabilia. The retired postal worker has become well known as the unofficial authority on *GWTW*.

It all started in the early 1960s when he began to collect various editions of *GWTW*. He obtained several foreign editions and then wanted to buy an autographed first edition in its dust jacket. Besides the first edition, his collection has expanded into other *GWTW*-related items.

As the collection grew, he began to receive invitations to speak at various clubs about his hobby. He usually took posters or other items from his collection. During the years that followed, he added to his memorabilia. In 1967, to celebrate the release of the film in 70 mm, he arranged a display for Rich's (one of Atlanta's prestigious department stores).

Bridges's hobby has taken him across the United States, to France, and to Japan. He has also published books on his favorite subject. His first was *Scarlett Fever* in 1976. Since then he has published *The Filming of Gone with the Wind* (1984) and *Frankly, My Dear* (1986).

Bridges is working on a *GWTW* project at the CNN Center in Atlanta. He estimates that it will be ready by the time of the 1996 Olympics. For him, *accuracy* is the important word when designing posters or brochures about the event.

For this man from a small town in Georgia, what began as an interest in obtaining various editions of one novel has grown into a full-time hobby. He hopes that ultimately he can set up a permanent exhibition of his collection. In the meantime, Bridges is still collecting.

weighed less than a hundred pounds and stood at an even five feet tall. Someone said, "She was a petite lady, but she produced a giant of a book."

In 1922, Peggy Mitchell got a job as a reporter on the *Atlanta Journal Sunday Magazine* for $25 a week. A sprained ankle refused to heal, so she continued to write a column from her home. She stayed with the magazine a little more than four years.

Mitchell married her second husband, John R. Marsh, in 1925 (an earlier marriage had lasted less than two years). Because of a long illness, John was heavily in debt when they married. They moved into a small apartment (they called it the Dump) at 979 Crescent Ave. They had no car, little money, but many books and a lot of friends. The Dump became a place where many Atlantans gathered.

In 1926, still not recovered from her ankle problems, Mitchell began to write a novel set in the Civil War period. She wrote parts of it, then set it aside to work with her husband who had become manager of the advertising department of Georgia Power Company. By 1929, she had practically completed the novel. But it remained almost untouched for the next six years.

In 1932, her friend Lois Cole, who had been connected with the Atlanta branch of Macmillan Publishing Company, transferred to the New York branch. She asked Mitchell about the book but received no reply about its progress.

In the spring of 1935, Harold Latham, trade editor and vice president of Macmillan, visited the larger cities of the South in search of new writers and manuscripts. Cole urged Mitchell to show her manuscript to him. Cole wrote to another friend, Medora Perkerson, who was with the *Atlanta Journal Sunday Magazine,* and urged her to cooperate in finding new writers. She immediately thought of Margaret Mitchell, with whom she had worked on the newspaper.

When Latham and Mitchell met through the introduction of Perkerson, the writer said she had nothing she wanted to show him. He asked to read her manuscript anyway. No one had read it except John Marsh. Her husband persuaded her to allow Latham to read the manuscript.

She consented and took him the manuscript that was dusty, dog-eared, and covered with penciled-in changes. She said that she had written the first chapter more than 70 times and was still not happy with it. She did write a synopsis—hastily—of the first chapter that included a conversation between the Tarleton twins after they left Scarlett. That part has remained almost as she wrote it, but she did not complete the rest of the first chapter until after she had sold the book.

When Mitchell took the manuscript to the hotel, the material was so bulky that Latham bought a suitcase to put it in. He left for San Francisco and began to read her manuscript on the train. Before he had finished half of it, he realized he had in his possession one of the most important novels he had ever read.

Weeks later, Margaret Mitchell reluctantly signed a contract. Despite the publisher's optimism, she doubted the success of the book.

After she signed the contract, Mitchell worked, retyping and polishing the material. She also carefully checked for historical accuracy. She changed character names and the title many times. One of her early titles was *Bye, Bye Black Sheep,* and she called her heroine Pansy.

In an interview, she once explained how

she arrived at the published title. She read Ernest Dowson's poem "Cynara" and came across the line: "I have forgot much, Cynara—gone with the wind."

In January 1936, she sent the finished manuscript to the publisher. Macmillan released it simultaneously in the United States and Canada, June 30, 1936. Because of the high cost of printing, the book carried a $3 price tag, $0.50 higher than usual for fiction.

Immediately, critics and the public hailed it as a masterpiece. It sold more than 500,000 copies in less than four months. In September, it went into British editions and eventually editions throughout the world. In 1994, a Margaret Mitchell–autographed first edition sold in an Atlanta bookstore for $4,500.

On August 11, 1949, a speeding car driven by Hugh Gravitt, a 29-year-old off-duty taxi driver, struck Margaret Mitchell while she was standing on a Peachtree corner. Five days later, on August 16, 1949, she died as a result of her injuries. Gravitt was convicted of involuntary manslaughter and sentenced from 12 to 18 months in prison.

Margaret Mitchell Marsh is buried with other family members in Atlanta's Oakland Cemetery.

THE MOVIE

Produced by David O. Selznick and released through Metro-Goldwyn-Mayer,

the film lasts 222 minutes. Among the ten Oscars won: best picture of 1939, Vivien Leigh for best actress, Hattie McDaniel for best supporting actress, Victor Fleming for direction, Sidney Howard for screenplay, and Max Steiner for musical score. The cast includes Vivien Leigh, Clark Gable, Leslie Howard, Olivia de Havilland, Thomas Mitchell, Barbara O'Neil, Victor Jory, Laura Hope Crews, Hattie McDaniel, Ona Munson, Harry Davenport, Ann Rutherford, Evelyn Keyes, Carroll Nye, Paul Hurst, Isabel Jewell, Cliff Edwards, Ward Bond, Butterfly McQueen, William Blakewell, Violet Kemble-Cooper, Eric Linden, and George Reeves.

When the book first hit the public scene, it immediately caught the attention of people in the motion picture world, particularly the women. Apparently, Kay Brown of Selznick International wired David Selznick about the novel when she was only halfway through reading it. Kay Brown continued to badger Selznick to read the synopsis of the book that she had written. (Eventually, he bought the movie rights for $50,000.)

In 1936, Elsa Neuberger, at that time with Universal Studios, wired her new boss, Charles Rogers, about it, only to be turned down because he didn't want to do a costume picture. Jack Warner, head of Warner Brothers studio, considered his top star, Bette Davis, for the role of Scarlett. She refused it because she had already signed for a Civil War–era movie called *Jezebel* (for which she won her second Oscar in 1938). After she refused the role, Warner lost interest in the book. Ironically, when Selznick bought the rights and began a talent search for the actress to play Scarlett in "the part of a lifetime," Bette Davis was one of the hundreds of actresses who tested for the role. Other top actresses who took screen tests included Lana Turner, Susan Hayward, Paulette Goddard, and Evelyn Keyes (who did win the role of Scarlett's sister, Suellen).

Selznick spent two and a half years searching for the right actress to play Scarlett. In the meantime, he had sets constructed and did the preliminary filming. He had already signed Clark Gable to play the role of Rhett Butler. In 1938, Vivien Leigh, a relatively unknown British actress, visited the set with her later-to-be husband, Laurence Olivier. The actor had come to Hollywood to play the title role of Heathcliff in *Wuthering Heights*. Selznick's brother, Myron, then a top agent in Hollywood, saw Leigh on the set when they filmed the burning of Atlanta. He supposedly said to David, "This is Scarlett." Selznick met Leigh, tested her, and signed her for the role.

Filming officially began on January 26, 1937. Before Selznick finished the film, he had used three major directors (although only Victor Fleming was recognized) and 15 screenwriters. Selznick himself wrote much of the final script and directed some of the scenes. The script contained 20,107 words of dialogue and 685 script scenes. He used 4,400 people to make the film, which cost a then-unheard-of $4 million. It won 10 Academy Awards—a record unbeaten for twenty years until the release of *Ben Hur*. Two women in the cast won Oscars. The first, Vivien Leigh (best actress), also won the New York Critics Award for best actress. Hattie McDaniel (best supporting actress) won for her role as Mammy. McDaniel holds the distinction of being the first African-American to win Hollywood's most coveted acting award.

The world premiere of *GWTW* took place on December 15, 1939, at Loew's Grand Theatre on Peachtree Street in Atlanta. The governor of Georgia declared a three-day holiday before the opening. Schools and public buildings closed by order of the mayor. More than 300,000 people turned out to greet the arriving stars. Atlanta celebrated with parties, costume balls, and receptions for the visitors from Hollywood. Four days later, *GWTW* had its New York premiere, and two days after Christmas, it premiered in Hollywood. Many critics hailed it as the greatest motion picture ever made. It has achieved the status of a classic film.

METROPOLITAN ATLANTA

One of the first things you'll learn is that Atlanta has nearly 40 streets named Peachtree. It could be West Peachtree or Peachtree Battle. But when someone gives you directions, don't fear if she says, "Turn left at Peachtree." In Atlanta, there is only *one* street when the word is used by itself. It's Peachtree Road NE—the main street that runs from midtown Atlanta to Buckhead.

Why Peachtree? After all, even though Georgia does grow some of the finest peaches in the world, the tree isn't native to the state. We're not sure why, but here is one possible answer. In 1782, explorers discovered a Cherokee village on the Chattahoochee River called Standing Peachtree. Historians, however, think the Cherokee named their village because of the *pitch* tree (a resinous pine). But the name held. During the War of 1812, when a young America fought against England, the former village became the location of Fort Peachtree, a small frontier outpost. About that time, Peachtree Road began. It connected Fort Peachtree to Fort Daniel (Gwinnett Co., northeast of Atlanta).

Besides the overuse of Peachtree, another thing you'll notice if you look at the map is all those streets with the word *Ferry* as the second word. You'll find Paces Ferry, Montgomery Ferry, Bakers Ferry, and on they go. Before the Civil War, ferries carried passengers to and from roads on either side of the Chattahoochee River. The ferries no longer exist, but their names remain. The location of the ferries largely determined the character of the battle of Atlanta campaign in the Civil War (1861–65), say historians, because General William T. Sherman's forces had to use the crossings. By the way, Sherman did say that the fortifications protecting the ferries were the best he had ever seen.

We have a lot of nicknames for our city. One of the most common is the Big A. Another used once in a while is the Big Apple. Hot-lanta is another often-used term. Some refer to it as Dogwood City. That's because every spring the city comes alive with pink-and-white dogwood blossoms. The sight becomes even more dazzling with a variety of azaleas and the fragrant pristine white blooms of the mag-

nolia. This can happen as early as February, but it's usually March or early April when Atlanta takes on its verdant spring colors.

A BRIEF HISTORY OF ATLANTA

In 1826, during the early days of the railroads, surveyors suggested the present site of Atlanta as a practical spot for a railroad connecting Georgia's cotton and other crops with the northern markets. It took ten years before it happened. In 1837, the state legislature approved starting the Western & Atlantic Railroad. Today, Underground Atlanta has a marker known as Zero Milepost. It marks the W&A Railroad site around which the city called Terminus grew.

In the early 1800s, the northern part of Georgia was still Native American territory belonging to the Creek. More settlers arrived on the eastern shores and pushed westward. In the 1820s, the Creek signed treaties ceding millions of acres to settlers.

■■   **ATLANTA WEATHER**   ■■

During the spring and fall, you can expect temperatures to stay between 50°F and 70°F. The months of June through August are warm and humid. Temperatures sometimes exceed 90°. January and March are usually the wettest.

From November to late March, temperatures range between a low of 25° to a high of 60°. It occasionally gets into the teens. Snow is infrequent.

TRIVIA ABOUT ATLANTA

- Atlanta is the state capital, but not the first. In fact, it is the fifth city to have that honor and the third official capital:

1. Savannah in colonial days
2. Augusta in 1786
3. Louisville (pronounced Lewis-ville) in 1796 (the first official capital)
4. Milledgeville in 1804 (a more central location) for 61 years
5. Atlanta since 1868, after the Civil War

- Terminus? Marthasville? Those were the first two names of the city that we call Atlanta—since 1847, that is.
- But why the name *Atlanta*? It was a feminized version of the Atlantic.
- Lenox in the Buckhead area is the largest mall in the Southeast.
- The Westin Peachtree Plaza boasts of being the tallest hotel in North America with 73 stories, and it's 723 feet high.
- Hartsfield International Airport is the second (sometimes listed as third) busiest airport in the world, beaten consistently only by Chicago's O'Hare.
- The first streetlights in Atlanta burned whale oil.
- Maxwell House Coffee's "Good to the last drop" was originally a slogan of Coca-Cola.
- Atlanta had a net growth of 70,000 in 1993, according to the Chamber of Commerce.
- Atlanta is corporate headquarters for Coca-Cola, Delta Airlines, Chick-fil-A, Lockheed, Days Inns, Ritz-Carlton, Holiday Inn, Georgia-Pacific, Turner Broadcasting System, and Scientific Atlanta.

In 1830, with the support of President Andrew Jackson, the U.S. Congress passed a bill that forced all southern Native American tribes to move to lands hundreds of miles away on the western side of the Mississippi River. Even though the Supreme Court ruled against the order, Jackson ignored its ruling and sided with Georgia settlers.

In 1832, the state set up a land lottery system for settlers. The first settler built a log cabin in 1833. Many of the winners had to claim their prize with guns, forcing the Native Americans off the land. In 1838, federal soldiers rounded up 17,000 Native Americans and forced them to walk westward. It was part of the infamous Trail of Tears. During the 800-mile journey, they suffered from cold, hunger, and disease. Nearly one-fourth of the Native Americans died.

Atlanta Skyline

With the original inhabitants gone, Terminus was in the hands of the settlers. It soon became a meeting point of major rail lines. By 1843, Terminus had become Marthasville. The first locomotive, called the Kentucky General, reached Marthasville in 1845. Because of the town's burgeoning growth, many considered the name too provincial. The railroad's chief engineer, J. E. Thomson, is credited with calling it Atlanta. In 1848, Atlanta held its first mayoral election.

Atlanta and the South prospered, largely because of the production of cotton and other agricultural crops. The economics of the South, however, depended on slave labor. In contrast, those in the northern states railed against slavery. Tensions grew, and by 1859, it was obvious that a civil war would occur. (*Real* Southerners, they say, have never acknowledged it as the Civil War. For them it was the War of Northern Aggression, or the more refined referred to it as the War Between the States.) Two years later, in 1861, the Georgia legislature voted for secession and joined the Confederate States of America.

Atlanta became the Southern supply depot and the medical center of the Confederacy with makeshift hospitals set up around the city. By 1862, about 4,000 soldiers convalesced in the city. A smallpox epidemic broke out, which made the situation worse.

In 1864, Major General William T. Sherman came south with 100,000 troops against the Southern force of 60,000, who were not well armed. More than 8,000 Confederates died in the battle of Atlanta on July 22, whereas the Union army lost 3,722. On July 28, the Confederates lost another 5,000 troops and the Federals only 600. The siege continued until September 1, when Confederate troops pulled out (after first burning vast stores of ammunition and anything else that might benefit the Yankees). The next day, the city surrendered. The U.S. Army occupied Atlanta, and Sherman forced all Atlantans to evacuate. Before the troops left in November, they leveled railroad facilities and burned most of the city.

The war ended the following year. It was followed by the period known as Reconstruction. President Lincoln had taken a benevolent attitude toward the South, but after his assassination, those in Washington reversed his policies. Troops stayed in Atlanta until 1876. Despite the military occupation, Atlanta began to rebuild and grow.

Atlanta University was chartered in 1867, and today it is the world's largest predominantly African-American institution of higher learning.

In 1868, Atlanta became the new capital of the state. The following year, the city adopted the symbol of a phoenix rising from the ashes for its official seal—called *Resurgens*. The *Atlanta Constitution* began to print a daily paper in 1886 under the editorship of Henry Grady, who inspired readers with his vision of an industrialized and culturally advanced New South.

By 1900, Atlanta had grown to a population of 90,000 and doubled that within the next 20 years. A massive fire in 1917 swept through the city and destroyed almost 2,000 buildings, but the city, true to its concept of a phoenix rising from the ashes, rebuilt once again. In 1929, the city opened its first

PHOENIX SCULPTURE: *RESURGENS*

The bronze sculpture symbolizes the spirit of Atlanta. It depicts a mythical Egyptian bird of the heron type. In Greek mythology, the phoenix became a symbol of resurrection, reappearing periodically after its self-destruction ended each life span.

Atlanta rose again from the ashes of the Civil War when General Sherman's Northern troops burned the city (1864). The city refers to itself as "Atlanta from the ashes."

The sculpture came to the city as a gift from the Rich Foundation in 1969 to commemorate the 100th anniversary of Rich's Department Store. An unknown artist in Rich's marketing department drew the original sketch. An Italian artist, Gamba Quirino, did the actual sculpture. *Resurgens* first rested at the viaduct of Martin Luther King, Jr., Drive and Spring Street. Because of construction for the Olympics, the city had it moved. It is now permanently located in Woodruff Park at Five Points, a well-known Atlanta intersection.

airport—later to become Hartsfield International. The same year, Delta Airlines began to spread its wings.

Like the rest of the South, Atlanta remained segregated until the early 1960s and had its share of race riots. Unlike many other cities of the South, however, Atlanta adopted a progressive attitude about race by hiring African-American police officers and electing African-Americans to the Atlanta board of education. In 1955, the city desegregated a public golf course and did the same with public transportation in 1959. Mayor Hartsfield, who held the office almost 30 years, called Atlanta "a city too busy to hate." In 1961, without riots or mobs, Atlanta peacefully desegregated its public schools and Georgia Institute of Technology (Georgia Tech). In 1974, Atlanta elected Maynard Jackson as its first African-American mayor. (Since then two other African-Americans have been elected: Andrew Young and the current mayor, Bill Campbell.)

In 1966, Atlanta moved into the big-time sports league when the Braves and Falcons came. The city went wild when Hank Aaron broke Babe Ruth's home-run record.

Growth has continued in the Big A. In the 1960s, the million-square-foot Merchandise Mart became the nucleus for the nationally renowned Peachtree Center complex. Today Peachtree Center is a 13-city-block pedestrian village with megahotels, the Atlanta Market Center, 200,000 square feet of retail space, a row of restaurants, and six large office towers that connect with covered walkways and bridges.

Metropolitan Atlanta Rapid Transit Authority (MARTA)—Atlanta's transport system—began its rapid-transit trains in 1979. Today just about every part of Atlanta is accessible by subway or bus.

In 1980, a revitalized 10-block African-American neighborhood called Sweet Auburn became a National Historic District. The notable sites include Martin Luther King, Jr.'s boyhood home, his crypt, the church where he preached, a museum, and the Center for Nonviolent Social Change. This is the major African-American history attraction in the nation.

Ted Turner started Superstation TBS in the late seventies and followed it with CNN (1980), Headline News, TNT, and his 1995 venture, Turner Romance Classics. Turner's Castle Rock Entertainment makes theatrically released films and has won acclaim for the quality of made-for-TV films. Turner announced the sale of TBS to Time-Warner in 1995.

The 1996 Olympics are expected to generate $3.5 billion with new hotels, tour packages, and megastadiums. Spectators will sit in the 70,500-seat Georgia Dome and the 10,000-seat open-air Olympic Velodrome. The Olympic Village, built on the campus of Georgia Tech, will be used for student housing after the Olympics.

Emergency   911
Fire   404-659-5600
Major Hospitals in Midtown Atlanta:
   Crawford Long   404-686-4411
   Georgia Baptist   404-653-4000
   Grady Memorial   404-616-4307
   Piedmont   404-605-5000
Visitor Information:
   Atlanta Convention and Visitors Bureau, 233 Peachtree St. NE, Atlanta,
      30303; 404-521-6600.
   Atlanta Chamber of Commerce, 235 International Blvd. NW, P.O. Box
      1740, Atlanta, 30301; 404-880-9000.

AN EXTRA TOUCH OF ATLANTA: ALONZO HERNDON

Alonzo Herndon had a true rags-to-riches story. Born a slave in Social Circle (about 30 miles northwest of Atlanta) in 1858, he received his freedom during his youth. He worked in the fields until he was 20 years old. During that time, he also began to learn how to be a barber, for which he seemed to have a natural talent. He perfected his skills as a barber, and he soon owned and operated three barbershops in Atlanta. All were successful. One of his barbershops came to be considered the place where anyone who was anyone went for haircuts.

By 1895, the remarkable man, with only a year of formal education and out of slavery less than 40 years, was the richest African-American in the U.S.

He took his entrepreneurial skills into the field of real estate, and he had great success. Beginning in 1905, he acquired various benevolent societies and protective associations and created the Atlanta Mutual Insurance Company (later Atlanta Life Insurance Company), America's largest African-American owned stockholder insurance company.

Herndon and his first wife, Adrienne McNeil, built what is now known as the Herndon Home in 1910. The house, built in the Beaux Arts Classical style, was just being completed when Adrienne passed away. Her death cut short her teaching and drama career.

Two years later, Herndon remarried. His second wife, Jesse Gillespie, a socially prominent figure in Chicago and also a hairdresser, served as vice president of Atlanta Life for many years. She passed away in 1947. Herndon died in 1927.

Completely restored, the Herndon Home provides a showplace for son Norris Herndon's collections of antique furniture and glass. It serves as a wonderful reminder of the inspiring life of Alonzo Herndon.

WHERE TO GO AND WHAT TO SEE

 Alonzo Herndon Home. 1910 Beaux Arts Classical home of the founder and president of Atlanta Life Insurance Company. Tue.–Sat. 10 a.m.–4 p.m. Admission: free. 587 University Place NW. 404-581-9813.

Apex Museum. History of African-American heritage in the Sweet Auburn area. Tue.–Sat. 10 a.m.–5 p.m.; Sun. 1–5 p.m. 135 Auburn Ave. NE. 404-521-APEX.

Atlanta African-American Tours. Contact Atlanta Preservation Center. 404-876-2041.

Atlanta Cyclorama. **Don't Miss.** This Civil War museum is located in Grant Park. Created in 1866 by 15 artists, it was renovated in the 1980s at a cost of $11 million. First listen to a 20-minute sight and sound narration that explains the battle of Atlanta

and the Cyclorama. You are on a revolving platform and view the battle of Atlanta as you face a 360°, 42-foot-high painting that uses sound and light for special effects with 3-D figures. The locomotive, Texas, is also housed there. Daily 9:30 a.m.–5:30 p.m. June–September; 9:30 a.m.–4:30 p.m. October–May. Admission: $3.50; senior and youth discounts. 800 Cherokee Ave. SE. Take exit 26 off I-20 E. Go south on Boulevard, turn right on Berne St., and follow it into Grant Park. Cyclorama is located next to Zoo Atlanta in Grant Park. 404-658-7625.

Atlanta History Center. One of the country's largest history museums, it's worth going for the exhibitions on the many facets of Atlanta's history. Besides the museum exhibits, you can see the gardens and two historic houses on the National Register: Swan House (a 1928 mansion) and Tullie Smith Farm (built about 1840), a plantation farmhouse with traditional outbuildings. Mon.–Sat. 10 a.m.–5:30 p.m.; Sun. noon–5:30 p.m. Ticket sales stop at 4:30 p.m. Closed major holidays. Library/Archives closed Sun. Admission: adults $7; students 6–17 and seniors $5. Admission includes museum, all exhibitions, and garden. $1 admission to the historic houses. 130 W. Paces Ferry Rd. NW. 404-814-4000.

Atlanta History Center Downtown. Take time to visit this downtown center that provides exhibits and videos on Atlanta history and helpful information on things to do and see in Atlanta. Admission: free. Mon.–Sat. 10 a.m.–6 p.m. 140 Peachtree St. (at Margaret Mitchell Square). 404-814-4000.

Atlanta Life Insurance Building. The history of the organization is exhibited in the lobby and Heritage Room. The company was founded in 1927 by Alonzo Herndon, a slave born in Georgia who opened the first insurance company owned by an African-American. Mon.–Thu. 8 a.m.–4:30 p.m. 100 Auburn Ave. NE. 404-659-2100.

Atlanta University Center Historic District. This cluster of higher learning institutions was established for African-Americans. It is the largest predominantly African-American higher education complex in the world. Atlanta University (1865) was originally the graduate school for the complex; also included are Clark College (1869); Morris Brown College (1885); Morehouse College (1867), a male undergraduate college; Spellman College (1881), a female undergraduate college; and Interdenominational Theological Center (1957). The merger of Clark College and Atlanta University has given it the new name of Clark Atlanta University, which now offers graduate and undergraduate degrees. Area bounded by Ashby St., Martin Luther King, Jr., Dr., and Northside Dr. Self-guided tours. 404-880-8000.

Ben W. Fortson, Jr., State Archives and Records Building. At this 17-story building, you'll see historical exhibits, state documents, and records of the Civil War. Don't miss the auditorium's stained glass windows depicting the Confederacy. Mon.–Fri. 8 a.m.–4:15 p.m.; Sat. 9:30 a.m.–3:15 p.m. Admission: free. 330 Capitol Ave. SE. 404-656-2393.

Carter Presidential Center and Museum of the Jimmy Carter Library. **Don't Miss.** The Center is located at Copen Hill, the site from which General Sherman directed the battle against Atlanta in the Civil War. You'll be at the scene of 30 acres that let you view a Japanese garden, a waterfall, and two lakes. The four interconnected buildings contain nearly 30 million documents. You can hear a 30-minute documentary narrated by actor Cliff Robertson.

The Center also houses the offices of the Task Force for Child Survival, Global 2000, the Carter Center of Emory University (not open to public), and the Carter-Menil Human Rights Foundation, Carter's blueprint to assist Atlanta's disadvantaged citizens. There is also a public restaurant. Mon.–Sat. 9 a.m.–4:45 p.m.; Sun. noon–4:45 p.m. Closed major holidays. Admission: $4; over 55 $3; under 16 free. One Copenhill Ave. Off I-75/85, Highland and Cleburne Aves. 404-331-3942.

Ebenezer Baptist Church. See *Martin Luther King, Jr., National Historic Site.*

Fernbank Museum of Natural History. **Don't Miss.** This is the largest natural history museum in the Southeast. You'll be overwhelmed with dioramas, films, and exhibits. Take time to view "A Walk Through

Time in Georgia" that uses the distinct land forms of Georgia to tell the story of the earth's history. Children love the Fantasy Forest (ages 3–5) and the Georgia Adventure (ages 6–10). You also can walk among 65 acres of beautifully preserved woodland. Mon.–Sat. 9 a.m.–6 p.m.; Sun. noon–6 p.m. Closed major holidays. Admission: $5.50 for museum or IMAX theater; discounts for seniors and youth. Combination tickets available. 767 Clifton Rd. NE. 404-370-0960.

Fernbank Science Center, Planetarium, and Observatory. The state-of-the-art planetarium is the third largest in the U.S. 156 Heaton Dr. NE. 404-378-4311.

Georgia State Capitol. The building was patterned after the national capitol, and the 75-foot exterior dome is covered in gold leaf that was mined in North Georgia. It is topped by a statue of *Freedom*. Inside is the Georgia State Museum of Science and Industry where you can see minerals, rocks, fossils, Native American artifacts, and displays of commercial products. General Assembly in session January–March. Mon.–Fri. 8 a.m.–5:30 p.m. Guided tours Mon.–Fri. at 10, 11, 1, and 2. Closed holidays. Admission: free. On Washington St. between Martin Luther King, Jr., Dr. and Mitchell St. Tour desk: 404-656-2844.

Hammonds House Galleries of African-American Art. The Victorian house was the home of Dr. Otis T. Hammonds, an African-American anesthesiologist and art pa-

tron. It is now a national center for the exhibition, preservation, research, and documentation of African-American art. Exhibits change. Tue.–Fri. 10 a.m.–6 p.m.; Sat.-Sun. 1–6 p.m. Admission: $2; seniors and students $1. 503 Peeples St. SW. 404-752-8730.

Georgia State Capitol

Henry W. Grady Monument. This bronze statue is of the late 19th-century editor of the *Atlanta Constitution,* who is credited with coining the phrase "the New South." On Marietta St. near Forsyth St.

Heritage Row, Underground Atlanta. The entire Underground Atlanta complex occupies 12 acres in the center of downtown. It's the historic hub that marked the end of the Western & Atlantic Railroad. At this highly entertaining attraction, you'll learn the story of Atlanta from its beginning as a wilderness village to the present and even get a view of the city's projected future. Tue.–Sat. 10 a.m.–6 p.m.; Sun. 1–6 p.m. Closed Mon. Admission: $3; seniors and youth ages 6–17 $2; children under 6 free. 55 Upper Alabama St. 404-584-7879.

Herndon Home. See *Alonzo Herndon Home.*

High Museum at Georgia-Pacific Center. Exhibits of folk art and photography change regularly. Tours, lectures, and films. Mon.–Fri. 11 a.m.–5 p.m. Closed holidays. Enter through Georgia Pacific Bldg. at 133 Peachtree St. NE, or enter directly at 30 John Wesley Dobbs Ave. NE. Admission: free. 404-577-6940.

High Museum of Art. The museum was founded in 1926. The present award-winning building opened in 1983 at a cost of $20 million. This four-story building is a work of art itself with its white porcelain tiles and an equally white interior. The permanent collection of more than 10,000 pieces includes a group of 19th- and 20th-century American paintings. Tue.–Sat. 10 a.m.–5 p.m. (Fri. 10 a.m.–9 p.m.); Sun. noon–5 p.m. Admission: $5; senior and youth discounts. No charge Thu. 1–5 p.m. 1280 Peachtree St. NE. 404-733-4400. (Note: There is a small branch of the museum at the Georgia-Pacific Center downtown.)

Historic District Tours. Contact Atlanta Preservation Center for information on guided tours of Atlanta's historic districts. 404-876-2040.

Martin Luther King, Jr., Center for Non-Violent Social Change. (See *Sweet Auburn.*) **Don't Miss.** This organization continues the work of MLK to reduce violence within the community and among nations. Located in the Freedom Hall Complex. Daily 9 a.m.–8 p.m. early April–late October; 9 a.m.–5:30 p.m. other times. Admission: free. 449 Auburn Ave. 404-524-1956.

Martin Luther King, Jr., National Historic Site. Don't Miss. (See *Sweet Auburn.*) This encompasses 23 acres. You can visit the King Center and the grave site at 449 Auburn Ave. NE. Daily 9 a.m.–5:30 p.m. Tour MLK's birth home at 501 Auburn Ave. NE—available every 30 minutes daily 10 a.m.–5 p.m. Ebenezer Baptist Church, 407 Auburn Ave. NE, where MLK preached, is open for touring daily 10 a.m.–4:30 p.m., except Sun. All closed Thanksgiving Day and Christmas Day. Admission: free. King Center: 404-524-1956.

Michael C. Carlos Museum of Emory University. You'll see a collection of artifacts from the Middle and Far East. Exhibits change regularly. Tue.–Sat. 10 a.m.–4:30 p.m.; Sun. noon–5 p.m. Closed major holidays. Admission: $3. 1380 S. Oxford Rd. NE. 404-727-4282.

Rhodes Hall, Buckhead. Built in 1903, this is one of the few existing pre–World War I Peachtree St. mansions. It was built for

Atlanta businessman A. G. Rhodes with granite from nearby Stone Mountain. Inspired by German castles, the granite exterior has Romanesque windows, battlements, buttresses, parapets, towers, and turrets. Nine stained glass windows depict the rise and fall of the Confederacy. After Rhodes's death in 1928, the mansion was given to the state of Georgia. It is on the National Register of Historic Places. Mon.–Fri. 11 a.m.–4 p.m. Closed holidays. Admission: $2; children under 12 $0.50. 1516 Peachtree St. 404-881-9980.

Road to Tara Museum. This is one of the largest collections of *Gone with the Wind* memorabilia, with its collection of Scarlett dolls. You can also view a documentary film on the life of Margaret Mitchell. Mon.–Sat. 10 a.m.–6 p.m.; Sun. 1–5 p.m. Closed holidays. Admission: $5; student and senior discounts. 659 Peachtree St. Suite 600 in the Georgian Terrace. 404-897-1939.

Robert W. Woodruff Arts Center. This four-story center is a center for entertainment and education in performing and visual arts. The Atlanta Symphony, Alliance Theater, and headquarters of Atlanta College of Art are also located in the complex. 1280 Peachtree St. NE. 404-733-4200.

SciTrek, the Science and Technology Museum of Atlanta. Opened in 1988, SciTrek offers a hands-on adventure for adults and kids in science and technology. You'll see more than 100 exhibits. The Kidspace has simple exhibits for 2- to 7-year-olds. Tue.–

Sat. 10 a.m.–5 p.m.; Sun. noon–5 p.m. Closed major holidays. Admission: $6.50; student and senior discounts. 395 Piedmont Ave. NW. 404-522-5500.

Robert W. Woodruff Arts Center

***Sweet Auburn (Martin Luther King, Jr., National Historic Site).* Don't Miss.** Allow yourself a day to explore Auburn Ave., known as Sweet Auburn. It includes the Martin Luther King, Jr., National Historic District, about 12 blocks along Auburn. You'll see King's birthplace. Parts of the street are in an ongoing process of restoration. Through this walking tour, you can gain an insight into African-American history and urban culture in the South as well as the civil rights movement. Administered by the National Park Service. Scheduled tours conducted year-round, 9 a.m.–5 p.m. Visitors Center open daily Mon.–Fri. 9 a.m. –5 p.m. 443 Edgewood Ave. NE. 404-524-1956.

Telephone Museum. Exhibits, tapes, and

slides commemorate the first century of U.S. telecommunications. Southern Bell Center, Plaza level. 675 W. Peachtree St. NE. 404-529-7334.

Welcome South Visitors Center. This museum-style center will promote southeastern states and feature interactive exhibits sponsored by private corporations, eight state governments, and the Atlanta Convention and Visitors Bureau. Expected to be fully operational by May 1996.

World of Coca-Cola. Adjacent to Underground Atlanta, this is a three-story museum of Coca-Cola products. Take a self-guided tour and see exhibits that trace the history of the soft drink from its beginnings in 1886 to the present. There are interactive displays and multimedia exhibits. Sample Coca-Cola products not available in the U.S. Mon.–Sat. 10 a.m.–8:30 p.m.; Sun. noon–5 p.m. Closed major holidays. Admission: $3.50; senior and youth discounts. 55 Martin Luther King, Jr., Dr. at corner of Central Ave. 404-676-5151.

Wren's Nest, Atlanta. National Historic Landmark. This 1870 farmhouse was named for the family of wrens that once nested in the mailbox. (The Queen Anne Victorian facade was added in 1884.) It is the historic home of Joel Chandler Harris, famous for writing the Uncle Remus tales of Brer Rabbit and Brer Fox. It has been open to the public since 1913. You can see original Harris family furnishings, books, photographs, memorabilia; diorama from Walt Disney's 1948 film *Song of the South.* Guided tours. Special storytelling sessions Tue.–Sat. 10 a.m.–5 p.m.; Sun. 1–5 p.m. Last tour at 4 p.m. Closed major holidays. Admission: adults $4; senior citizens and teens $3; children 4–12 $2. 1050 R. D. Abernathy Blvd. SW. 404-753-8535.

EATING

Recipes

Although the world of food in the international city that Atlanta has become is different from years ago, certain recipes are part of Atlanta (and of Georgia) no matter what the year. So here are a few old southern standbys.

Grits. This southern staple was relatively unknown in some parts of the U.S. before President Jimmy Carter went to Washington. Grits (ground, dried, hulled corn) are cooked with boiling water until the mixture is creamy and thick. Most people serve them with butter, salt, and pepper. For some reason, this simple dish seems to strike terror in the heart of the uninitiated, as evidenced by the story of a visitor from the North. When she ordered breakfast on her first morning in Atlanta, someone asked her if she wanted grits (which she had never seen), and she declined. Her hosts urged her to try them, and finally, she agreed but insisted, "Oh, all right, but just one!"

Grits are also delicious topped with bacon bits or grated cheese. For a real treat, add butter and grated cheese to the grits while they're still cooking.

If there should be some grits left over, pour them into a loaf pan and let them set for several hours in the refrigerator. Then turn out of the pan, slice, and fry in melted butter.

Praline Grits. This recipe is another variation on grits.

To your cooked grits (about 2 cups), add a beaten egg, 1/4 cup brown sugar, 1/8 cup chopped pecans, 1 tablespoon margarine, and 1/4 teaspoon cinnamon. Pour into a greased baking dish and bake in 350° oven until knife inserted in center comes out clean (about 50 minutes). Garnish with whipped cream if desired.

Peach Cobbler. This is the Peach State, so you definitely want to try a recipe for peach cobbler.

Peel and slice 2 quarts of fresh peaches. Combine 2 cups flour, 2 teaspoons salt, 1/2 teaspoon soda, 1/4 cup cooking oil, 2 tablespoons buttermilk, and 1/2 cup water. Mix into a dough, and roll out very thin.

Cut into strips and place 1/3 in bottom of large baking dish (buttered), then add 1/2 of the fresh peaches, dot with margarine, and sprinkle with 3/4 cup sugar. Add another layer of dough strips, rest of peaches with about 2/3 cup sugar, and end with final layer of dough strips on top. Bake in 350° oven for 1 hour.

Heavenly Hash. It's a favorite for the Christmas holidays.

Cut into small pieces 1/4 pound marshmallows, 1 large can of sliced pineapple (minus 3 slices and juice), 1 small bottle red maraschino cherries (drained), and 1 cup any kind of nuts. Whip 1/2 pint whipping cream until it peaks, then combine with ingredients above. Chill thoroughly.

Where to Eat

Metropolitan Atlanta offers a tremendous number of restaurants, representing a wide range of cultural and ethnic tastes. There's something for everyone, from the family looking for an inexpensive meal out to folk ready to dine in the grandest manner. We're listing only a few of them.

Also, look in the "Leisure" section of Saturday's edition of the *Atlanta Journal/Atlanta Constitution*. The large section is made up mostly of ads, but the selections vary from fondue to New England or vegetarian.

Ask someone who lives in Atlanta for recommendations.

Explain to your concierge what kind of dining you want. The concierge usually knows places to suggest and can give you directions.

Bone's.*** Prime steaks, fresh seafood. Call for reservations. 3130 Piedmont Rd. NE. 404-237-2663.

Boston Sea Party.*** Seafood lover's delight in elegant setting. Fine seafood buffet. Reservations requested. 3820 Roswell Rd. in Buckhead. 404-233-8766.

The Colonnade.** It may not have the outward charm of more modern restaurants, but it's been around since 1927. To many, it is an Atlanta institution. It offers some of the South's most authentic specialties. 1879 Cheshire Bridge Rd. NE, between Wellborne Dr. and Manchester St. 404-874-5642.

The Country Place.** Across from the Woodruff Arts Center, its quiet atmosphere and good food have made it a favorite for many who attend the theaters in the area. 1197 Peachtree St. NE at 14th St. in the Colony Square complex. No reservations. Validated parking in the Colony Square lot. 404-881-0144.

Downtown City Grill.*** French. Reservations recommended; jacket necessary. 50 Hurt Plaza. 404-524-2489.

Kudzu Cafe.* Maybe we just like the name, but it has a reputation for simple southern cooking. If you'd like to try fried green tomatoes, this is a good place to eat them. No reservations. Complimentary valet parking. 215 Peachtree Rd. at E. Shadowlawn Ave. 404-262-0661.

57th Fighter Group Restaurant,* Chamblee. Enjoy a superb meal with a great view in a gracious restaurant with World War II ambience. Patio and dance floor. Serves lunch, dinner, and Sunday brunch. Dinner reservations recommended. 3829 Clairmont Rd. next to Peachtree-DeKalb Airport. 770-457-7757.

The Mansion.** Elegant dining in an old home. 179 Ponce de Leon Ave. NE. 404-876-0727.

Mary Mac's Tearoom.* **Don't Miss.** This quaint restaurant has been operating since 1945 and is a bastion of classic southern cuisine. Socialites to bus drivers eat in the four interconnected dining rooms. The walls are covered with photographs (they alone make it worth seeing, including the original house used for Tara in *Gone with the Wind*). Warning: If you want leisure dining, don't go. This is fast, fast service. A glass of pencils on the table is there for you to write the items you want. You'll be in and out in half an hour. Free parking. No reservations.

224 Ponce de Leon Ave. NE at Myrtle St. 404-876-6604.

103 West. *** It is what someone has called unrestrained Victorian opulence. Its porte cochere entranceway is lit by 19th-century coach lights. Notice its interior rose silk moiré walls and you'll get the idea. Besides the ambience, 103 West has received a number of awards for its excellent food. Reservations recommended. 103 W. Paces Ferry Rd. off Peachtree Rd. 404-233-5993.

Pittypat's Porch. ** A perennial Atlanta favorite. Traditional southern food. 25 International Blvd. NW. 404-525-8228.

Pricci, ** Buckhead area. Italian and contemporary. 500 Pharr Rd. 404-237-2941.

Savannah Fish Company. ** Seafood. Reservations not necessary; jacket advised. 210 Peachtree St. Westin Peachtree Plaza. 404-589-7456.

The Varsity

The Varsity. * **Don't Miss.** If you don't know about the Varsity, you don't know about Atlanta—the inexpensive fast-food restaurant that Atlanta has grown with since 1928. Owners call it the world's largest drive-in restaurant. There is a 150-foot stainless steel counter with 200 red-shirted employees rushing out hundreds of orders. Yeah, five large TVs blare at you, the food is greasy, and the cuisine violates all the new health rules, but it's an Atlanta experience. 61 North Ave. at Spring St. 404-881-1706.

SLEEPING

Atlanta Hospitality. This reservation service places you in accommodations of your choice (whenever possible) and includes homes, inns, condos, and farms. The service tries to accommodate special needs. Listings throughout Georgia. 404-493-1930.

Bed & Breakfast Atlanta. This has been a professional service since 1979 and offers lodging in homes, cottages, inns, and B&Bs. Listings throughout Georgia. 404-875-0525; 800-96-PEACH.

International Bed & Breakfast Reservations. Represents historic, licensed, and inspected B&Bs in Metro Atlanta and around the state. 404-875-9449; 800-473-9449.

Obviously, Atlanta has many places for you to spend the night or a week, some of which are national chains or well advertised. We've listed some of the B&Bs in the area.

Belmont Bed & Breakfast, midtown Atlanta.

Restored 1891 mansion in theater, restaurant, and cultural district. 404-872-9290.

Beverly Hills Inn, Buckhead. European-style inn; five-minute drive to enjoy dining, shopping, nightlife, and entertainment in Atlanta. 404-233-8520; 800-331-8520.

Oakwood House, Atlanta. Historic home (about 1911) in Inman Park. Each bedroom has a private bath. Entire house available to guests. 951 Edgewood Ave. NE. 404-521-9320.

Shellmont Bed & Breakfast, midtown Atlanta. An 1891 mansion listed on National Register and Atlanta Landmark Buildings. Furnished with antiques. 821 Piedmont Ave. NE. 404-872-9290.

Virginia Highlands House, Atlanta. A 1940s home. Spacious three-room suite has private entrance. 879 Los Angeles Ave. NE. 404-876-0226.

Woodruff Bed & Breakfast Inn, Atlanta. A restored 1906 Victorian home, decorated with antiques; 12 bedrooms with private baths. Full southern breakfast. Learn the history of the Bessie Woodruff Inn while you're there. 223 Ponce de Leon Ave. NE. 404-875-9449.

SHOPPING

Cumberland Mall. Spend all day shopping in northwest Atlanta. Mon.–Sat. 10 a.m.–9 p.m.; Sun. 12:30–6 p.m. At I-75 and I-285. 770-435-2206.

Lenox Square. Largest mall in the Southeast. In addition to major department stores, it has movie theaters, restaurants, and more than 200 specialty shops, plus a wide range of service shops. Mon.–Sat. 10 a.m.–9:30 p.m.; Sun. 12:30–5:30 p.m. 3393 Peachtree Rd. NE. 404-233-6767; 800-344-5222.

Macy's Close-out, Decatur. Avondale Mall. 3588 Memorial Dr. 404-286-0829.

Northlake Mall. Congregation of shopping facilities gathered in the same area in addition to the mall itself. Across the street at the Northlake Festival are movie theaters, shops, and restaurants. Mon.–Sat. 9 a.m.–10 p.m.; Sun. 12:30–5:30 p.m. LaVista Rd. off I-285 on east side of Atlanta. 770-938-3564.

Outlet Square of Atlanta. 4166 Buford Hwy. NE. 404-633-2566.

Peachtree Center Mall. Downtown. Stores, restaurants, and service shops. Mon.–Sat. 10 a.m.–6 p.m.; some stores Sun. noon–5 p.m. Peachtree St. at International Blvd. 404-614-5000.

Perimeter Mall. It's advertised as the "family shopping center northeast of Atlanta." 4400 Ashford-Dunwoody Rd. Exit off I-285. 770-394-4270. (Technically, this is outside I-285 and should be with North Georgia, but it's such a close call, we've included it with Atlanta.)

Phipps Plaza. Upscale shopping. Lord & Taylor, Parisian, Saks Fifth Avenue. First-class restaurants and multiple movie theaters.

Mon.–Sat. 10 a.m.–6 p.m. (except Thu. 10 a.m.–9 p.m.); some stores Sun. 12:30–5 p.m. 3500 Peachtree Rd. NE. 404-262-0992.

Rich's Finale. Greenbriar Mall. 2841 Greenbriar Parkway SW. 404-346-2615.

Underground Atlanta. Historical setting full of places to shop for just about everything. Mon.–Sat. 10 a.m.–9:30 p.m.; Sun. noon–6 p.m. Alabama St. between Central Ave. and Peachtree St. 404-523-2311.

ANTIQUES AND CRAFTS

Atlanta Flea Market, Chamblee. Its 80,000 square feet house goods from 140 merchants. Fri.–Sat. noon–8 p.m.; Sun. noon–7 p.m. 5360 Peachtree Industrial Blvd. Inside I-285. 770-458-0456.

Broad St. Antique Mall, Chamblee. Antiques and collectibles; 30 dealers. In Chamblee's Antique Row. 3550 Broad St. 770-458-6316.

Chamblee's Antique Row. More than 100 dealers in one of the South's largest and most unusual antique areas. Take Peachtree Industrial Blvd. exit off I-285 E (just north of I-85), and go south on Peachtree Industrial. Turn on Broad St. and follow to Antique Row.

Clocks "Antique Haus Mall," Chamblee. Antiques, collectibles, deco, and depression glass. In Chamblee's Antique Row. 3510 Broad St. 770-458-7131.

Eugenia's Place, Chamblee. Antique collectibles, vintage toys, and antique hardware. In Chamblee's Antique Row. Fri.–Sun. 11 a.m.–7 p.m. at 5360 Peachtree Industrial Blvd. 770-458-0682. Mon.–Sat. 10 a.m.–6 p.m. at 3522 Broad St. 770-458-1677.

The Family Jewels, Decatur. Antique jewelry and accessories, estate pieces, toys, collectibles, paintings, books, and glassware. Tue.–Sat. 11 a.m.–5:30 p.m.; or by appointment. Inside I-285 in downtown Decatur. 114 E. Ponce de Leon Ave. 404-377-3774.

Old Blanton House, Chamblee. American furniture, accessories, and collectibles. Mon.–Fri. 10:30 a.m.–5 p.m.; Sat. 10:30 a.m.–5:30 p.m.; Sun. 1–5 p.m. In Chamblee's Antique Row. 5449 Peachtree Rd. 770-458-1453.

Out of the Attic Antiques, Atlanta. Kitchen collectibles, nostalgia, furniture, pottery, and primitives. Daily 11 a.m.–7 p.m. In the Cottage House. 1830 Cheshire Bridge. 404-876-0207.

Rust N' Dust Antiques, Chamblee. Mon.–Sat. 10:30 a.m.–5 p.m.; Sun. 1–5 p.m. 5486 Peachtree Rd. 770-458-1614.

Scott Antique Market, Atlanta. Second weekend of every month. More than 1,000 exhibitor booths. Expo Center, two miles east of Atlanta Airport. I-285, exit 40 to airport.

Scottdale Flea Market and Antique Center, Scottdale. Indoor and outdoor sections. It's 1.7 miles inside I-285 on E. Ponce de Leon. 3110 E. Ponce de Leon. 404-294-4726.

(Note: See **North Georgia** for many antique shops located outside, but near to, Metro Atlanta.)

OUTDOORS

Canoeing and Rafting

Take a trip down the Chattahoochee River (*real* Atlantans call it the Hooch). This is the focal point of the Chattahoochee River National Recreation area. Everything you'll need, including shuttle service, is provided by the Chattahoochee Outdoor Center: 404-394-6622.

Golf

Atlanta International Golf and Golf Course, Decatur. 404-981-1400.

Bobby Jones, Atlanta. 404-355-1009.

Browns Mill, Atlanta. 404-366-3573.

Candler Park, Atlanta. 404-373-9265.

Clifton Springs Par 3, Decatur. 404-241-3636.

College Park, College Park. 404-761-0731.

Cross Creek, Atlanta. 404-352-5612.

Lakeside Golf Club, Atlanta. 404-344-3629.

North Fulton, Atlanta. 404-255-0723.

Sugar Creek, Atlanta. 404-241-7671.

"Tup" Holmes, Atlanta. 404-753-6158.

ENTERTAINMENT

Like any large, cosmopolitan city, Atlanta offers a wide variety of entertainment. Your best bet is to buy the Saturday edition of the *Atlanta Journal/Atlanta Constitution* (two daily newspapers that combine on weekends) and pull out the "Leisure" section. You'll find all the top current entertainment of the week listed by categories. Especially check out the sidebar called "Week's Best." Several pages follow called "Calendar" for all the ongoing events of the Metro area.

What about the nightlife? Atlanta is a city that's alive at night, and it offers a wide variety of places to spend the evening and even into the wee hours of the morning. These tend to change rather frequently. Check with people who have visited some of the local nightspots and get their recommendations, or check with your hotel's concierge for information.

Agatha's—A Taste of Mystery. Dinner theater production features audience participation. 693 Peachtree St. NE. 404-875-1610.

Alliance Theater. Musicals to both new and classic dramas. Most productions $14–$34; senior and student discounts. In the Robert W. Woodruff Art Center. 1280 Peachtree St. NE. 404-733-5000.

Atlanta Ballet. One of the oldest civic ballet companies in the country. Performs September–April at Civic Center Auditorium. Special holiday presentation of "The Nutcracker." Box office: 404-892-3303.

Atlanta Boat Show. Five-day event produced by the National Marine Manufacturers Association, held at the Georgia World Congress Center. Features houseboats, yachts, cabin cruisers, saltwater craft, pleasure craft, rowboats and canoes, fishing gear, waterskiing equipment, and other water-related items. September. Admission: adults $6; children 12 and under $3. Florida office: 305-531-8410.

Atlanta Botanical Gardens. Vegetables, herbs, gardens, and walking trails cover 30 acres. Glass-enclosed Fuque conservatory. Tue.–Sun. 9 a.m.–7 p.m. Conservatory Tue.–Sun. 10 a.m.–7 p.m. Closed major holidays. Admission: $6; senior and student discounts; under 6 free. Piedmont Park in midtown Atlanta. 1345 Piedmont Ave. NE. 404-876-5859.

Atlanta Chamber Players. Performs wide range of classical and contemporary pieces. Season runs fall through spring. Tickets about $12. 404-651-3618.

Atlanta Home and Garden Show. Sponsored by the Southern Exposition Management Company (SEMCO). Four-day event in mid-March at the Georgia World Congress Center. Display gardens and landscaping ideas; seminars on variety of subjects. Admission: adults $7; seniors $6; children 7–12 $4; under 7 free. 404-998-9800.

Atlanta Symphony Orchestra. Celebrated 50th anniversary in 1995. Extensive annual schedule. Features world-renowned guest artists. Themed programs. Family concerts. Holiday concerts. Concert series in Chastain Park in summer. Free evening concerts at selected Atlanta parks during summer. Woodruff Arts Center. 1280 Peachtree St. NW. Concert hotline: 404-733-4949. Box office: 404-733-5000.

Baseball. National League's Braves play from early April to early October at the Atlanta-Fulton Co. Stadium. Tickets and information: 404-249-6400.

Basketball. Catch the National Basketball Association's Hawks at the Omni Coliseum downtown. 100 Techwood Ave. Tickets and information: 404-827-DUNK.

Cathedral Antiques Show. Four-day event in mid-February; displays by more than 30 dealers of high-quality antiques at the Cathedral of St. Philip. Sit-down lunch each day. Admission: $6 per day, or $25 for preview party, includes all four days. 2744 Peachtree Rd. NW. 404-365-1000.

Center for Puppetry Arts. History of puppets. Multicultural exhibits. Open year-round Mon.–Fri. 9 a.m.–5 p.m. 1401 Spring St. at 18th. 404-873-3391 or 874-0398.

Chastain Park Amphitheatre. Outdoor facility seats 7,000. Outdoor concerts May–October. Picnic on the grass before the concert. Features big-name performers. Order tickets well in advance. 4469 Stella Dr. NW. 404-817-8700. (Atlanta Symphony tickets: 404-733-5000; Atlanta Symphony Information: 404-733-4900; Concert/Southern Promotions: 404-296-6400.)

CNN Studio Tours. Guided walking tour lasts 45 minutes. You can see network operations and observe aspects of CNN, Headline News, CNN International, and TBS Collection; also weather demonstrations occur. Reservations recommended, although some tickets available on daily basis. 9 a.m.–5 p.m. Closed holidays. Admission: adults $7; senior and youth discounts. One CNN Center (Marietta St. and Techwood Dr.). 404-827-2300.

Coca-Cola Lakewood Amphitheatre. This $15 million building accommodates nearly 20,000, including 7,000 reserved seats and a sloping lawn for 12,000. Not a top facility for headliners, but the amphitheatre has featured Elton John, the Allman Brothers, Janet Jackson, and others. It's 3.5 miles from downtown, Fair Dr. at the Lakewood exit of I-85. Get tickets through Ticketmaster: 404-627-9704 or 249-6400.

Decatur's Neighborhood Playhouse, Decatur. Main stage play plus another play in the Discovery Arena. 430 W. Trinity Place. 404-373-5311.

Football. The National Football League's Atlanta Falcons play in the Georgia Dome from early September to mid-December. One Georgia Dome Dr. (at International Blvd. and Northside Dr.). 404-223-8000.

Fox Theater. **Don't Miss.** Atlanta landmark built in 1927; exotic interior. Offers a "Best of Broadway" season with major shows from New York; summer Broadway series; "The Nutcracker" performed Christmas season by Atlanta Ballet. Major film festival in the summer. 660 Peachtree St. NE. (at Ponce de Leon Ave.). Administrative Office: 404-881-2100. Tickets: 404-249-6400.

Georgia Dome. Opened in the early 1990s, this 71,500-seat facility presents headliner concerts and country music shows when it isn't offering sports events. One Georgia Dome Dr. on south side of Atlanta.

Grant Park. The home of Atlanta Cyclorama and Zoo Atlanta covers 144 acres. You can also enjoy Old Fort Walker and scenic trails. Daily 6:30 a.m.–1 a.m. Admission: free. Exit 26 off I-20 E.

Historic Air Tours. Provides aerial tours of area (antebellum homes, Civil War battlefields, landmarks). Daily 10 a.m.–6 p.m. Closed Christmas Day. Cost: $40–$95; senior and youth discount. 1954 Airport Rd. (exit 32 off I-85). 404-457-5217.

Martin Luther King Week. This may not properly be labeled entertainment, but it's important to list. This event occurs the second week of January and offers an inter-faith service, plays, musical tributes, semi-nars, films, a parade, and speeches. Each year major performers present concerts. 404-524-1956.

Racing. (See *Entertainment* sections in **North Georgia** and **Middle Georgia**.)

Ringling Brothers Barnum & Bailey Circus. Early February each year at the Omni Coli-seum for about 20 performances. 404-681-2100. Ticketmaster: 404-249-6400.

St. Patrick's Day Parade. March 17. A major event for more than 7,000 marchers and more than 150,000 viewers. Mayor and other politicians attend, along with sports celebrities, high school bands, clowns, clog-gers, drill teams, and bagpipers. It all ends with a concert of Irish music, plus dance and other festivals. The parade begins at Peachtree and Ralph McGill Blvd. and ends near Underground Atlanta. Check newspa-per for details.

Six Flags Over Georgia. See listing in **Mid-dle Georgia** under *Entertainment*.

Southeastern Flower Show. A significant five-day gardening event, usually around Valentine's Day, but may be as late as early March. Landscape and garden displays with flowers and vegetables fill 100,000 square feet. Gardening ideas demonstrated. Admis-sion: $10; discounts for seniors and children. Proceeds benefit the Atlanta Botanical Gar-dens. 650 Ponce de Leon Ave. 404-888-5638.

Stone Mountain. See listing in **North Georgia** under *Entertainment*.

Zoo Atlanta. Animals live in habitats de-signed to look and feel like their homes in the wild. Home of famous gorilla, Willie B. Visit the World of Reptiles, OK-to-Touch Corral, and Zoo Train. You can watch animal shows and feedings. Weekdays 10 a.m.–4:30 p.m.; weekends 10 a.m.–5:30 p.m. during daylight savings time. Closed major holidays. Admis-sion charged. 800 Cherokee Ave. SE (in Grant Park). Exit 26 off I-20 E. General information: 404-624-5600.

FESTIVALS

February

Atlanta Storytelling Festival. Folk tales, legends; multicultural; evening concert. At-lanta History Center. 404-814-4000.

Hispanic Festival of the Arts. February or March. Multimedia festival held at Geor-gia Tech Center for the Arts. 770-938-8611.

Southeastern Flower Show. At Ponce Square in midtown Atlanta. 404-876-5859.

April

Dogwood Festival. Parade, driving tours, hot-air balloon races, and other events. 404-892-0538.

Inman Park Festival. Streets are blocked off for a time of music and crafts. Celebrates southern heritage. Tour of Victorian homes in neighborhood. 404-242-4895.

Sweet Auburn Festival. Tours of African-American historical neighborhood, parades, ethnic foods, and music. 404-577-0625.

May

Decatur Arts Festival, Decatur. 404-371-8386.

Music Midtown Festival. Live performances by big-name performers. Sponsored by Midtown Alliance. Admission: $11–$17. 404-892-4782.

June

Atlanta Jazz Festival. Free concerts at Grant Park featuring talented artists. 404-653-7160.

Georgia Shakespeare Festival. Shakespearean classics staged under an open-air tent. Oglethorpe University. 4484 Peachtree Rd. NE. 404-688-8008.

July

National Black Arts Festival. Dance, theater, music, folklore, and heritage programs.

Only during even-numbered years. 404-224-1142.

September

Arts Festival of Atlanta. Paintings, sculpture, photography, crafts, puppets, workshops for children, and performances in dance, music, and theater. Piedmont Park. 404-885-1125.

Atlanta Greek Festival. Since 1974, always held the last week of September. Greek Orthodox Cathedral of the Annunciation. 2500 Clairmont Rd. NE. 404-633-6988.

Chamblee Fall Antique Festival, Chamblee. Peachtree Industrial Blvd. exit off I-285 E. 770-458-1614.

Georgia Music Festival. Underground Atlanta. 404-523-2311.

Montreaux/Atlanta International Music Festival. Features European performers with other known artists; variety of musical styles. Starts Labor Day for one week. Piedmont Park. 404-953-3278, ext. 225.

October

Festival of Cultures. Downtown. 404-817-0800.

Folklife Festival. Tours of house and gardens; demonstrations of 19th-century crafts, pottery making, and dulcimer music. The Tullie Smith House, Atlanta History Center. 404-814-4000.

Great Halloween Caper. Zoo Atlanta. 404-624-5000.

Habitat for Humanity Birdhouse Artfest. Lenox Square. 404-264-3999.

Halloween in the Alley. Underground Atlanta. 404-523-2311.

Heritage Festival. Decatur. 404-371-8386.

Little Five Points Halloween Festival. 404-681-2831.

Martin Luther King, Jr., Street Festival. 404-522-3249.

Olde English Festival. St. Bartholomew's Episcopal Church. 404-634-3336.

Ormewood Park Fall Festival and Tour of Homes, Atlanta. 404-622-9323.

Vinings Jubilee Fall Festival, Vinings. 770-438-8080.

November

Christmas at Callanwolde. November–December. Callanwolde on Briarcliff Rd. 404-872-5338.

Lighting of the Rich's Great Tree, Underground Atlanta. 404-523-2311.

Mideastern Festival. St. Elias Antiochian Orthodox Church. 404-687-9266.

December

Bonfire and Marshmallow Roast, Decatur. Downtown. 404-371-8386.

Christmas at the Wren's Nest. 1050 R. D. Abernathy Blvd., SW. 404-753-7735.

Egleston Christmas Parade. Peachtree St. 404-264-9348.

Festival of Trees. Decorated trees; holiday activities. Ten-day event starts first Sat. in December. World Congress Center. 404-264-9348.

First Night Atlanta. Begun in 1993, it is a New Year's Eve nonalcoholic, family-oriented event. The event showcases art, entertainment, and music, with everything from Cajun to folk, from gospel to opera. December 31 in midtown Atlanta, 3:00 p.m.–12:30 a.m. Admission: $10 in advance or $12 at event. 404-881-0400.

Holiday Candlelight Tour of Homes, Decatur. 404-371-8386.

Kwanzaa. December 26–January 1. This African-American celebration, which originated in 1966, is based on celebrations from West and East Africa, and it is now celebrated in more than 100 major cities. (*Kwanzaa* comes from the Swahili word for "first." It is a time to celebrate African heritage, reinforce positive family values, reflect on past accomplishments, and express hope for the future.) 404-730-4001, ext. 110, or 404-521-9014.

Olde Christmas Storytelling Festival. The Southern Order of Storytellers celebrates the traditional Christmas season. Begins

Christmas Day. Callanwolde (Gothic Tudor-style mansion). 404-872-5338.

Peach Drop and New Year's Eve Party. December 31. World's Largest Tailgate Party on eve of Peach Bowl game. Underground Atlanta. 404-523-2311.

An Underground Christmas. November–December. Underground Atlanta. 404-523-2311.

CHAMBERS OF COMMERCE

(Italics indicate a county name.)

Atlanta	404-880-9000
Buckhead & Int'l	404-266-9867
DeKalb	404-378-8000
Hapeville-Airport	404-209-0910
North *Fulton,* Greater	404-993-8806

CHAPTER
TEN

NORTH GEORGIA

Cities of North Georgia

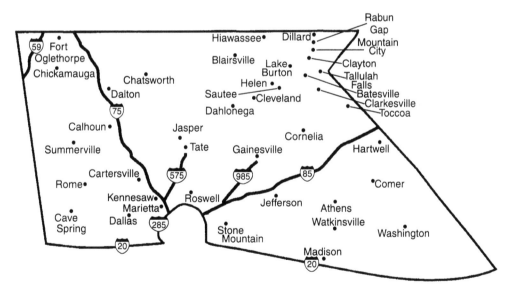

	NORTH GEORGIA AT A GLANCE			
LOCATION	**TO SEE/DO**	**EATING**	**SLEEPING**	**OTHER**
Athens	Chestnut Grove School Church-Waddel-Brumby House Double-barreled cannon Georgia Museum of Art Morton Theater Taylor-Grady House West Hancock District White oak	The Grill Trumps		
Batesville		Batesville General Store		

Blairsville	Margarita Morgan miniature
	   collection
		Tucker's Inn Family
		   Restaurant
				Quilt Patch

Calhoun	New Echota	BJ's Restaurant		Antique Mall
Cartersville	Etowah Indian Mounds Lowry Covered Bridge William Weinman Mineral Museum	Morrell's		Antique Mall
Cave Spring	Historic sites		Tumlin House B&B	
Chatsworth	Chief Vann House	Edna's Cafe		
Chickamauga			Gordon-Lee Mansion	
Clarkesville		Taylor's Trolley	Glen Ella Springs Inn	Burton Gallery Mark of the Potter

Clayton	Four Winds Village		Old Clayton Inn	Lofty Branch Arts
				   & Crafts
				Main St. Gallery
				Timpson Creek
				   Gallery

Cleveland			Villagio De Montagna Rusharon	Gourdcraft Babyland General
Comer	Watson Mill Bridge			
Cornelia		Appletree Farms		Hartford House
Dahlonega	Gold Museum Indian princess grave	Smith House	Mountain Top Lodge Smith House	Pan for gold
Dallas	Pickett's Mill Battlefield			
Dalton	Crown Gardens & Archives	Cellar Restaurant Dalton Depot Oakwood Cafe		Carpet outlets

LOCATION	TO SEE/DO	EATING	SLEEPING	OTHER
	NORTH GEORGIA AT A GLANCE			
Dillard		Dillard House	Copecrest Resort Dillard House	Craft Stores Hambidge Center Minimall Village Weaver
Ft. Oglethorpe	Chickamauga Battlefield		Captain's Quarters	
Hartwell	Jackson Morrison House			
Helen	Alpine village theme	Courtyard Restaurant		Anna Ruby Falls Oktoberfest Outlet stores Tekakwitha
Hiawassee		Fieldstone	Deer Lodge Fieldstone	Always Christmas/ Hen's Nest Georgia Mountain Fair
Jasper		Woodbridge Inn		
Jefferson	Crawford W. Long Museum			
Kennesaw	Big Shanty Museum Kennesaw Battlefield			
Lake Burton		Laprade's		
Madison	Antebellum homes Morgan Co. African-American Museum		Boat House B&B Burnett Place	Old Madison Antiques Step Back in Time
Marietta	National Cemetery and Confederate Cemetery		Stanley House Whitlock Inn	Antique shops White Water & American Adventures
Mountain City	Foxfire Museum		York House	
Rabun Gap				Mountain Sounds
Rome	Berry Museum Oak Hill Plantation Chieftains Museum	Tiberio	Claremont House	
Roswell	Bulloch Hall			Shops of Distinction Antiques

		NORTH GEORGIA AT A GLANCE		
LOCATION	TO SEE/DO	EATING	SLEEPING	OTHER
Sautee	Nora Mill Granary Old Sautee Store Sautee Bridge	Stovall House	Stovall House Lumsden Homeplace	
Summerville	Paradise Gardens			
Tate			Tate House	
Toccoa	Travelers Rest			Toccoa Falls
Washington	Robert Toombs House Kettle Creek Battleground (Revolutionary War)			
Watkinsville	Eagle Tavern			

Special
Mention:
	Stone Mountain Park
	Wineries
	Cloudland Canyon
	    (northwest Georgia)
	Amicalola Falls (Dawsonville)
	Tallulah Gorge
	Vines Botanical Gardens
	    (Logansville)			

Georgia sits at the southern tip of the Appalachian Mountain chain. It has two separate sections: the Blue Ridge Mountains in the east, and the Cohuttas in the west, which are a continuation of the Great Smoky Mountains.

Georgia's mountains are always beautiful, especially when the leaves change in the fall and you gaze at a brilliant array of red, orange, and gold surrounded by holly, laurel, or a variety of evergreen trees. Some say it's even more spectacular when the wildflowers bloom and fill the hillsides with a myriad of hues. Warm summer colors of purple, blue, and yellow seem to be everywhere. Even winter's chill leaves the landscape bursting with the greenery of native magnolias and Burford holly.

Everything in North Georgia is accessible. Interstates 75 and 575 are the two major highways into the northwest, but US 411 and US 278 are also heavily traveled. Interstates 85 and 985 and GA 400 are the primary routes into northeastern Georgia.

Stop to view the many historical and natural wonders. Especially pause to see the mountain and foothill region of northwestern Georgia that once belonged to the Cherokee. You'll drive right into the heart of Cherokee County, the location of most of the Native American historical sites in the state.

In the northeasternmost corner of Georgia lie the Blue Ridge Mountains, the oldest chain on the North American continent. If you're a nature lover, you'll marvel at the effects of eons of wear on the mountains. Innumerable hardwood and evergreen trees, bluebells, rhododendron, and native fauna decorate the landscape. The number of rivers, creeks, and waterfalls along the well-watered Blue Ridge may surprise you. This is the eastern continental divide that separates waters to the Gulf of Mexico, the Atlantic Ocean, and the Mississippi River.

The natural beauty and bounty of northeastern Georgia attracted many of America's first pioneers. They moved into the wilderness with their unique Appalachian folk traditions. Despite the effects of urbanization, you can still see this folk tradition alive in northeastern Georgia.

Continental Divide Marker

AN EXTRA TOUCH OF NORTH GEORGIA: HOWARD FINSTER

Howard Finster may well be one of the most talked-about individuals in the state. Depending on who you ask, they'll describe him as visionary or a true folk artist, or they may say, "He's very different."

The Reverend Howard Finster, whose formal education ended with the sixth grade, is a self-taught artist—in addition to following 22 other vocations. Certainly one of the most flamboyant figures in Georgia, he established his Paradise Gardens near Summerville as his own wonderland of all types of art.

With his individual philosophy about life, Finster has filled the gardens with everything from plants growing wild near small creeks to painted angels (the word gaudy is the way some folk put it), surreal images, a structure made from old Coke bottles, and another from discarded bicycles. He displays Bible passages everywhere in the garden. Of course, you'll have to decide for yourself whether you agree with gallery owners who consider Finster a major talent.

The gardens have been there since the 1940s and are worth seeing. Open daily. Admission: free. Paintings and wooden figures are for sale. About three miles north of Summerville, off US 27 on Rena St. 706-857-2926.

WHERE TO GO AND WHAT TO SEE

Here are some of our favorite places that will give you a touch of the real North Georgia. We've included directions to get there. You won't be able to see everything on your first visit. But don't worry, you'll have plenty of places to visit on your return trip.

Alexander H. Stephens State Historic Park, Crawfordville. Named for the vice president of the Confederacy during the Civil War (1861–65). Stephens returned to Washington after the war as a U.S. senator. His residence, the two-story Liberty Hall, was built in 1875. Take a guided gaslight house tour any time during the year. The adjacent Confederate museum houses a large collection of Confederate artifacts. Exit 55 on I-20. 706-456-2602.

Athens. This city was incorporated in 1806. Of more than 40 Athenses in the U.S., this is the best known. It was named after the capital of Greece, the "mother of arts of eloquence." The University of Georgia, the nation's first state-chartered university, was established there in 1785. It is the site of Georgia's official art museum.

Walking and driving tours lead you to many of the city's historic sites such as impressive Civil War homes, especially the *Taylor-Grady House,* 634 Prince Ave., 770-549-8688, an 1840s Greek Revival mansion. Once home to the voice of the New South, *Atlanta Constitution* editor, Henry Grady, it covers an entire city block.

Be sure to see the famous *white oak.* Often referred to as the richest tree in the world, the tree owns itself. It is located in the center of a cobblestone street at Dearing and Finley Streets, and a former owner deeded the land around it to the tree! (A 1942 storm destroyed the original tree, but it was replaced by growth from one of its own acorns.)

The *West Hancock Historic District* was originally a separate settlement on the western outskirts of Athens. It was a complete cross section of the African-American society with a mixture of architecture and economics. Dr. Thomas J. Elder, a well-known educator, is counted among its prominent citizens. Bounded by Glenhaven and Hancock Avenues and Reese, Billups, Rock Springs, and Indale Streets. Self-guided tours.

Berry Museum, Rome. See *Oak Hill Plantation* and the *Martha Berry Museum,* located at Berry College. Wealthy Martha Berry left Oak Hill Plantation to begin a school for Appalachian children. If you want to see a classic southern plantation, Oak Hill (built 1847) is one of the best in the state. The museum structure (1972) is Greek Revival architecture. Museum and Oak Hill open Tue.–Sat. 10 a.m.–5 p.m.; Sun. 1–5 p.m. Admission: nominal. From Atlanta, take I-75 and US 41 to intersection US 411 north of Cartersville, and then on US 411 to Rome. 770-291-1883.

Big Shanty Museum, Kennesaw. The original Great Locomotive Chase began at Big Shanty. On April 12, 1862, Andrew's Raiders stole the locomotive with plans to head north and destroy supply lines to Confederate armies. The plan was thwarted by the conductor, Capt. William A. Fuller, and his band of pursuers. You can see the locomotive, named the General, housed in a museum that was an authentic cotton gin. Exit 117 or 118 off I-75 N, 25 miles from Atlanta. 770-427-2117.

Bulloch Hall, Roswell. Named after Mittie Bulloch, the mother of President Theodore Roosevelt, this historic house shows the magnificence of antebellum homes. Tue.–Fri. 11 a.m.–2 p.m. Admission: $3. 180 Bulloch Ave. 770-992-1731.

Canton. This town in Cherokee Co. was first called Cherokee Court House with the start of the post office in 1832. It was first incorporated as Etowah in 1833, but town officials changed it to Canton the following year because Judge Joseph Donaldson brought in 100,000 silkworms from China and planted many mulberry trees. He hoped to develop a thriving silk industry. (He didn't.) Canton was also the home of Joseph Brown, who served as governor in Georgia during the Civil War era (1857–67).

Chestnut Grove School, Athens. One of the few remaining one-room schoolhouses in Georgia. Built in 1896, the school also served as a community and religious center for the African-American community. 610 Epps Bridge Rd. Tour information: 706-548-1741.

Chickamauga Battlefield, Fort Oglethorpe. This is the largest and oldest military park in the country. Chickamauga and Chattanooga National Military Park is headquartered at Chickamauga Battlefield on US 27 south of Fort Oglethorpe. It was established 25 years after the Civil War ended in 1865 because veterans on both sides wanted to commemorate the 35,000 soldiers who died in two days of fighting for control of Chattanooga and Atlanta. It was the most costly battle of the Civil War.

Chickamauga Battlefield Visitors Center

To get a feel of the battle, don't do anything until you see the slide show of the battle at the Visitors Center. You can also pick up trail maps and guides. As you tour the park, you'll sense the troop movements and the fighting. You'll also see 1,500 historical markers and monuments. You'll want to listen to self-guided audiotape tours and ranger-interpreted programs. During the summer, the park offers living history reenactments.

Chickamauga Battlefield

Do you want to hike at the park? The hiking trails are quiet and well kept. Center is open 8 a.m.–5:45 p.m. from Memorial Day to Labor Day; the rest of the year it closes at 4:45 p.m. Take exit 141 (GA 2) off I-75 W to Fort Oglethorpe, then turn south on US 27 to the park. 706-866-9241.

Chieftains Museum, Rome. This splendid white clapboard plantation house is the site of the Chieftains, where the Cherokee built a commercial empire. As you tour the museum, especially see the exhibits about Major Ridge, the prominent Cherokee leader who struggled to adapt to white culture while retaining his own heritage. Tue.–Fri. 11 a.m.–4 p.m.; Sun. 2–5 p.m. Closed on all national holidays. 80 Chatillion Rd. 770-291-9494.

Chief Vann House, Chatsworth. State historic site. Joseph Vann, one of the Cherokee Indian chiefs, built this two-story brick mansion in 1804. It is the only mansion in America built by a Native American. Be sure to pause at the elaborately carved stairway, the oldest example of cantilevered construction in Georgia. Vann House Days, third weekend in July, demonstrate living history. Candlelight tours second weekend in December, Fri.–Sat. 6–9 p.m. Other activities scheduled throughout year. Contact Chatsworth-Murray Co. Chamber of Commerce for information: 706-695-6060.

Chief Vann House

Church–Waddel Brumby House, Athens. Believed to be the oldest surviving residence in the city, this Federal period house was built in 1820 for Alonzo Church. He later became president of the University of Georgia. Shortly after its construction, Dr. Moses Waddel bought it and lived there as university president (1820–29). In 1834, Mrs. Stephen Harris bought the house. Her descendants were the Brumby family. This striking symbol of Athens's history now houses a Welcome Center, museum, and headquarters for the Heritage Foundation. Mon.–Sat. 9 a.m.–5 p.m.; Sun. 2–5 p.m. 280 E. Dougherty St. 770-546-1805.

Crawford W. Long Museum, Jefferson. This is tagged "the birthplace" of anesthesia because Dr. Crawford Long (b. 1815) used ether for surgical anesthesia—a first in medicine—in an operation on James Venable on March 30, 1842. At the museum, you'll see displays of Dr. Long's personal items and documents. Other buildings present the history of the area. Of special interest are the antebellum general store and a re-created doctor's office and apothecary shop of the 1840s. Exit 50 off I-85 N; US 129 south five miles to Jefferson. Located 60 miles northeast of Atlanta. 706-367-5307.

Crown Gardens and Archives, Dalton. You'll discover fine examples of early chenille bedspreads among the exhibits. After the mill could mass-produce the chenille bedspread, workers eventually adapted machinery to manufacture carpeting. Other features are historical displays, an African-American heritage room, an outdoor spring, and picnic areas. At original Crown Cotton Mill. 715 Chattanooga Ave. 706-278-0217.

Dahlonega. In Lumpkin Co., the city received its name from the Cherokee *Tau-la-ne-ca* (golden color) or *Atela-dalanigei* (yellow money). A branch of the U.S. mint was established there in 1838 until the outbreak of the Civil War (1861). During that time, the mint produced $6 million worth of gold coins from the locally mined ore. North Georgia College now occupies the site. In 1958, the citizens of Lumpkin Co. donated 43 ounces of gold leaf to gild the state capitol dome.

Visit the town square, built in 1838 of Greek Revival architecture, and you'll find it lined with two-story Victorian storefronts. The windows of the shops display the town's heritage. Besides the *Dahlonega Gold Museum* (see below), you can also visit the *Consolidated Gold Mine* with its railcar system to pull gold out. You start a 40-minute tour by going down through a stone passageway and descend 125 feet below the water table. Admission charged. On US 19 connector, just east of the square. 706-864-8473.

Dahlonega Gold Museum, Dahlonega. **Don't Miss.** (State historic site.) Dahlonega is the place of America's first major gold rush in 1828. (It was 20 years before the California gold rush began.) Located in the foothills of the Blue Ridge Mountains, Dahlonega became a thriving town by 1833. Through slides and exhibits, you can learn the history of Dahlonega's gold discovery. Authentic 19th-century buildings circle the courthouse museum. Gold Museum is in an old courthouse that graces the center of the town square. One hour north of Atlanta on GA 400. 706-864-2257.

Double-Barreled Cannon, Athens. This novel double-barreled cannon was made for Civil War fighting in 1862. In theory, this unusual weapon was to simultaneously fire two cannonballs connected by an eight-foot iron chain. The balls were supposed to pull the chain taut and sweep across open fields and strike Northern soldiers. In practice, they rarely fired at the same time. The chain inevitably broke when the cannon was fired, and the balls spun off in two directions. The cannon was never used in battle. After the war, it was placed outside Athens City Hall. Some say it points north just in case Yankees decide to invade again.

Eagle Tavern, Watkinsville. Here's a chance to get a touch of the frontier. Eagle Tavern opened in 1802 as a stagecoach stop and tavern. Built in the late 1700s, it is one of the oldest surviving structures in Oconee Co. from when Watkinsville was a frontier town on the edge of Creek and Cherokee Indian territories. In 1956, Lanier Billups donated the tavern to the Georgia Historical Commission for restoration. The commission decided that the 16 rooms added by 1847 should be removed, and it should be restored to its earliest form, called a two-up, two-down Plain Style structure—the type of house built along Georgia's up-country before Greek Revival architecture became fashionable.

The tavern remains on its original site in the center of Watkinsville on the historic Antebellum Trail. The state operated the tavern as a Welcome Center during the 1960s and then deeded it to the county in the mid-1970s. Today it is the Oconee Co. Local State Welcome Center. You can view a variety of handcrafted chests, tables, beds, and other artifacts typical of the furnishings of Georgia's early days. 770-769-5197.

Etowah Indian Mounds, Cartersville. **Don't Miss.** State historic site. They consist of three grass-covered mounds used for religious rites by chiefs and priests. They were also the graves of those dignitaries. You'll find an excellent small museum and reception center where dioramas and artifacts from the mounds tell the story of a mysteriously vanished tribe. Especially look for the priest's burial chamber and carved busts of a woman and a warrior. You can also enjoy a film that traces the history of the Etowahs. 813 Indian Mounds Rd. SW. Exit 124 off I-75 N; take GA 113/61. 770-387-3747.

Four Winds Village, near Clayton. This was a Native American museum–trading post. You'll find a variety of antiques, crafts, and gifts. Don't miss the enchanting display of ancient pottery and beadwork, paintings, relics, and oddities. Six miles south of Clayton on old US 441. 770-782-6939.

Foxfire Museum

Foxfire Museum, Mountain City. If you've read or heard about the Foxfire series, you won't want to bypass this area. Students at Rabun Gap–Nacoochee School were sent into the hills to preserve their endangered heritage, and these books present their research in readable form. At the museum you'll see examples of Appalachian living through toys, a rope bed, farming tools, and even a gristmill. Three miles north of Clayton on US 441. 706-746-5828.

Georgia Museum of Art, Athens. In 1945, Alfred H. Holbrook donated his collection of 100 American paintings to the University of Georgia. This permanent collection has grown to more than 7,000 works of art. Linger over the permanent collection in the south gallery. The museum also schedules temporary exhibitions that feature prints and drawings from the permanent collection as well as those from private and public schools. Admission: free. Mon.–Sat. 9 a.m.– 5 p.m.; Sun. 1–5 p.m. Museum shop: Mon.–Sat. 11 a.m.–4 p.m.; Sun. 1:30–4 p.m. Closed on most university holidays. Located at University of Georgia. 706-542-3255; 706-542-3254 exhibition line; 706-542-0447.

Helen. **Don't Miss.** This Blue Ridge Mountain village in White Co. has taken on the look of an Alpine village. It didn't incorporate until 1913 when it became a site to mill pine trees from the surrounding slopes. When residents wanted a name for the town, a lumber official suggested Helen—his daughter's name. The people agreed, which may have had to do with the fact that most of them worked for the lumber company. By the 1940s, the timber had been cut and the lumberjacks had moved on. In 1969, Main St. had only five places of business left when John Kollock suggested they make the town over to look like the Bavarian Alps. The people agreed. Today, nearly 200 businesses serve four million tourists who come to town each year. Visit the Museum of the Hills in the castle on Main St., and the Doll and Toy Museum with a collection of more than 2,000 antique dolls. Welcome Center: 706-878-2181.

Town of Helen

Jackson Morrison House, Hartwell. Morrison, a carpenter, farmer, and real estate broker who contributed to the growth of the area, was also one of the most prominent African-Americans of Hart Co. He designed and completed his house about 1902. 439 Rome St. Exterior showing only.

Kennesaw Battlefield, Kennesaw Mountain. After the Northern troops defeated the Southern troops at Chattanooga in 1863, the Confederates retreated to Kennesaw Mountain, 25 miles north of Atlanta. For two weeks in June 1864, 60,000 soldiers fought in and around the 1,808-foot mountain. Finally, Union General William T. Sherman forced the Southern army to flee. They retreated to Atlanta, the site of another historic battle.

If you're a hiker, you'll want to take time to leisurely explore the miles of wooded trails around the Civil War fortress. Don't pass up a highly entertaining and educational slide presentation at the National Park Service Visitors Center. Take in the exhibits and see the authentic cannons outside. The park also provides excellent picnic facilities. Mon.–Fri. 8:30 a.m.–5 p.m.; Sat.–Sun. 8:30 a.m.–6 p.m. Exit 116 off I-75 N; go west 4.5 miles. 770-427-4686.

Lowry Covered Bridge, near Cartersville. See **Covered Bridges and Gristmills of Georgia**.

Madison. Located in present-day Morgan Co., the town was first settled in 1809 and incorporated in 1866. It was named in honor of President James Madison.

Lancelot Johnson developed the process of pressing oil from cotton seed, which was a big boon to the southern economy.

If you feel disappointed at not seeing the antebellum homes as depicted in the film *Gone with the Wind,* you can find them by taking an hour's ride from Atlanta to Madison. You can see more than 35 antebellum homes with a variety of architecture from

gingerbread to Grecian columns. Visitors Center: 706-342-4454.

Margarita Morgan Miniature Collection, Blairsville. It's a small, small world of thousands of miniature tables, chairs, pianos, chandeliers, and other furnishings. See a diminutive southern mansion, a manor, and a palace—all inside the Union Co. Historical Society Museum at the old courthouse in Blairsville. Wed.–Sat. 10 a.m.–4 p.m. Closed during winter. Admission: $2 donation. 706-745-5493.

Marietta National Cemetery and Confederate Cemetery, Marietta. Marietta has both a Confederate and a Union cemetery. The Marietta National Cemetery, located off Washington Ave. east of the downtown square, is on land donated by Henry Cole in 1866. He intended that dead from both sides be buried there as a symbol of peace. Citizens of Marietta didn't agree, however, and they created a Confederate Cemetery, located on Cemetery St. south of downtown.

Morgan Co. African-American Museum, Madison. Founded to study, preserve, and interpret the heritage of African-Americans. Local history emphasized. Tue.–Fri. 10 a.m.–4 p.m.; Sat. noon–4 p.m. 156 Academy St. 706-342-9191.

Morton Theater, Athens. Built in 1910, it has since been renovated. The theater was a meeting place for the African-American community and a showcase for the performing arts. 199 W. Washington St. 706-613-3770.

New Echota Cherokee Capital, Calhoun. State historic site. The state has carefully reconstructed this to reflect the 1820s when New Echota became the capital of the Cherokee Nation. You can see that the Cherokee Indians assimilated the lifestyle of white settlers. After an orientation slide show and exhibits, take the self-guided walking tour. 1211 Chatsworth Hwy. NE. One mile east of exit 131 off I-75 N, via GA 225. 706-629-8151.

Nora Mill Granary

Nora Mill Granary, Sautee. It's almost impossible to leave the 120-year-old Nora Mill Granary without buying a bag of something. Tables are heaped high with cloth bags of grains: whole wheat flour, buckwheat flour, mountain batter mix, and three-grain pancake mix.

Then you find new things, too—such as popcorn meal ground from corn meant for popping, and pioneer's porridge made of equal parts yellow and white grits, rice, and

cracked Georgia wheat (just heat and eat). Mon.–Sat. 9 a.m.–5 p.m.; Sun. 10 a.m.–5 p.m. Sautee is located on GA 17 and 75, eight miles north of Cleveland. 800-927-2375.

Oak Hill Plantation, Rome. See *Berry Museum.*

Old Sautee Store, Sautee. National Register of Historic Places. This country store museum with its large collection of memorabilia dates to the 1870s. Located in the mountains of northeastern Georgia on the old Unicoi Turnpike at the junction of the Nacoochee and Sautee Valleys, it was once the center of the Cherokee Nation. You can browse through the Scandinavian Gift Shop and an international Christmas shop.

While you're at Sautee, pause to gaze over the valley and the headwaters of the Chattahoochee River. You'll see Mount Yonah (called Crouching Bear Mountain by the Cherokees). Junction of GA 17 and 255. 706-878-2281.

Paradise Gardens, Summerville. See *An Extra Touch of North Georgia: Howard Finster.*

Pickett's Mill Battlefield, Dallas. State historic site. For Civil War buffs, this is a don't-pass-it-up site because Pickett's Mill is one of the best-preserved Civil War battlefields. Living history programs authentically demonstrate Civil War weapons firing and military drills. Take a walk along the roads once traveled by both Union and Confederate forces. 2640 Mount Tabor Rd.

Five miles northeast of Dallas. 770-443-7850.

Robert Toombs House, Washington. State historic site. Toombs was called Georgia's unreconstructed rebel. He served as both a U.S. senator and secretary of state of the Confederacy during the Civil War. After the war, he refused to pledge his allegiance to the United States, and he died still a rebel. Watch a film and take a guided tour of Greek Revival house. 216 E. Robert Toombs Ave. 706-678-2226.

Rome. The city began in 1834 when five travelers met at a spring and decided to start a city. Each suggested a name, then they put them into a hat and drew out the name of Rome.

Go by Berry College, which claims to be the largest campus in the world. You can learn about Martha Berry, who devoted her life to bringing education within the reach of poor Appalachian children. (See *Berry Museum.*)

Sautee-Nacoochee Indian Mound

Sautee-Nacoochee Indian Mound, near Helen. A gazebo marks the burial place of

two young lovers, separated because of the warring Cherokee and Chickasaw tribes. Legend says that Nacoochee's father threw Sautee off the mountain so the young man could not marry his daughter. Heartbroken, she leaped after him. The two lovers managed to drag their bodies to each other at the foot of the cliff. They died in an embrace. They were buried, still locked in that embrace.

The Nacoochee Mound (on property that belongs to L. G. Hardman estate) is the site of a burial mound used by tribes long before the Cherokee arrived. The mound is on the State Register of Historic Places. Intersection of GA 17 (east) and GA 75 (north), two miles south of Helen.

Traveler's Rest

Traveler's Rest, Toccoa. State historic site. Built in 1833 as plantation home of Devereaux Jarrett, it once became a 19th-century B&B. (It's no longer a B&B.) Authentic antiques fill the rooms. Marvel at the white oak tree believed to be well into its third century. You'll also see several crepe myrtles that are at least a century old. US 123, six miles northwest of Toccoa. 706-886-2256.

Washington. This town was named in honor of George Washington and was the first city chartered in America by that name, as the president himself acknowledged on his trip through the town in 1791. The town is more associated with battles of the Revolutionary War than the Civil War. However, Washington was the last city to hide the elusive Confederate treasury of a half million dollars in gold, which was moved to the town in 1865 from Richmond, Virginia.

If you visit Washington, stop at the Kettle Creek Battleground that marks a battle in the Revolutionary War. In 1779, Elijah Clark led patriots against the British and saved the colony from British occupation.

Watson Mill Bridge State Park, Comer. The park has an original-site covered bridge 229 feet in length. (See **Covered Bridges and Gristmills of Georgia.**) This hundred-year-old bridge is supported by a Town lattice truss system, which is held together with wooden pins. Six miles south of Comer off GA 22. 706-783-5349.

William Weinman Mineral Museum, Cartersville. The purpose of the museum is to educate visitors about the earth sciences, rocks, minerals, fossils, and gemstones. The educational videos and lectures are worth taking in. In three exhibit halls, you'll see more than 2,000 specimens. Special features

you won't want to miss include a simulated cave and waterfall.

This is one of the most modern museums in Georgia and dates only to 1983. The family of William J. Weinman, a pioneer in barite mining in Bartow Co., donated funds to establish a museum in his honor. In 1986, Frank Mayo, a prominent chemical manufacturer, added the Frank and Winnifred Mayo Wing and Library. Tue.–Sat. 10 a.m.–4:30 p.m.; Sun. 2–4:30 p.m. Closed Mon. Admission charged. Exit 126 off I-75 and US 411. 770-386-0576.

AN EXTRA TOUCH OF NORTH GEORGIA: WINERIES

Georgia's history of wine production dates to the 1730s. Since the 1980s, wineries have increased in the state. Sand, quartz, and mica in the soil of North Georgia make the land fertile for growing grapes.

Chateau Elan

Chateau Elan, Braselton, is a winery and resort and resembles a 16th-century French chateau. Guests can sample local wines and wander through the interior plazas of shops and restaurants, and enjoy the artwork or walk along one of the nature trails and enjoy a picnic. Free winery tours and tastings. Daily 10 a.m. Closed Christmas Day. Take exit 48 (GA 211) off I-85 N. 800-233-WINE (9463).

Chestnut Mountain Winery offers free tasting, a wine-cellar tour, rooftop patio, observation tower, and nature trails on its 30-acre grounds. Tue.–Sat. 10 a.m.–6 p.m.; Sun. 12:30–6 p.m. Exit 48 off I-85, then follow signs along GA 211 S. 706-867-6914.

Fox Vineyards makes a pleasant stop on a wine-tasting tour. Its vineyards and winery are set attractively on a hillside. Mon.–Sat. 10 a.m.–6 p.m.; Sun. 1–6 p.m. 225 Hwy. 11 S, Social Circle. One mile south from exit 47 on I-20 E. 770-787-5402.

Georgia Wines, outside the town of Chickamauga, occupies a beautiful site that overlooks the lower slopes of Lookout Mountain. The winery features wine tasting and tours. The specialty is peach muscadine wine. Mon.–Sat. noon–6 p.m. Exit 141 off I-75 N, then follow signs. 706-923-2177.

Habersham Winery specializes in white muscadine wine but also produces other kinds of wine. Daily 10 a.m.–6 p.m.; Sun. 1–6 p.m. GA 365 in Baldwin. 706-778-9463.

Recipes

Fried Apple Pies. Mention fried pies to some folk today, and they think of the desserts available at fast-food restaurants. But what we're talking about here are the real things—individual fruit pies with a flaky crust. Not deep fried, but skillet fried in just enough shortening to cook the crust. Most popular are fried apple pies.

For your crust, mix together 2 cups flour, 2 teaspoons salt, 3/4 cup shortening, and 4 tablespoons water. Knead to make a smooth dough, then roll out and cut into rounds about 4 inches in diameter. (Slightly larger is okay, too.) For the filling: peel, core, slice, and cook 4 to 6 apples (depending on size) in a little water until translucent. Mash slightly, add sugar to taste, with a little butter, nutmeg, and cinnamon. Put 1-1/2 tablespoons of this mixture on half of a pastry round, then fold pastry in half so that other side covers filling. Pinch edges together with fingers or tines of a fork. Fry in a little shortening in a skillet, turning once. Drain on paper towels. Delicious warm or cooled.

Johnnycakes. Can be substituted as a side dish instead of cornbread.

Combine 2-1/2 cups cornmeal, 1 teaspoon salt, 2-1/4 cups milk, and 1 egg (beaten) in a bowl. Blend well. Drop by tablespoonfuls onto a hot greased griddle. Fry until golden brown, turning once (just like pancakes). Serve hot with butter or margarine. Also can be served with maple-flavored syrup if you like.

Apple Cake. Apples are a major crop in North Georgia. Apple cake is a specialty of this area.

Mix together 1-1/2 cups sugar, 1 stick butter or margarine, and 2 eggs. Sift together 1-3/4 cups flour, 1 teaspoon soda, 2 teaspoons baking powder, 1 teaspoon cinnamon, 1 teaspoon nutmeg, then add to first mixture. Stir in 3 cups finely chopped apples, 1 cup chopped English walnuts, 1 teaspoon vanilla, 1/2 teaspoon almond flavoring, and 1/2 teaspoon salt. Bake in buttered tube pan at 350° for 50 to 60 minutes. Serve with whipped cream if desired.

⋅⋅

Perhaps you'd like to try recipes handed down from Native Americans in Georgia. Here are two recipes provided by Governor Zell Miller (*The Legend of Hiawassee* [Franklin Springs, GA: Advocate Press, 1977], pp. 16, 19).

Squaw Bread. Ingredients include 5 cups plain flour, 2 tablespoons baking powder, 1 teaspoon salt, cooking oil for frying the bread, 1 tablespoon melted butter or margarine, and 2 cups milk.

Sift 4 cups of the flour with the baking powder and salt.

Combine milk and melted margarine or butter.

Place flour–baking powder mixture in a large bowl, and add the liquid ingredients, a little at a time, beating them in at first with an egg beater.

When the 4 cups have been worked into a soft dough with the milk, lightly flour a board with part of the remaining 1 cup of flour. Turn the dough out onto the board, and knead lightly, working in the rest of the flour.

Divide the dough into three parts, and shape each into a round pone about 1/8 inch thick and a diameter to fit the skillet. Pour oil in skillet 1/4 inch deep.

Heat the oil, and brown the breads quickly, one at a time, until golden on both sides.

Spread with any meat mixture or jam or stewed dry fruits. Cut into wedges and serve at once.

Indian Pudding. Ingredients include 1 quart milk, 1/4 cup water, 1/2 cup molasses, 1/2 cup stone-ground cornmeal, 2 tablespoons sugar, 1/2 teaspoon salt, 1 tablespoon butter, 1 egg (beaten), and dash of ginger, nutmeg, and cinnamon.

Scald milk. Mix water, molasses, and cornmeal, and blend this mixture into milk and bring to a boil. Remove from heat and add sugar, butter, salt, and seasonings. Cool and add egg. Bake 1 hour in baking dish in 325° oven.

Where to Eat

Here are some sample places to get a taste of North Georgia.

Appletree Farms, * Cornelia. Have you ever eaten fried pies? Don't leave Georgia without this southern experience. Plan to eat lunch at the Tree House Cafe for your first one because Appletree Farms is the place to sample this treat. Appletree Farms grows more than 20 varieties of apples. Get the fruit fresh or as cider, jams, and jellies. Located in the Blue Ridge Mountains of Habersham Co., it's about an hour's drive north of Atlanta on GA 365, south of Cornelia and Duncan Bridge Rd. (GA 384 to Helen). Open year-round. 706-776-8381.

*BJ's Restaurant,** Calhoun. You'll find real southern cooking that includes barbecue, country fried steak, and more vegetables than you knew they produced in the South. In shopping center at 102 Bryant Parkway (US 41), south of downtown Calhoun. 706-629-3461.

*Batesville General Store,** Batesville. Great stop for country food, famous for its hot biscuits. Breakfast and lunch year-round; dinner served April–October. GA 197 in northwest Habersham Co. 706-947-3434.

*Cellar Restaurant,*** Dalton. Perhaps for a dress-up dinner you'd like to try the Cellar in its downtown location. It features more traditionally American foods. Moderate-to-high prices. Mon.–Sat. 101 E. Crawford St. 706-226-6029.

*Courtyard Restaurant,** Helen. If you'd like to try casual dining on the river in the lovely town of Helen, the Courtyard is definitely worth a visit. Open seven days. Seasonal hours. 706-878-3117.

Courtyard Restaurant in Helen

*Dalton Depot,** Dalton. Enjoy anything from burgers to steaks in the ambience of what was once a Confederate Army ordnance depot. It dates back to 1850 when it was a Western & Atlantic rail depot. Mon.–Sat. 11 a.m.–11 p.m. 110 Depot St. 706-226-3160.

*Dillard House,** Dillard. **Don't Miss.** You'll want to linger over the family-style dining that provides southern cooking at its best. Unless you can say you've eaten here, even Georgians won't believe you visited North Georgia. US 441 (close to North Carolina–Georgia border). 706-746-5348; 800-541-0671.

*Edna's Cafe,** Chatsworth. Give yourself a big treat. Go by Edna's and order the coconut and peanut butter pie. US 411. 706-695-4951.

*The Grill,** Athens. This is the hangout for

students from the University of Georgia. Open 24 hours a day, seven days a week, for burgers, fries, shakes, and breakfast. 171 College Ave. 706-543-4770.

Laprade's, * Lake Burton. Once there was a town named Burton, but the site is now under Lake Burton. Stop at Laprade's for family-style genuine southern meals at a restaurant that dates back to 1925. GA 197 N. 706-947-3312.

Morrell's, * Cartersville. This informal family-run restaurant is a delightful place to eat your first grits and other southern breakfast items. If you're there for other meals, don't pass up the southern fried chicken. 1120 N.Tennessee St. 706-382-1222.

Oakwood Cafe, * Dalton. In the Dalton area, you get some of the best southern-style cooking here. 201 W. Cuyler St. 706-278-4421.

Smith House, * Dahlonega. There's nothing fancy at this rustic mountain inn and restaurant that serves family style. The Smith House has developed an excellent reputation and a faithful following. The variety of vegetables will overwhelm you—and it's an all-you-can-eat place—but leave room for the cured ham and southern fried chicken. Smith House was built in 1884 atop a vein of gold ore that wasn't mined because of its proximity to the town. 202 S. Chestatee St. 770-864-3566.

Stovall House, * Sautee. National Register of Historic Places. This country inn and restaurant began about 1837. Interesting menu. Nonsmoking. Reservations recommended. GA 255 N. 706-878-3355.

Taylor's Trolley, * Clarkesville. Stop by for a turn-of-the-century atmosphere. The special feature in this old drugstore is its soda fountain that can easily take you backward in time. Lunch Mon.–Sat.; dinner Tue.–Sat. US 441 at the town square. 706-754-5566.

Tiberio, * Rome. In a nicely refurbished turn-of-the-century bank building, owner Piero Barba, who comes from Capri, serves truly classic Italian cooking. 201 Broad St. 706-291-2229.

Trumps, * Athens. If you want more formal-but-comfortable dining, try Trumps. It's located in the old Georgia Hotel building. Continental lunches and dinners 11:30 a.m.–2:30 p.m. and 5–10 p.m. (later on Fri.–Sat. nights); Sun. 10:30 a.m.–2 p.m. Make reservations for weekend evenings. 247 E. Washington St. 706-546-6388.

Tuckers' Inn Family Restaurant, * Blairsville. Here is an excellent place to eat mountain trout in an antique dining room. We think you'll like the country buffet, which is truly southern-style cooking, served 4:30–9:30 p.m.; Sun. buffet 11 a.m.–4 p.m. GA 19 and 129 N. 706-745-6474.

Woodbridge Inn, * Jasper. If you'd like a

European flavor when you're in the North Georgia mountains, try this inn. You can drive there from Atlanta in about an hour. 706-692-6293.

SLEEPING

See **Georgia's Gorgeous Outdoors** for a list of parks with campsites, lodges, and cottages.

Boat House Bed & Breakfast, Madison. A B&B that was a sea captain's home in 1850, it was also the home of Woodrow Wilson's wife, Ellen. If you like antiques, you'll rave over this B&B, which has been restored in true Victorian style with clawfoot tubs and 12-foot ceilings. No pets; no children; non-smokers only. 383 Porter St. 706-342-3061.

Burnett Place, Madison. Located in Madison's Historic District, this restored Federal-type house dates to 1830. The owners have nicely blended the atmosphere of a bygone era with modern comforts. Private baths and full breakfast. 317 Old Post Rd. 706-342-4034.

Captain's Quarters, Fort Oglethorpe. Take a 15-minute drive from Lookout Mountain or downtown Chattanooga and you're there. Adjacent to the Chickamauga-Chattanooga National Military Park, it was originally part of Fort Oglethorpe. 13 Barnhardt Circle. 706-858-0624.

Claremont House, Rome. Built in 1882, it has Empire Victorian architecture; breakfast is served in a formal dining room. No smoking; no children under 10. Champagne and pastries at check-in. Second Ave. in east Rome. 800-254-4797; 706-291-0900.

Copecrest Resort, Dillard. This B&B has become famous for western square dancing. Betty's Creek Rd. 706-746-2134 or 746-6535.

Deer Lodge, Hiawassee. Located near the junction of GA 66 and GA 75, secluded cabins in woods for two or four persons are available. 706-896-2726.

Fieldstone Inn and Restaurant, Hiawassee. You'll find this upscale, full-service hotel on the western shore of Lake Chatuge. US 76. 706-896-2262; 800-545-3408.

Glen-Ella Springs Inn and Conference Center, Clarkesville. This hundred-year-old hotel has been converted into a 16-room country inn. US 441/23 between Clarkesville and Tallulah Falls. Rt. 3, Box 3304, Bear Gap Rd. 706-754-7295; 800-552-3479.

Gordon-Lee Mansion, Chickamauga. National Register of Historic Places. Stay at this B&B antebellum plantation house with its formal gardens and early southern aristocracy atmosphere dating to 1847. During the battle of Chickamauga, the Union army used it for its headquarters and a hospital. Private baths. 217 Cove Rd. 706-375-4728; 800-487-4728.

Lumsden Homeplace, Sautee-Nacoochee.

This 1890 farmhouse has been converted into a country inn with period furnishings. Private baths. Breakfast. GA 255. 706-878-2813.

Mountain Top Lodge, Dahlonega. About an hour's drive north of Atlanta, Mountain Top features wonderful views from the decks, antique-filled rooms, private baths, and whirlpool tubs. A special feature is the full country breakfast. 706-864-5257; 800-526-9754.

Old Clayton Inn, Clayton. A country inn with views of the mountain, it is located in downtown Clayton. No pets or smoking. S. Main St. 706-782-7722.

Rusharon, Cleveland. 1896 Logan-Henley House, moved to current location in 1980. Combined Victorian-Eastlake styles. Functioning fireplaces. Old Clarkston Hwy. (nine miles south of Helen). 706-865-5738.

Stanley House, Marietta. Why not stay at a Victorian inn that dates to 1895? It's within walking distance of historic Marietta Square, shops, restaurants, and theater. 236 Church St. 770-426-1881.

Stovall House, Sautee. National Register of Historic Places. Country inn and restaurant that began about 1837. Staff have a reputation for being friendly and helpful. GA 255 N. 706-878-3355.

Tate House, Tate. Resort and restaurant. National Register of Historic Places. Widely accepted as one of Georgia's historic treasures, the Pink Marble Mansion was built in 1926 by Georgia Marble Company president Colonel Sam Tate as a residence and showcase for the unique products of his nearby quarries. Especially look at the rare Etowah marble exterior and marble walks, fountains, and statuary. You'll be dazzled by the marble floors, baths and fireplaces. One hour north of Atlanta. From I-565 (GA 515) exit GA 108 (stoplight), east to GA 53. Outside GA: 770-735-3122. GA toll-free: 800-342-7515.

Tumlin House, Cave Spring. National Register of Historic Places. Victorian house built in 1842. Fruit and cheese at check-in. Southern breakfast. 38 Alabama St. 706-777-0066.

Villagio De Montagna, Cleveland. With its Mediterranean art deco, you'll wonder if you've gone to the French or Italian Alps. This expensive but one-of-a-kind inn was built by Xavier Roberts of the Cabbage Patch Kids industry. 706-865-7000.

Whitlock Inn, Marietta. Don't overlook this beautiful Victorian mansion, which is one block from the historic Marietta Square. Five guest rooms with private baths; you can relax on rocking chair porches or in the roof garden. Three miles west of I-75. 57 Whitlock Ave. 770-428-1495.

York House, Mountain City. National Register of Historic Places. Located in the northeast Georgia mountains, this 1896-built B&B has a country atmosphere. As you enjoy the period antiques, eat a hearty breakfast served on a silver tray. Between Mountain City and Dillard, one-fourth mile off US 441. 800-231-9675.

York House

SHOPPING

In North Georgia, there are plenty of places to shop for everything from clothes to furnishings for the home. The following list does not include all the great places to shop in North Georgia, but it gives you some places to start. You'll find numerous shopping opportunities everywhere you travel.

Alpine Village Factory Outlets, Helen. The stores advertise savings up to 70 percent on brand-name merchandise. Men's and women's clothing, shoes, kitchen items, linens, fragrances and cosmetics, rain gear, cards, and books. Open year-round. Ample parking. Main St.

Babyland General, Cleveland. An "adoption" center for soft sculpture dolls. Mon.–

Sat. 9 a.m.–5 p.m.; Sun. 10 a.m.–5 p.m. Off US 129 south of Cleveland. 706-865-2171.

Bavarian Alpine Village, Helen. Cobblestone plazas and Bavarian-style shops make this a different kind of shopping experience. GA 75 N. 706-878-2181; 800-858-8027.

Bill's Dish Barn and Billy Bob's Flea Market, Clarkesville. Pictures, pottery, dishes, sculptures, lamps, and birdbaths. Wed.–Mon. 9 a.m.–6 p.m. Closed Tue. Historic GA 441. 706-754-2048.

Dalton "Carpet Capital of the World." More than 100 carpet outlets, many located along the interstate. Exit 136 off I-75 N.

Dixie 400 Flea Market, Cumming. More than 200 inside booths plus outside spaces. Open year-round. Sat.–Sun. 9 a.m.–6 p.m. GA 400 and Bottoms Rd. at the 40-mile marker. 706-889-5895.

Georgia Antique Center and International Market. Combination antique and gift center and weekend flea market. See listing under *Antiques and Crafts*.

Lakeshore Mall, Gainesville. Mon.–Sat. 10 a.m.–9 p.m.; Sun. 1–6 p.m. Washington St. and Pearl Nix Parkway.

Mountain Casuals, Blue Ridge. Misses' and women's discount brand fashions. Mon.–Sat. 10 a.m.–5 p.m. GA 5 (Business Rt.). 706-632-7820.

Old Sautee Store, Sautee. Scandinavian ski

sweaters, trolls, crystal, sterling, gold, enamel, jewelry, embroidery, books, and gourmet foods—all of this in among old store memorabilia. Junction GA 17 and GA 255. 706-878-2281.

Penny's Garden, Mountain City. Gourmet herbal food products, herb plants, aromatherapy products, dried arrangements, and wreaths. Herbal workshops. Mon.–Sat. 9 a.m.–5 p.m. April–December. Blacks Creek Rd. 706-746-6918.

Sherry's Women's Wear Outlet, Blue Ridge. Women's discount fashions direct from factory, 50 percent off. Mon.–Sat. 10 a.m.–5 p.m. GA 5 (Business Rt.) and E. 1st St. 706-632-7420.

Shops of Dillard, Dillard. Antiques, crafts, Christmas decorations, and clothes. US 441.

Shops of Dillard

Silks for Le$$, Blue Ridge. Silk flowers and arrangements up to 50 percent less than retail. Mon.–Sat. 9 a.m.–5 p.m. E. Main St. 706-632-2161.

Tanger Factory Outlet, Commerce. This outlet has 45 stores. Mon.–Sat. 9 a.m.–9 p.m.; Sun. noon–6 p.m. Exit 53 off I-85 N. 706-335-4537.

Windy Hill Flea Market, Smyrna. This is Cobb County's largest indoor flea market with its 20,000-square-foot building. Fri. 12–7 p.m.; Sat. 10 a.m.–8 p.m.; Sun. 12–7 p.m. 1000 Windy Hill Rd., next to Belmont Hills Shopping Center.

AN EXTRA TOUCH OF NORTH GEORGIA: DALTON CARPETS

At the turn of the century, a farm girl from Whitfield Co. named Catherine Evans made a hand-tufted chenille bedspread that she had copied from an old family heirloom. She sold the bedspread and decided to make some more of the colored cotton spreads. Tourists, as well as local homemakers, bought them. Seeing a good thing, other women began making bedspreads at home, and in the next 20 years chenille bedspreads became a flourishing cottage industry. In addition to the usual patterns, some bedspreads featured the brilliant plumes of the male peacock. This pattern became such a favorite that the highway leading into Dalton (US 41) was known as Peacock Alley. Then in the 1920s, someone invented a machine to make the bedspreads in mass production. Later, someone else decided that the same machinery might be adaptable to making carpet—he was right, and the manufacture of carpet began. Today Dalton supplies more than half the world's tufted carpets.

Always Christmas/Hen's Nest, Hiawassee. If you're into crafts, this is the place to go. Drool over craft ideas, fabrics, and hard-to-find notions and Faye Wine's McCall's patterns, collectibles, old-world-style ornaments, and animated displays. Closed Sun. 706-896-3559.

Burton Gallery and Emporium, Clarkesville. Fine art prints, folk art, wood carvings, wind chimes, folk pottery, collectibles, crafts, oil paintings, bronze sculptures, and handmade jewelry. Mon.–Sat. 10 a.m.–6 p.m.; Sun. 1–6 p.m. Closed Tue. GA 197 at Burton Dam Rd. 706-947-1351.

Calhoun Antique Mall, Calhoun. The mall of 10,000 square feet holds the wares of more than 70 dealers. Mon.–Sat. 10 a.m.–6 p.m.; Sun. 1–5 p.m. Exit 130 off I-75 N. 1503 Redbud Rd. NE (GA 156). 706-625-2767.

Cartersville Antique Mall, Cartersville. Browse through 12,000 square feet of antiques. Closed Mon. 1277 Joe Frank Harris Parkway (US 41). Exit 125 off I-75 N, west to US 41, then one-eighth mile north. 770-606-0035.

Co-Op Craft Stores, Tallulah Falls and Dillard. The first store was founded in 1969 to increase the income of local people and preserve the mountain craft heritage. At both stores, you'll find thousands of authentic mountain crafts at reasonable prices. Shop either store seven days a week, year-round, for quilts, pillows, soft sculpture, toys, wood crafts, jewelry, pottery, and more. Mon.–Sat. 10 a.m.–5 p.m.; Sun. 12:30–5 p.m. Old Train Depot in Tallulah Falls; 706-754-6810. On the square in Dillard; 706-746-5990.

Dillard Minimall, Dillard. Antiques and decorator items. US 441. 706-746-2127.

Georgia Antique Center and International Market. This combination seven-days-a-week antique and gift center and weekend flea market showcases an assemblage of 200 merchants, restaurants, furniture, jewelry, collectibles, gold, silver, Oriental rugs, pottery, rare coins, books, and more. Some merchants open daily; market open Fri. noon–7 p.m.; Sat. 10 a.m.–8 p.m.; Sun. noon–7 p.m. On the I-85 access road just north of I-285. From Atlanta, take I-85 N, exit at Northcrest-Pleasantdale Rd. (exit 36), and go north on the access road. 6624 I-85 Northeast Expressway Access Rd. 770-446-9292.

Gourdcraft Originals and Co., Cleveland. This unique place offers useful and whimsical items made from nature. You'll marvel at things made from gourds. Gourd museum art from all over the world, and other nature-related shops and exhibits. Mon.–Sat. 10 a.m.–5 p.m.; Sun. 1–5 p.m. May–December. Open weekends and by appointment January–April. Highway 384 (Duncan Bridge Rd). 706-865-4048.

Grandma's Stuff, Stone Mountain Village. Affordable country and primitive antiques, unusual accessories and boxes. Mon.–Sat. 10 a.m.–5 p.m.; Sun. 1–5 p.m. 994 Main St. 770-498-9078.

Hambidge Center

Hambidge Center, Dillard. National Register of Historic Places. Founded in 1934 by Mary Crovatt Hambidge to preserve traditional Appalachian crafts, this is Georgia's only residential center for the creative arts. Check in at the office and then roam around the grounds. Gaze at the works of art, crafts, and folk art. The Hambidge Gallery exhibits May through October. Barkers Creek Mill at Hambidge, a water-powered gristmill, is open the first weekend of each month. Center is open Mon.–Fri. 9 a.m.–5 p.m. Located 3.5 miles off US 441 on Betty's Creek Rd. 706-746-5718.

Hartford House, Inc., near Cornelia. Quality handcrafted furniture and accessories. Mon.–Sat. 10 a.m.–5:30 p.m.; Sun. 1–5 p.m. On I-985/GA 365, three miles south of Cornelia. 706-778-3449.

Lofty Branch Art and Craft Village, Clayton. Works by more than 200 artisans. On US 441 S. Lakemont, six miles south of Clayton. 706-782-3863.

Main Street Gallery, Clayton. Contemporary crafts, folk art, paintings, rustic furniture, weavings, jewelry, and pottery. Main St. 706-782-2440.

Marietta Antique Shops, Marietta. Twenty-one shops, more than 200 dealers in and around Marietta. 770-429-0434.

Mark of the Potter, Clarkesville. Handmade crafts and pottery by 40 artists. This is the oldest craft shop in northeastern Georgia. You'll like the location in Grandpa Watts's Mill on picturesque Soque River. Daily 10 a.m.–6 p.m. GA 197, 10 miles north of Clarkesville. 706-947-3440.

Mountain Sounds, Rabun Gap. Handcrafted mountain and hammered dulcimers, Autoharps, psalteries, and other traditional instruments. Home of Thornton Dulcimers. You might want to buy recordings of a select group of beautiful traditional music or instruction books. Don't overlook the hand-carved songbirds by Orchid David.

Hours vary with seasons. US 441. 706-746-3244.

Olde Town Gallery, Blue Ridge. Antiques, home furnishings, and accessories. Valley Village Shopping Center. 706-632-6116; 800-523-7443.

Old Hotel Antique Mall, Ellijay. Collectibles and wood furniture. 11 North Ave., just off the square. 706-276-2467.

Old Madison Antiques, Madison. Antique furniture, glass, collectibles, baseball cards, and comics. Mon.–Sat. 10 a.m.–5:30 p.m.; closed Sun. 184 S. Main St. 706-342-3839.

Quilt Patch, Blairsville. South's largest selection of handmade quilts. Tue.–Sat. 10 a.m.–5 p.m. May–October. 1112 Gainesville Hwy. S. 706-745-5349.

Shops of Distinction, Roswell. Antiques and collectibles fill 6,500 square feet. Mon.–Sat. 10 a.m.–6 p.m.; Sun. 1–5 p.m. 11235 Alpharetta Hwy. 770-475-3111.

Step Back in Time, Inc., Madison. Antiques and collectibles, linens, glass, and furniture. Mon.–Sat. 10 a.m.–5:30 p.m. Closed Sun. 130 W. Washington St. 706-342-3311.

Tekakwitha, Helen. Native American leatherwork, jewelry, beadwork, paintings, drums, baskets, carvings, and pottery arts and crafts from several tribes. S. Main St. 706-878-2938.

Timpson Creek Gallery, Clayton. Antiques; American folk and decorative arts. Pause to look at the furniture made from bark, twig, heart pine, and antler. US 76. 706-782-5164.

Unicoi Craft Shop, Unicoi State Park. High-quality crafts cooperative in the Unicoi State Park main lodge. One mile northwest of Helen via GA 356.

Village Weaver, Dillard. Owner Sharon Grist was chosen as one of 200 best crafters in America for 1995 by *Early American Life* magazine. Her specialty is tartan weaving. You can tour her studio. Mon.–Fri. 9 a.m.–noon December–May; Mon.–Sat. 10 a.m.–4 p.m. June–November. US 441. 706-746-2287.

OUTDOORS

Within the northwest mountains lie some of Georgia's most valuable natural treasures. The Department of the Interior Bureau of Mines lists Georgia as America's number one producer of granite. These mountains also contain the world's largest deposits of marble. Although the fact is not widely publicized, Georgia marble adorns the New York Stock Exchange, the U.S. Capitol, and the Lincoln Memorial. Of the 198 minerals mined in Georgia today, 50 come from the Bartow Co. area, more than any other comparable area in the nation.

The northeastern mountains defy description. Someone has said that "spring spends the summer among them." The 360-

degree panorama from the tower atop 4,784-foot Brasstown Bald covers four states. The ravine at Tallulah Falls—the oldest natural gorge in America—plunges breathtakingly to a depth of 1,100 feet, second only to the Grand Canyon.

Waterfalls

Niagara Falls might get the publicity, but the waterfalls in North Georgia are as beautiful and much more scenic.

Cloudland Canyon, a Georgia state park, located in northwestern Georgia, was an unknown treasure and almost inaccessible until roads came into the area in the 1930s. Even today, it remains quite isolated.

Hiking in the area offers magnificent views. Rim Trail is five miles long and crosses Daniel's Creek. The Falls Trail goes down hundreds of steps and into the canyon. You'll be rewarded with the view of two fantastic waterfalls. The East Rim Trail (seven miles) requires a permit. Take I-75 N, exit at GA 2, go west on GA 2, turn left at GA 193, go south to GA 136, and then right.

Amicalola Falls, Dawsonville. The name is a Cherokee Indian word meaning "tumbling waters"—quite appropriate for these 729-foot falls, which are the highest in Georgia.

Amicalola Falls State Park, 16 miles northwest of Dawsonville. See **Georgia's Gorgeous Outdoors.**

Anna Ruby Falls, Helen. A 1,600-acre scenic area next to Unicoi State Park that features twin waterfalls of 50 and 153 feet,

an observation platform, fishing and hunting with permits, and picnic facilities.

Amicalola Falls

AN EXTRA TOUCH OF NORTH GEORGIA: STONE MOUNTAIN

We think there's something awesome about getting your first glimpse of Stone Mountain, just east of Atlanta. Its 1,683-foot-tall dome is the largest piece of exposed granite in the East. Part of the dramatic effect comes because of the stark contrast to the forested hills all around.

The first written record of Stone Mountain goes back to 1567 when the Spaniard Juan Pardo reported discovering what he called Crystal Mountain. In the 1830s, the state built a 160-foot wooden observation tower on top, but with nothing to anchor it, a storm blew it away. Quarrying began in the mid-1840s and continued for more than 100 years. The U.S. Capitol Building, the Panama Canal, Tokyo's Imperial Hotel, and the Fulton Co. (Atlanta) Courthouse all used Stone Mountain granite in their construction.

Stone Mountain

The most awesome moment comes when you see the carving. The memorial carving is one of the world's largest sculptures. Started in 1923, it took 47 years to complete. The figures are three prominent Confederates of the Civil War on horseback. Jefferson Davis, Robert E. Lee, and Stonewall Jackson are as tall as a nine-story building. They rest against a niche the size of a city block. Some have called this the southern version of Mount Rushmore.

***Tallulah Gorge.* Don't Miss.** This really is one of the most spectacular gorges in the eastern U.S., with its chasm two miles long and nearly 1,000 feet deep. The common word we hear from first-time visitors is *breathtaking*. This is a favorite stopping point along US 441.

At one time you could see Tallulah Falls, but they disappeared when the Georgia Power Company installed hydroelectric dams. However, the gorge itself is worth the visit. When you take in the sight, imagine walking a tightrope across the gorge. In 1886, Professor Leon (despite a stumble) did it. Almost a century later, in 1970, the flying Karl Wallenda made his heart-stopping tightwire walk across the chasm on a two-inch-thick, thousand-foot-long wire. Hollywood featured the almost sheer cliffs in the film *Deliverance* when actor Jon Voight climbed them.

Tallulah Gorge

Take a few minutes to browse through the crafts in the cooperative store inside the old railroad station of the Tallulah Falls Gallery (operated by the students of Tallulah Falls school, a coed boarding school sponsored by the Georgia Federation of Women's Clubs).

Tallulah Gorge has no Loch Ness monster, but from time to time, someone claims to spot the Yunwi Tsudini (little people)—

Native Americans who were supposed to have lived in the hidden nooks and crannies underground.

At the privately owned overlook concession stand, the outside view is free. The North Rim Trail reaches an overlook about a quarter mile from Terrora Park. The quarter-mile South Rim Trail leads out of Tallulah Gorge Park; an admission charge of $2 for adults and $0.75 for children benefits the local school district.

Toccoa Falls, Toccoa. A 186-foot waterfall on the campus of Toccoa Falls College. 8 a.m.–7 p.m. Two miles northeast of Toccoa off GA 17.

(Note: These aren't the only falls, but they are our favorites. You'll find many lesser-known waterfalls throughout the area. Local Welcome Centers provide information about local waterfalls.)

Biking

Pavement Ends Mountain Bike Tours. These are GT and Raleigh rental mountain bikes from rigid fork to full suspension. Multiple-day and group rental discounts available. Rentals include helmet, bike car rack, and instruction on equipment operation as well as riding techniques. Mountain bike tours offer a variety of terrain and skill levels. On GA 400 in the Long Branch Station Mini Mall just south of GA 60. 706-864-8525.

Fishing

Andy's Trout Farm and Wilderness Camp, Dillard. Would you like to catch rainbow trout? Try Andy's where you'll have 350 acres of well-stocked ponds and lakes. Bait and poles available. Fish cleaned. No license. No limit. Pay by pound. Cabins also available. Five miles west of Dillard on Betty's Creek Rd. 706-746-2550.

Golf

You can swing your clubs at the following North Georgia state parks (senior discounts available, and weekday specials usually offered year-round).

Hard Labor Creek, Rutledge. 706-557-3006.

Victoria Bryant, Royston. 706-245-6770.

Other places for golf include the following:

BEAA CC, Lindale. 706-234-8010.

Big Canoe Resort, Big Canoe. 706-268-3323.

Big Sandy, Trenton. 706-657-6738.

The Boulders at Lake Acworth, Acworth. 770-917-5151.

Butternut Creek, Blairsville. 706-745-5153.

Calhoun Elks, Calhoun. 706-629-4091.

Cedar Lake, Loganville. 770-466-4043.

Cedar Valley, Cedartown. 770-748-9671.

Centennial, Acworth. 770-975-1000.

Champions Club at Apalachee, Dacula. 770-822-9220.

Champions Club of Atlanta, Alpharetta. 770-343-9700.

Champions Club of Gwinnett, Snellville. 770-978-7755.

Chateau Elan Golf Club, Braselton. 800-233-WINE.

Chatooga/Trion, Trion. 706-734-2712.

Chattahoochee, Gainesville. 770-532-0066.

Chicopee Woods, Gainesville. 770-534-7322.

City Club, Marietta. 770-528-0555.

Countryland, Cumming. 770-887-0006.

Cumberland Creek CC, Marietta. 770-422-3800.

Deer Trail CC, Commerce. 706-335-3987.

Eagle Watch, Woodstock. 770-591-1000.

Fields Ferry, Calhoun. 706-625-5666.

Fieldstone Golf and CC, Conyers. 770-483-4372.

Fox Creek Golf Range and Exec. Course, Smyrna. 770-435-1000.

Gold Creek, Dawsonville. 706-265-2700.

Goodyear, Rockmart. 770-684-9343.

Green Acres, Rome. 706-235-7104.

Greene County CC, Union Point. 706-486-4513.

Green Hills CC, Athens. 706-548-6032.

Green Valley Greens, Cartersville. 770-382-8510.

Green-Way, Maysville. 706-652-2385.

Greystone, Douglasville. 770-489-9608.

Hamilton Mill, Buford. 770-945-1345.

Harbor Club, Greensboro. 800-505-GOLF.

Hartwell, Hartwell. 706-376-8161.

Heritage, Clarkesville. 706-754-8313.

Highland, Conyers. 770-483-4235.

Hollywood Hills, Cornelia. 706-754-2255.

Honey Creek Golf and CC, Conyers. 770-483-6343.

Horseleg Creek, Rome. 706-290-1982.

Idlewood, Lithonia. 770-987-0731.

Indian Trace, Chatsworth. 706-695-7353.

Innsbrook, Helen. 800-642-2709.

Jones Creek, Evans. 706-860-4228.

Kraftman Club, Coosa. 706-235-9377.

La Fayette, La Fayette. 706-638-9095.

Lake Lanier Island Hilton Resort, Lake Lanier Islands. 770-945-8787.

Lane Creek, Bishop. 800-842-6699.

The Legacy, Smyrna. 770-434-6331.

The Links at Brasstown Valley, Young Harris. 706-379-9900.

Meadow Lake, Cedartown. 770-748-4942.

Metropolitan Golf and Tennis Club, Lithonia. 770-981-5325.

Monroe Golf and CC, Monroe. 770-267-8424.

Mystery Valley, Lithonia. 770-469-6913.

Nob Nort, Cohutta. 706-694-8505.

Olde Atlanta, Suwanee. 770-497-0097.

Piedmont, Demorest. 706-778-3000.

Pine Hills, Winder. 770-867-3150.

Port Armor, Greensboro. 706-453-4564.

Prospect Valley, Rockmart. 770-684-5961.

Rabun County, Clayton. 706-782-5500.

Ridge Valley, Adairsville. 706-291-9049.

River Pines Golf, Alpharetta. 770-442-5960.

Royal Lakes CC, Chestnut Mountain. 770-535-8800.

Royal Oaks, Cartersville. 770-382-3999.

St. Andrews CC, Winston. 770-489-2200.

St. Marlo, Duluth. 770-495-7725.

Skitt Mountain, Cleveland. 706-865-2277.

Sky Valley Golf and Ski Resort, Sky Valley. 706-746-5303.

Springbrook Public, Lawrenceville. 770-822-5400.

Stonebridge, Rome. 706-236-5046.

Stonemont, Stone Mountain. 770-498-5715.

Stouffer Renaissance Pine Isle Resort, Lake Lanier Islands. 770-945-8922.

Sugar Hill, Sugar Hill. 770-271-0519.

Toccoa Golf and CC, Toccoa. 706-886-6545.

Towne Lake Hills, Woodstock. 770-592-9969.

Tunnel Hill, Tunnel Hill. 706-673-4131.

University of Georgia, Athens. 706-369-5739.

Weslyn Hills, Chatsworth. 706-695-9300.

Westchester Golf and CC, Dallas. 770-445-7655.

West Pines, Douglasville. 770-920-0850.

Whispering Pines, Colbert. 706-788-2720.

White Columns, Alpharetta. 770-343-9025.

Whitepath, Blue Ridge. 706-276-3080.

Windstone Golf and CC, Ringold. 615-894-1231.

Woodmont/Lakemont, Stone Mountain. 770-498-5715.

Hang Gliding

Did you know that North Georgia has

the best hang-gliding sites on the East Coast? You have 60 miles of ridgeline and the thermal-producing valley floor to make this not only the best in the East but one of the tops in the nation. You can see activity going on just about every day, and the area regularly hosts national and regional competitions. You can take off from Lookout Mountain Flight Park on McCarty Bluff. Located between GA 136 and Rock City on GA 189. 706-398-3549.

Horseback Riding

Eagle Mountain Equestrian Center, Ellijay. Stables and chalet; buggy rides; daily guided trail rides. GA 382. Call for reservations. Stables: 706-276-1014. Chalet: 706-276-1075.

Horseshore Bend Stables. Trail rides along the Ellijay River, 45 minutes from Marietta, at the Cornett Ranch. 706-276-3900.

Ranch at Coker Creek. Overnight horseback packages. A 99-minute drive from Atlanta. 800-288-3245.

Lake Sports

Lake Lanier Islands. There is something for everyone. You can boat, ride horses, camp, play minigolf, or cool off on the beaches and at the water park that features special water thrills. You can shop, eat, and spend the night. Less than 45 minutes northeast of downtown Atlanta. Take I-85 N to I-985 to either exit 1 or exit 2, then follow signs. Or take GA 400 to GA 20 and follow signs. 6950 Holiday Rd. 770-932-7200.

Lakes Rabun, Seed, and Burton. In the 1920s, Georgia Power constructed several dams to control the once-raging Tallulah River. The resulting lakes now offer beautiful mountain scenery easily glimpsed from a slow-moving drive or a bicycle tour. Maybe you'd like to have a scenic flatwater canoeing adventure and cross the three lakes west to east, with short portages past two dams. Contact Appalachian Outfitters at 706-864-7177 for canoe rentals and shuttle information. To reach the lakes from US 441, drive two miles north of Tallulah Falls, cross the gorge bridge, then a second bridge, and turn left immediately before the third bridge. Continue 2.5 miles (crossing yet another bridge), and turn left onto Lake Rabun Rd. One of the best Forest Service recreation areas in the Blue Ridge. All sights are accessed from Lake Rabun Rd.

Lakes at State Parks

A. H. Stephens Historic Park, Crawfordville.

Black Rock Mountain Park, Mountain City.

Bobby Brown Park, Elberton.

Elijah Clark Park, Lincolnton.

Fort Mountain Park, Chatsworth.

Fort Yargo Park, Winder.

Hard Labor Creek Park, Rutledge.

Hart Park, Hartwell.

James H. "Sloppy" Floyd Park, Summerville.

Moccasin Creek Park, Clarkesville.

Red Top Mountain Park, Cartersville.

Richard B. Russell Park, Elberton.

Tallulah Gorge Park, Tallulah Falls.

Tugaloo Park, Lavonia.

Victoria Bryant Park, Royston.

Vogel Park, Blairsville.

Watson Mill Bridge Park, Comer.

Rafting

Amicalola River Rafting Outpost, Dawsonville. Whatever your age, you'll find something you like: rafting, tubing, hiking trails, cabins, and hot tubs. One hour north of Atlanta, six miles west of Dawsonville. GA 53. 706-265-6892.

Canoe-The-Hooch, Cleveland. Whitewater canoeing and rafting on the Chattahoochee River. Near Helen. 46 Portwood Dr. 706-865-5751.

Chattooga River Rafting, Rabun Co. Whether you're a beginner or an experienced rafter, Chattooga can provide for you. Nantahala Outdoor Center: 800-232-7238; Wildwater Limited: 800-451-9972; Southeastern Expeditions: 800-868-7238.

Whitewater Rafting, Canoeing, and Kay-

aking on the Chattooga. This is Georgia's wildest river, so why not try the six-mile stretch? For a raft trip call Southeastern Expeditions: 770-329-0433. For a whitewater canoe or kayak trip call Buckhead Mountain Shop in Gainesville: 770-536-0081; or Wildwood Shop in Helen: 770-878-2541.

Skiing

Sky Valley Skiing, Sky Valley. Southernmost ski slopes in U.S. Season: December–February. 706-746-5302; 800-437-2416.

Spelunking

For cave explorers, the northwestern corner of Georgia, the northeastern corner of Alabama, and the southern part of Tennessee (which they call TAG) is a region linked by the Cumberland Plateau and a vast network of caves cut through limestone. Ellison's Cave with its 586-foot-deep Fantastic Pit is the deepest cave east of the Mississippi River.

A few caves are commercial and charge a fee, such as Cave Spring, which is west of Rome. Contact local guides, or call the National Speleological Society (in Alabama) at 205-852-1300.

Tennis

The following North Georgia state parks offer tennis courts. Other public recreation areas' availability will vary from town to town.

Cloudland Canyon Park, Rising Fawn.

Fort Yargo Park, Winder.

Red Top Mountain Park, Cartersville.

Terrora Park and Campground at Tallulah Gorge Park, Tallulah Falls.

Tugaloo Park, Lavonia.

Unicoi Park, Helen.

Trails for Hiking

See **Georgia's Gorgeous Outdoors** for additional information. Most parks offer walking trails.

Appalachian Trail. The internationally famous trail of 2,050 miles goes northward through 15 states, two national parks, and eight national forests. But it starts at Georgia's Springer Mountain. Take the 8.5-mile Appalachian Trail Approach from Amicalola Falls State Park. Contact the all-volunteer Georgia Appalachian Trail Club, P.O. Box 654, Atlanta, GA 30301, or the U.S. Forest Service. 706-536-0541.

Cloudland Canyon. See the discussion in the **Waterfalls** section.

Cohutta Wilderness Area. For hikers, we highly recommend Cohutta. An Act of Congress classified 34,100 acres of National Forest land as the Cohutta Wilderness Area. To preserve the wilderness isolation, access to the interior is by footpath only. (See *Chattahoochee National Forest* under **Georgia's Gorgeous Outdoors**.)

Whether you want to rough it or walk casually over rocky terrain, Georgia offers

plenty of opportunities for a summer outing. For more specific information on trails, write Forest Supervisor, Chattahoochee-Oconee National Forest, 508 Oak St. NW, Gainesville, GA 30501. 770-536-0541.

ENTERTAINMENT

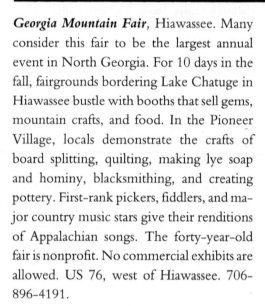

Georgia Mountain Fair, Hiawassee. Many consider this fair to be the largest annual event in North Georgia. For 10 days in the fall, fairgrounds bordering Lake Chatuge in Hiawassee bustle with booths that sell gems, mountain crafts, and food. In the Pioneer Village, locals demonstrate the crafts of board splitting, quilting, making lye soap and hominy, blacksmithing, and creating pottery. First-rank pickers, fiddlers, and major country music stars give their renditions of Appalachian songs. The forty-year-old fair is nonprofit. No commercial exhibits are allowed. US 76, west of Hiawassee. 706-896-4191.

Oktoberfest, Helen. It's like a trip to an Alpine village that takes place Thu.–Sun. in September. In October, it's daily except Sun. Helenites wear lederhosen and dirndls. Often genuine oompah bands direct from the mother country entertain the crowds. Spend some time gazing at the red-tile roofs, flower boxes, biergartens, and stucco-fronted shops selling cuckoo clocks, Christmas ornaments, Tyrolean hats, and leather coats. Helen also schedules a number of other events. For a complete list, call the Helen Welcome Center: 706-878-2181.

Panning for Gold, Dahlonega. Crisson Gold Mine, the oldest family-owned and -operated mine in Georgia. Learn the art of panning and find out how to screen for gemstones. 706-864-6363. Consolidated Gold Mine, underground gold mine tour. Display of 1800s equipment. 706-864-8473.

"The Reach of Song," Young Harris. Georgia's official state historic drama tells the story of mountain folk with fiddling, gospel singing, dancing, tale swapping, and problem sharing. Early June–early August. Clegg Auditorium on the campus of Young Harris College. On US 76, seven miles east of Blairsville. 800-262-7664.

Road Atlanta. Sports car, Formula One, motorcycle, and motocross events on its road circuit, April–November. Exit 49 off I-85 N, 39 miles northeast of Atlanta. 770-967-6143.

Stone Mountain Park, Stone Mountain. **Don't Miss.** This is the world's largest exposed granite mountain. Take a day to discover a 3,200-acre world where excite-

ment is carved in stone. A magnificent mountain monument of Confederate leaders is surrounded by recreation, entertainment, and leisure. It boasts of having the world's largest high-relief sculpture. The Confederate memorial carving, which measures 90 by 190 feet, took almost 50 years to complete. Ride the skylift or walk up the mountain. Enjoy a ride on the railroad, and don't pass up a trip on the paddle-wheel riverboat. Don't forget the antebellum plantation, antique auto and music museum, and wildlife trails. During the summer months, it features a highly popular laser show every night. Be sure to see the much-photographed covered bridge, which was moved from Athens in 1964. (See **Covered Bridges and Gristmills of Georgia**.) Gates open year-round 6 a.m.–midnight. Attraction hours: Summer: 10 a.m.–9 p.m.; other seasons: 10 a.m.–5:30 p.m. Go 16 miles east of Atlanta on US 78, off I-285. 770-498-5600.

Vines Botanical Gardens, Loganville. North Georgia's newest and most spectacular regional attraction will dazzle your senses every season of the year. Enjoy 25 acres of botanical gardens, beautiful gazebos, and 18,000-square-foot Vines Manor House. Be sure to take in the exquisite black swans, white swans, Indian running ducks, and other wildlife. Hours vary according to season. Admission: adults $2; children 5–12 $1; under 5 free. 3500 Oak Grove Rd. 770-466-7532.

White Water and American Adventures, Marietta. For family fun, visit this scenic water park that provides a wave pool and special area for young children. More than 40 attractions and rides and five restaurants. Lockers and shower rooms. Cobb Parkway. Take exit 113 on I-75 N. 770-424-WAVE.

 **March**

Cherry Blossom Festival, Conyers. International crafts, food, arts, exhibits, and games. 770-918-2169.

Daffodil Festival, Adairsville. 770-773-7480.

Roswell Antebellum Spring Festival and Colors Cultural Arts Festival, Roswell. Fine arts, crafts, and a barbecue. 800-776-7935.

April

Big Shanty Festival, Kennesaw. Celebrates April 12, 1864. 770-427-2117.

Granite City Arts and Crafts Festival, Elberton. Children's events, parade, 5K race/walk, barbecue, and vendors. 706-283-7499.

May

American Indian Festival, Lawrenceville. Native American foods, crafts, music, and demonstrations. Covered arena. 770-795-5743.

Bluegrass Festival, Adairsville Barnsley Gardens. 770-773-7480.

Howard Finster Arts Festival, Summerville. 706-857-4033.

New Salem Mountain Festival, Rising Fawn. (Also in October.) 706-398-1988.

Prater's Mill Country Fair, Dalton. Second weekend in May. (Also in October.) Centers on Benjamin Prater's 1859 gristmill. 706-275-6455.

Resaca Festival/Civil War Battle of Resaca Reenactment, Calhoun. 706-625-3200.

Rhododendron Festival, Hiawassee. Last weekend in April and first weekend in May. Arts and crafts show. 706-896-4966.

Snellville Days Festival, Snellville. Arts, crafts, concerts, and parade. 770-985-3500.

Springfest, Stone Mountain Park. Barbecue competition, live entertainment, arts, and crafts. 770-498-5702.

Spring Music Festival, Hiawassee. Hill music. 706-896-4191.

Sweetwater Fever Fine Arts and Crafts Festival, Mableton. Mother's Day weekend. Arts and crafts, Native American art, children's events, and live music. 770-739-0189.

Wildflower Festival of the Arts, Dahlonega. Fine art. 706-864-7449.

Winefest, Helen. Free wine tasting from

Georgia wineries and live entertainment. 800-858-8027.

June

Cave Spring Arts Festival, Cave Spring. Second weekend. Contact City of Cave Spring: 706-777-3382.

Marigold Festival, Winterville. Arts, crafts, antiques, and antique cars. 706-742-8600.

Native American Festival, Sweetwater Creek State Park, Lithia Springs. 770-732-5876.

July

Homespun Festival, Rockmart. Arts, crafts, parade, road race, fireworks, and entertainment. 770-684-8774.

August

Georgia Mountain Fair, Hiawassee. Twelve days. Bluegrass fiddlers, gospel singers, clog dancers, craft makers in woodworking, pottery, painting, leatherwork, furniture, jewelry, basket weaving, needlework, quilting, macramé, and dolls. Fairgrounds. 706-896-4191.

Theater Festival, Madison. Mid-August. Tour of 35 antebellum homes during festival. Contact Chamber of Commerce, P.O. Box 826, Madison, GA 30659. 706-342-4454.

September

Art in the Park, Marietta. Glover Park. 770-429-1115.

Arts on the Courthouse Square, Duluth. 770-822-5450.

Atlanta Jewish Festival, Dunwoody. Zaban Park. 770-875-7881.

Banks Co. Festival, Homer. Family fun downtown on the square. 706-677-2108.

Bartow Co. Fair, Cartersville. Fairgrounds. 770-382-4207.

Big Cedar Arts and Crafts Show, Cave Spring. Big Cedar Campgrounds. 706-777-8555.

A Blue Ribbon Affair, Marietta. More than 250 artists displaying their works. Jim R. Miller Park. 770-423-1330.

Chattahoochee Mountain Fair, Clarkesville. Fairgrounds. GA 17 N. 706-778-4654.

Cherokee Capital Fair, Calhoun. Cherokee Capital Fairgrounds. 706-629-2238.

Cotton Jamboree, Adairsville. Barnsley Gardens. 770-773-7480.

Creative Arts Guild's Festival, Dalton. Fine arts and crafts festival, and entertainment. 706-278-0168.

Duluth Fall Festival and Parade, Duluth. 770-476-3434.

Folk Festival for Preservation, Sautee-Nacoochee. Folk music outdoors, arts, crafts, and history museum. Sautee-Nacoochee Arts and Community Center. 706-878-3300.

Great Locomotive Chase Festival, Adairs-ville. September–October. 770-773-3451.

Gwinnett County Fair, Lawrenceville. Gwinnett Fairgrounds. 770-822-8000.

Historic Marietta Antiques Street Festival, Marietta. September–October. Marietta Square. 770-429-1115.

Madison Co. Agriculture Fair, Comer. Fairgrounds. 706-795-2096.

Monroe Crepe Myrtle Festival, Monroe. 770-267-4613.

New Manchester Days, Lithia Springs. Sweetwater Creek State Park. 770-732-5876.

North Georgia State Fair, Marietta. Live entertainment by top country music stars. Jim R. Miller Park. 770-423-1330.

Oktoberfest, Helen. September–October. Parade, music, and dances. 800-858-8027; Welcome Center 706-878-3677.

Old-Timers' Day, Blairsville. Vogel State Park. 706-745-2628.

Old Tyme Country Fest, Murrayville. Celebrate life the way it used to be. Go eight miles north of Gainesville on GA 60. 770-536-6828.

Paulding Meadows Arts and Crafts Festival, Dallas. 770-943-6793.

Pine Log Arts and Crafts Festival, Rydal. Pine Log United Methodist Church. 770-386-3324.

Pioneer Days Arts and Crafts Festival, Acworth. Acworth Beach. 770-775-6859.

Powder Springs Day, Powder Springs. Arts, crafts, games, road race, entertainment, and parade. 770-943-3912.

Raccoon Creek Bluegrass Festival, Dallas. 770-445-3574.

Riverfest Arts and Crafts Festival, Canton. Boling Park. 770-479-3017.

Roselawn Arts Festival, Cartersville. Rose-lawn Museum. 770-382-8277.

Roswell Arts Festival, Roswell. Historic town square. 770-640-3523.

Southern Appalachian Sampler Festival, Blue Ridge. Sugar Creek Music Park. 706-492-3819.

Southern Heartland Arts Festival, near Conyers. Entertainment, arts, and crafts. Salem Campground, exit 43 off I-20. 770-760-8846.

Taliaferro Co. Labor Day Fair, Crawford-ville. Arts, crafts, rides, amusements, and music. Alexander H. Stephens State Park. 706-456-2536 or 456-2140.

Yellow Daisy Festival, Stone Mountain Park. Arts, crafts, entertainment. 770-498-5702.

October

Alpenfest, Stone Mountain. Stone Mountain Park. 770-498-5702.

Banks Co. Halloween Festival, Homer. Hayride, contests, candy, and fun. Recreation Complex. 706-677-2108.

Calico Harvest Arts and Crafts Festival, Stone Mountain. Juried fine arts and crafts festival. 770-921-9440.

Carnesville Fall Festival, Carnesville. 706-384-4849.

Cherry Log Festival, Cherry Log. Go 10 miles north of Ellijay. 706-276-2200.

Chiaha Festival, Rome. 706-295-5576.

Coosa River Lighted Boat Parade, Rome. Downtown levee. 706-295-5576.

Dawson Co. Mountain Moonshine Festival, Dawsonville. 706-216-4089.

Fall Sugar Creek Bluegrass Festival, Blue Ridge. Sugar Creek Music Park. 706-632-2560.

Farm City Week Festival, Calhoun. Cherokee Capital Fairgrounds. 706-625-3200.

Festival of Life, Roswell. Roswell Municipal Auditorium. 770-594-6232.

Georgia Apple Festival, Ellijay. Two weekends. 706-635-7400.

Georgia Marble Festival, Jasper. 706-692-5600.

Ghostly Gatherings, Sandy Springs. Williams-Payne House. 404-851-9111.

Gold Rush Festival, Dahlonega. Rural pastimes such as a greased pig chase, tobacco spitting, and hog calling; Wild West shootouts; clogging; and especially gold panning. 706-864-3711.

Great Locomotive Chase Festival. See *September* listing.

Great Miller Lite Chili Cook-off, Stone Mountain Park. 404-872-4731.

Great Pumpkin Arts and Crafts Festival, Lake Lanier Islands. 770-932-7200.

Halloween Happenings, Marietta. Glover Park. 770-528-0616.

Heritage Holidays, Rome. 706-295-5576.

Hunt's Meadow Country Fair, Hiram. Arts, crafts, antiques, and music. 770-445-7166.

Lewis Memorial Fall Arts and Crafts Festival, Appling. 706-541-0156.

Lilburn Daze, Lilburn. Old Town Lilburn. 770-921-2210.

Mule Camp Market Festival, Gainesville. Folk art festival and entertainment. 770-531-0385.

Mule Day, Washington. Callaway Plantation. 706-678-2013.

New Salem Mountain Festival, Rising Fawn. See *May* listing.

North Georgia Folk Festival, Athens. Sandy Creek Park. 706-613-3620.

Oktoberfest, Helen. September–October.

Parade, music, and dances. 800-858-8027; Welcome Center 706-878-3677.

Olde Towne Fall Festival, Conyers. Games, arts, and crafts. 770-483-8615 or 929-0572.

Old Madison Days, Madison. Cotton Patch Craft Fair and Madison Agricultural Exposition. 706-342-4454.

Peach State Marching Festival, Rome. 706-236-5082.

Prater's Mill Country Fair, Dalton. Second weekend. See *May* listing.

Scottish Festival and Highland Games, Stone Mountain Park. Three-day event celebrating Scottish heritage. 770-498-5702.

Smyrna Jonquil Fall Festival, Smyrna. Village Green. 770-434-3661.

Snellville Arts in the Park, Snellville. 770-985-3535.

Sorghum Festival, Blairsville. 706-745-4745.

Tour of Southern Ghosts, Stone Mountain Park. Antebellum plantation. 770-498-5702.

Town and Country Arts and Crafts Festival, Lincolnton. 706-359-4300.

November

Alpenlights, Helen. November–February. Christmas lights. 706-878-2181.

Harvest Festival, Toccoa. Includes Civil War reenactment. 706-886-8451, ext. 269.

Holiday Celebration, Stone Mountain Park. November–December. 770-498-5702.

Lighting of the Chateau, Braselton. Chateau Elan. 770-932-0900.

Magical Nights of Lights, Lake Lanier Islands. November–January 1. 770-932-7200.

Tannery Row Festival of the Arts, Buford. 770-271-0436.

December

Apple Annie Christmas Craft Festival, Marietta. Catholic Church of St. Ann. 4905 Roswell Rd. 770-993-5640.

Christmas House, Mableton. Gift items and crafts. Historic Mable House. 770-739-0189.

Christmas in Dixie! Crawfordville. November–December. See 170,000 lights on Christmas display and hear Christmas music. Bennett Family Compound, six miles off I-20 (exit 55). 706-456-2265.

Christmas on Main Street, Lilburn. Old Town Lilburn. 770-921-2353.

Christmas Parade, Toccoa. 706-886-8451, ext. 269.

Festival of Trees, Rome. The Forum. 706-295-5576.

First Night Athens, Athens. December 31. 706-546-1805.

Historic Courthouse Tree Lighting Ceremony, Homer. Walking tour. 706-677-2108.

Marietta Pilgrimage: A Christmas Home Tour, Marietta. Tour of six beautiful homes decorated for the season. 770-429-1115.

A Merry Olde Marietta Christmas, Marietta. The square. 770-429-1115.

Old-fashioned Christmas in Dahlonega, Dahlonega. 706-295-5576.

Indian Princess Grave

AN EXTRA TOUCH OF NORTH GEORGIA: INDIAN PRINCESS TRAHLYTA

A pile of stones marks the grave site of this Cherokee princess. The people of her village (located on Cedar Mountain in Lumpkin Co.) found springs that reportedly halted the aging process. A rejected suitor named Wahsega kidnapped the princess and took her away from the springs. Without the magic water, she aged and became ill. Wahsega promised he would return her to the land of her people for burial. After she died, he kept his promise.

For years, anyone who passed her grave left a stone on the site for good luck. The grave site is on US 19, about nine miles north of Dahlonega. The springs (called Porter Springs today) are three-fourths mile northeast of the grave site but are overgrown, and you can't get to them for public viewing.

CHAMBERS OF COMMERCE

(Italics indicate a county name.)

Athens	706-549-6800
Banks	706-677-2108
Barrow	770-867-9444
Blairsville-*Union*	706-745-5789
Cartersville-*Bartow*	770-382-1466
Catoosa	706-965-5201
Chatsworth-*Murray*	706-695-6060
Chattooga	706-857-4033
Cherokee	770-345-0400
Cobb	770-980-2000
Conyers-*Rockdale*	770-483-7049
Cumming-*Forsyth*	770-887-6461
Dade	706-657-4488
Dahlonega-*Lumpkin*	706-864-3713
Dalton-*Whitfield*	706-278-7373
Douglas	770-942-5022
Elbert	706-283-5651
Fannin	706-632-5680
Franklin	706-384-4659
Gainesville-*Hall*	706-532-6206

Gilmer	706-635-7400	*Paulding*	770-445-6016
Gordon	706-625-3200	*Pickens*	706-692-5600
Gwinnett	770-963-5128	*Polk*	770-684-8760
Habersham	706-778-4654	*Rabun*	706-782-4812
Hart	706-376-8590	Rome, Greater	706-291-7663
Helen, Greater	706-878-3677	Royston-Franklin Springs	706-245-7868
Jackson	706-367-6300	Thomson-*McDuffie*	706-597-1000
La Fayette	706-375-7702	Toccoa-*Stephens*	706-886-2132
Lavonia	706-356-8202	*Towns*	706-896-4966
Lincolnton-*Lincoln*	706-359-7970	*Walker*	706-375-7702
Madison	706-795-3473	*Walton*	770-267-6594
Madison-*Morgan*	706-342-4454	Washington-*Wilkes*	706-678-2013
Oconee	706-769-7947	*White*	706-865-5356

CHAPTER
ELEVEN

MIDDLE GEORGIA

Cities of Middle Georgia

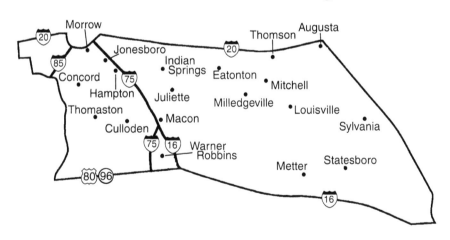

LOCATION	TO SEE/DO	EATING	SLEEPING	OTHER
	MIDDLE GEORGIA AT A GLANCE			

Augusta	Confederate Monument
	Cotton Exchange Building
	Discovery Center
	Gertrude Herbert Institute
	Laney-Walker Historical District
	Lucy Craft Laney Museum
	  of Black History
	Meadow Garden
	Morris Museum of Art
	Signers Monument
		Damon's, the Place for Ribs
		King George Pub
		LaMaison
		Sconyers Barbecue
		Word of Mouth Cafe
			Partridge Inn
			Telfair Inn
				Malls and outlets
				Masters Golf Tour
				Riverfront Marina
				Riverfront
				  Promenade

Concord			Inn Scarlett's Footsteps	
Culloden			Holmes Hotel	
Eatonton	Rock Eagle Effigy Uncle Remus Museum		Crockett House Rosewood B&B	Uncle Remus Attic
Indian Springs			Indian Springs Hotel	

Jonesboro	Ashley Oaks
	Confederate Memorial Cemetery
	Stately Oaks
				Juddy's Country
				  Store
				Atlanta Beach
				  Sports and
				  Entertainment
				  Park

Juliette	Jarrell Plantation Gristmill	Whistle Stop Cafe		
Louisville	Old Market			

Macon	Cannonball House and
	  Confederate Museum
	Garden Center
	Georgia Music Hall of Fame
	  (to open)
	Grand Opera House
	Harriet Tubman Historical
	  Museum
	Hay House
	Museum of Arts and Sciences
	Mark Smith Planetarium
	Ocmulgee National Monument
	Pleasant Hill Historic District
		Beall's 1860 Restaurant
		Len Berg's
		Natalia's
			1842 Inn	Cherry Blossom
				  Festival
				Mall

	MIDDLE GEORGIA AT A GLANCE			
LOCATION	**TO SEE/DO**	**EATING**	**SLEEPING**	**OTHER**
Macon (continued)	Rose Hill Cemetery Sidney Lanier Cottage Woodruff House			
Milledgeville	Historic District Tour Old Governor's Mansion Sally Davis House			
Statesboro			Statesboro Inn	
Thomaston	Auchumpkee Creek Covered Bridge			
Thomson	Upcountry Plantation Tours		1810 West Inn Four Chimneys B&B	Belle Meade Fox Hunt
Warner Robins	Georgia Aviation Hall of Fame Museum of Aviation	Pomos House of Barbecue		

Special Mention:	Atlanta Motor Speedway
	    (Hampton)
	Six Flags Over Georgia
	Hamburg State Park (Mitchell)
	Guideo Gardens (Metter)
	Spivey Hall (Morrow)
	Goodall Home (Sylvania)
	Georgia Golf Hall of Fame
	    (Augusta—to open)			

Middle Georgia is the area between the northern mountains and the southern plains and coastal region.

European immigrants first settled along the Georgia coast in the early 1700s. Soon the people of the then British colony spread from the first coastal settlement of Savannah upriver and established Augusta on the Savannah River in 1735. As they moved into Middle Georgia, they settled at Milledgeville (later the fourth capital of the state) on the Oconee River, Macon on the Ocmulgee, and Columbus on the Chattahoochee.

The Revolutionary War brought limited fighting to the colony. A century later, Middle Georgia suffered heavy losses during the Civil War. Union General Sherman's 1864 march to the sea with 50,000 Northern troops swept through the region, burning homes and towns as they marched onward. The destruction of Sherman's march devastated much of Middle Georgia.

Many residents still speak with regional pride of the glory days of the South. They point to the remaining antebellum architecture, monuments, and ghost towns as part of their heritage. If you drive through Middle Georgia, you'll pass courthouse squares, covered bridges, and monuments to the Confederacy—all reminders of a not-quite-faded past.

AN EXTRA TOUCH OF MIDDLE GEORGIA: SPRINGFIELD BAPTIST CHURCH, AUGUSTA

This is the oldest African-American congregation in the U.S. Although the church was organized in 1787, the current sanctuary dates to 1801.

Not only slaves had membership in the church, but free African-Americans as well. Some of them had bought their freedom. Others gained freedom through manumission.

From descendants of members of the Springfield church, churches and civic and charitable enterprises have come into existence throughout the region. 9 a.m.–2 p.m.

Sat. or by appointment. 114 12th St. at Reynolds. 706-724-1056.

WHERE TO GO AND WHAT TO SEE

Ashley Oaks Mansion, Jonesboro. Built about 1879, this planter's home took more than a million handmade bricks. Guided tours Tue.–Fri. 11 a.m., noon, and 1 p.m. 144 College St. 770-478-8986.

Auchumpkee Creek Covered Bridge, near Thomaston. See **Covered Bridges and Gristmills of Georgia**.

Augusta. This garden city of the South and America's golf capital began in 1735. Following Savannah, it is the next oldest settlement in the state. General Oglethorpe named it in honor of Augusta, the mother of King George III.

The Medical College of Georgia—the oldest in the state—started in 1828, and it is now part of the university system. The city also is home of Georgia's oldest academy.

Monuments honor outstanding citizens of the city. Be sure to see the one dedicated to four Georgia poets: Sidney Lanier, James R. Randall ("Maryland, My Maryland"), Father Ryan, and Paul Hamilton Hayne.

After the American Revolution, Augusta became the capital of Georgia for 10 years. George Washington visited in 1791. In 1806, Parson Weems published the famous cherry tree legend. (Washington cut down the tree, and when asked if he did it, he admitted his deed and said, "I cannot tell a lie.")

The only structure that still stands from the days of the Civil War is the 176-foot-tall chimney of the Confederate powderworks. It was then supposedly the world's largest munitions factory.

Take in the Cotton Exchange, the Morris Museum of Art, the Gertrude Herbert Institute of Art, the Springfield Baptist Church, and the Lucy Craft Laney Museum of Black History.

Don't bypass the Riverwalk promenade, which is really Augusta's major attraction, and walk around a mixture of modern and historic buildings. Entrance is at the end of 8th and Reynolds.

Cannonball House and Confederate Museum, Macon. This 1855 mansion of the Old South holds the distinction of being the only house hit by a cannonball in Macon during the Civil War—struck by the Northern forces of General George Stoneman on July 30, 1864. It is an authentic example of Greek Revival architecture and has since been restored with handsome furniture of the period.

Don't bypass the Confederate Museum, which is on the National Register of Historic Places. It is located in the former servants' house. Through the relics, you'll have a glimpse of old Macon and the Confederacy. Tue.–Fri. 10 a.m.–1 p.m. and 2–4 p.m.; Sat.–Sun. 1:30–4:30 p.m. Special rates for tours. 856 Mulberry St. 912-745-5982.

Confederate Memorial Cemetery, Jonesboro. This is the final resting place of more than 600 Confederate soldiers who died in the battle of Jonesboro, August 31–September 1, 1864. Open daily. McDonough and Johnson Streets.

Confederate Monument, Augusta. This 72-foot-high monument dates back to 1878. Life-size likenesses of Generals Robert E. Lee, Stonewall Jackson, Thomas R. R. Cobb, and W. H. T. Walker surround the bottom of the monument, but it memorializes a private at the top. 700 block of Broad St.

Cotton Exchange Building, Augusta. Built in 1886 for the business activities of cotton farmers, brokers, and buyers in what was one of the largest inland cotton markets in the world, the Cotton Exchange Building now houses the Historic Cotton Exchange Welcome Center, the Cotton Exchange Museum, and the Augusta-Richmond Co. Convention and Visitors Bureau.

The Augusta Cotton Exchange used the building until 1964. In 1978, it was entered into the National Register of Historic Places. After that, no one used the building, and by 1988, the neglect showed. Renovations began and included painstaking attention to details of the original structure. A local rumor said that a large blackboard used for posting daily market quotes existed behind a wall. It was correct. Renovators found the 45-foot wooden board intact and still chalked with cotton, currency, and commodities prices. The figures dated back to the early 1900s. 32 8th St. 706-724-4067; 800-726-0243.

Discovery Center, Augusta. A $16.2 million hands-on educational science and math museum. Opens spring of 1996 on the Riverwalk in central Augusta, only blocks from the Georgia Hall of Fame. It is a partnership between the National Science Center Foundation and the U.S. Army. They plan for it to become the cornerstone of a national network promoting math, science, electronics, and computer arts education.

Garden Center, Macon. In 1910, noted Georgia architect Neel Reid designed this 16th-century English-style four-story home for Joseph N. Neel. In 1957, the house became headquarters for the Federated Garden Clubs of Macon. The refurbished Neel House contains elaborate paneling, original fixtures, and furnishings. Accessibility for persons with disabilities. Garden Center house and grounds open Mon.–Fri. 9 a.m.– 1 p.m. September–May. 912-742-0921.

Garden Center in Macon

Georgia Aviation Hall of Fame, Warner Robins. The Wright brothers started their flying school in August in 1910. A special wing of the Museum of Aviation honors Georgia's pioneer aviators, men and women. (See *Museum of Aviation.*)

Georgia Golf Hall of Fame, Augusta. Located along the riverfront in central Augusta, this 60,000-square-foot museum will celebrate the history of golf in the city of the Masters Tournament. Plans call for the $24 million attraction to include an interactive theater where viewers can have their swings analyzed and also play some of the most famous holes in the golf course world. A holographic theater will show some of the world's greatest golfers in 3-D form. Scheduled for completion spring 1997.

Georgia Music Hall of Fame, Macon. This 38,000-square-foot, $6.5 million museum will showcase memorabilia of famous Georgia musicians, including Macon residents Otis Redding and "Little Richard" Penniman. The plan is to offer vintage listening rooms, a theater, and a library with archives. Scheduled to open mid-March 1996. Exit 4 off I-16, M. L. King Jr. Blvd.

Gertrude Herbert Institute of Art, Augusta. This house was built in 1818 for the then mayor, Nicholas Ware. The Federal-style mansion features an oval interior spiral staircase among its extravagant architectural details. Tue.–Fri. 10 a.m.–5 p.m.; Sat. 10

a.m.–2 p.m. Admission charged. 506 Telfair St. 706-722-5495.

Grand Opera House, Macon. It was built in 1884 as the Academy of Music, and the Macon Arts Council restored it in 1970. With a seating capacity of 1,057, the Grand Opera House once showcased leading stage and musical artists such as Will Rogers and Sarah Bernhardt. Tours Mon.–Fri. 10 a.m., noon, 2 p.m. Admission charged. 651 Mulberry St. 912-749-6580.

Hamburg State Park, Mitchell. You'll want to see the 1921 water-powered gristmill that continues to grind corn into hominy and meal (which you can buy at the country store) set against a wide bank of falls. A museum displays artifacts of rural country living. Hamburg Rd. (See **Georgia's Gorgeous Outdoors**.) 912-552-2393.

Harriet Tubman Historical and Cultural Museum, Macon. Named for the famed conductor on the Underground Railroad— a pre–Civil War method of smuggling slaves to freedom into the Northern states and Canada. View the mural *From Africa to America,* painted by local artist Wilfred Stroud, which depicts the history of African Americans from their capture in Africa to the present. Mon.–Fri. 9 a.m.–5 p.m.; Sat. 2–5 p.m. 340 Walnut St. 912-743-8544.

Hay House, Macon. Built 1855–59 and called the palace of the South, the Hay House is a National Historic Landmark. It is also one of the finest houses to survive from antebellum days (era prior to the Civil War). The Italian Renaissance Revival mansion is 18,000 square feet on four levels with a three-story cupola. It even holds a secret room where the Confederate treasury was supposed to have been hidden for a time. Mon.–Sat., 10 a.m.–5 p.m.; Sun. 1–5 p.m. Closed holidays. Admission charged. 934 Georgia Ave. From I-75 to I-16 E, exit at Spring St., turn right and go two and one-half blocks to Georgia Ave. and Hay House. 912-742-8155.

Indian Springs Hotel

Indian Springs Hotel, Indian Springs. Built in 1823 as a tavern and inn by Chief William McIntosh and Joel Bailey, it is the only surviving antebellum mineral springs hotel in Georgia. The hotel is being restored to its original condition, and the landscape is being re-created to the period of 1823–33. Take I-75 S to exit 67; proceed southeast on US 23 and then south on GA 42 to Indian Springs. Hotel is across from the entrance to Indian Springs State Park. Open on weekends and for special events, April–November.

Jarrell Plantation, Juliette. State historic site. This Georgia plantation will enable you to see an intact working farm from the 1850s with 20 historic buildings that date from 1847 to 1945. This is believed to be the largest and most complete collection of original family artifacts from this time period in Georgia. Tue.–Sat., 9 a.m.–5 p.m.; Sun. 2–5:30 p.m. Admission charged. It's 18 miles from I-75 and Forsyth (exit 61). 912-986-5172.

Laney-Walker North Historic District, Augusta. In the 19th century, a multiethnic working-class community of African-, Irish-, and Chinese-Americans settled in Augusta. Later, in the early 20th century, it became a flourishing African-American community. The Penny Savings Bank, built about 1922, is located in this area. Borders D'Antignac St. and Walton Way, 7th and Twiggs Streets, Laney-Walker Blvd., and Phillips and Harrison Streets. Self-guided tours.

Lucy Craft Laney Museum of Black History and Conference Center, Augusta. Community leader and educator Lucy Laney was born into slavery, but she went on to help shape the predominantly African-American neighborhood where businesses, theaters, and schools flourished at the turn of the century. A museum and conference center now occupy her former home. Tours by appointment only. (Pick up an African-American heritage tour pamphlet from the Visitors Center; 800-726-0243.) 1116 Phillips St. 706-724-3576.

Macon. The city was established in 1822. Its downtown Poplar Street is an "avenue of flags" with flags of all the U.S. states and territories displayed.

The city claims that the first Christian baptisms in the United States—done by a Spanish priest—took place in the Ocmulgee River in 1540.

Try to go in March, the most beautiful month of the year, with thousands of Yoshine cherry trees in bloom. (See *Cherry Blossom Festival.*) The city has 60 buildings on the National Register, of which the most notable is the Hay House (see above), an ornate Italian Renaissance mansion. You can also see a replica of an 1806 blockhouse called Fort Hawkins, which marks the birthplace of Macon. The Ocmulgee River became the southwestern boundary of the United States in 1805 after a treaty with the Creek. The government built the fort to put down uprisings by the Native Americans. (The Works Progress Administration—WPA—built this replica in 1938.) 912-743-3291.

Among other places to visit: Ocmulgee National Monument and the Pleasant Hill Historic District (see below). The Lamar Mound features a rare conically shaped mound with a spiral mount; to see it, you'll have to make arrangements with the Park Service (at the Visitors Center).

Meadow Garden, Augusta. This cottage of

George Walton was built in 1794. Walton signed the Declaration of Independence and later became a two-term Georgia governor. The cottage is the oldest documented house in the city and the first historic preservation project undertaken in Georgia. Mon.–Fri. 10 a.m.–4 p.m. Admission charged. 1320 Independence Dr. 706-724-4174.

Milledgeville Historic District Tour, Milledgeville. The city was the capital of Georgia (Act of 1804) until replaced by Atlanta in 1868.

Milledgeville was named for John Milledge, governor of Georgia (1802–6), U.S. senator (1806–9), and donor of the land for the University of Georgia in Athens. In 1861, the state declared secession from the Union, and from here, Governor Joe Brown directed Georgia's participation in the Civil War. When Northern General Sherman passed through Milledgeville in November 1864, he seized the town for two days, burned government buildings, but spared most of the city.

Historic District Tour signs designate the route, and the brochure describes each stop along the way. Some of the 37 stops are open to the public. Public guided trolley tours available on Tue. and Fri. 10 a.m. Group tours by appointment. Contact Convention and Visitors Bureau at 200 W. Hancock St. Mon.–Fri. 9 a.m.–5 p.m.; Sat. 10 a.m.–2 p.m. Closed holidays. 800-653-1804; 912-452-4687.

Morris Museum of Art, Augusta. These collections highlight paintings of southern artists. One 10th St. Tue.–Sat. 10 a.m.–5:30 p.m. Admission charged; free Sun. 706-724-7501.

Museum of Arts and Sciences, Mark Smith Planetarium, Macon. Nature trails and a whale fossil skeleton discovered near Macon are parts of the growing features of the Museum of Arts and Sciences. Different gem and mineral collections are displayed on a rotating basis. Two art galleries in a 22,000-square-foot addition change exhibits frequently.

Inside the museum building, the Mark Smith Planetarium is one of the largest in the state. Quadraphonic sound, 6,000 stars, lasers, and special effects bring space science to life. Shows change every two months. Admission covers museum and planetarium. Special planetarium shows include Cosmic Concert Fri.–Sat. 9 p.m. Free admission to museum and planetarium Mon. 9 a.m.–5 p.m. and Fri. 5–9 p.m. Also free is use of the observatory, open Fri. and Sat. evenings, weather permitting. 4182 Forsyth Rd. 912-477-3232.

Museum of Aviation, Warner Robins. The Museum of Aviation is home to more than 80 aircraft displays, and it is Georgia's official Aviation Hall of Fame. Daily 10 a.m.–5 p.m. Closed major holidays. GA 247 at the Russell Parkway exit. 912-926-6870.

Ocmulgee National Monument, Macon. You can see 12,000 years of Native American heritage. Several platform mounds and a prehistoric earth lodge form part of the largest archaeological development east of the Mississippi. The museum's permanent collection exhibits artifacts from the six Native American tribes that occupied the site at various times. Throughout the year you can see Native American arts, crafts, and demonstrations. Be sure to watch the brief film *People of the Macon Plateau,* which is shown throughout the day. Daily 9 a.m.–5 p.m. Visitors Center adapted for persons with disabilities. 1207 Emery Hwy. 912-752-8257.

Old Governor's Mansion, Milledgeville. This mansion was home for Georgia's governors 1838–68. This National Historic Landmark house is furnished in period antiques. Tue.–Sat. 10 a.m.–4 p.m.; Sun. 2–4 p.m. Guided tours begin on the hour. Admission charged. Closed Mon. and holidays. 912-453-4545.

Old Market, Louisville. The town was planned to duplicate the city of Philadelphia on a smaller scale and was named to honor France's King Louis XVI. It soon became the center of commerce when Louisville was capital of Georgia (1796–1804). Louisville was a stopover on the Georgetown-Savannah Trail.

This market where people traded slaves, lands, and goods started about 1795. You can still see the hand-hewn oaks that support the roof of the original slave market. US 1 and GA 24. Self-guided tours.

Pleasant Hill Historic District, Macon. Be-

gun in the 1870s, this African-American community is still active. Area covers College Street, Vineville Avenue, Rogers and Neal Streets. Driving tours permitted.

Rock Eagle Effigy

Rock Eagle Effigy, Eatonton. You'll want to pause and think about the 1,000-year-old aboriginal Rock Eagle effigy mound. It resembles a bird of prey standing upright with outstretched wings and measures 102 feet from wing tip to wing tip.

Experts believe the effigy is an eagle because of its significance in Native American mythology. The eagle takes its shape from thousands of rocks that were laboriously transported and heaped into a huge mound. *Rock Eagle is the only effigy site in Georgia.* Although now guarded by a tall wire fence, it looks as if no stone has been moved for centuries. The parting words of a Creek chief are inscribed on a marker at the site:

Tread Softly Here White Man
For Long Ere You Came
Strange Races Lived, Fought, and Loved
Located on US 441 seven miles north of

Eatonton in the Rock Eagle 4-H campground.

Tower at Rock Eagle Effigy

Rose Hill Cemetery, Macon. This is an excellent example of 19th-century landscape design that slopes toward the Ocmulgee River. It is one of the oldest surviving public cemetery-parks in the nation. It is listed on the National Register of Historic Places. Confederate Square encloses 600 Confederate and Union soldiers' markers. Self-guided tour. Open daily until sundown. 1091 Riverside Dr. 912-751-9119.

Sally Ellis Davis House, Milledgeville. Mrs. Davis was principal at the African-American Eddy School for more than 50 years. The school was a center for the community's educational, social, and religious events until 1945. Renovators plan to use the house as a museum of African-American heritage. Opening to be announced. 301 S. Clark St.

Sidney Lanier Cottage, Macon. Musician and poet Sidney Lanier was born in this Victorian cottage in 1842. Among Lanier's best-known poems are "The Marshes of Glynn" and "Song of the Chattahoochee." The cottage and furnishings show the architecture of the period. It is now the headquarters of the Middle Georgia Historical Society. Weekdays 9 a.m.–1 p.m. and 2–4 p.m.; Sat. 9:30 a.m.–12:30 p.m. Closed holidays. Admission charged. Guided tour. 935 High St. 912-743-3851.

Signers Monument, Augusta. The 1848 monument commemorates Georgia's signers of the Declaration of Independence—George Walton, Lyman Hall, and Button Winnett—with a 50-foot obelisk. Two of the three signers are buried underneath it. 500 block of Greene St.

Stately Oaks

Stately Oaks, Jonesboro. This 1839 plantation home was built of heart pine in the then popular Greek Revival architecture. You can walk into the original log kitchen and other rustic outbuildings. Wed.–Fri. 11 a.m.–3:30 p.m.; the second and fourth Sun. 2–4 p.m. On occasion, tour days canceled.

On Carriage Lane, off Jodeco Rd. south of Jonesboro. Exit 76 on I-75 south of Atlanta. 770-473-0197.

Uncle Remus Museum, Eatonton. The museum is a log cabin made from two original Putnam Co. slave cabins—similar to the one occupied by Uncle Remus, the character made famous by Joel Chandler Harris. Colorful scenes in each window depict the countryside of a southern plantation during antebellum days. The focal point is a large painting of Uncle Remus and the Little Boy. First editions of many of Mr. Harris's works and articles of interest fill a counter near the center of the museum. Turner Park, site of the museum, is part of the original home place of Joseph Sidney Turner, the Little Boy in the tales of Uncle Remus. Seek out the Uncle Remus marker near the center of town. Brer Rabbit's statue stands in front of the courthouse. Mon.–Sat. 10 a.m.–noon and 1–5 p.m.; Sun. 2–5 p.m. Closed Tue. in September–May. Admission charged. Three blocks south of the courthouse on US 441.

Uncle Remus Museum

Upcountry Plantation Tours, Thomson. As the name suggests, you can visit historic local homes. The most distinctive is the Rock House, one of the oldest dwellings still standing in Georgia. The fieldstone structure dates from around 1785. The interior house museum is open by arrangement with the Chamber of Commerce (111 Railroad St.). 706-595-5584.

Woodruff House, Macon. Of Greek Revival architecture, the house was built in 1836 for Jerry Cowles, a banker, by Macon's master architect and builder Elam Alexander. The ballroom once hosted a ball for Winnie Davis, daughter of Jefferson Davis, president of the Confederate States in the Civil War. The house was sold in 1847 to Colonel Joseph Bond, a wealthy cotton planter. It has been restored, and it is now owned and operated by Mercer University. Open for tours by appointment only. 958 Bond St. 912-744-2715.

EATING

Recipes

Fried Green Tomatoes. Recently made famous by the movie *Fried Green Tomatoes* (see *Whistle Stop Café*), this delicacy is something you may want to try at home.

Take several green tomatoes (number depends on how many people you're feeding, of course), wash and cut into 1/2-inch-thick slices. Mix together flour, salt, pepper, and just a little bit of sugar. Dip the tomato slices in the flour mixture, coating both sides, and fry in oil in skillet until browned. (Older recipes call for fat instead of oil.)

Southern-Style Fried Sweet Potatoes. Try them, you can't help but like them.

Wash 3 medium-sized sweet potatoes (about 1-1/4 pounds), and cook in boiling water about half an hour or until barely tender. Don't overcook. Remove from water, cool, then peel. Cut into 1/2-inch slices. Coat with flour on both sides. Fry in melted butter in moderately hot skillet, turning once. (Should be lightly browned on both sides.) Sprinkle with a little sugar. Serve as side dish with ham.

Collards. Buy fresh collard greens at the local supermarket if you haven't grown them.

Wash collard leaves; break off extra stem lengths, especially if they appear tough. Tear into pieces, and cook uncovered 15 minutes in boiling water. Pour off the water, add fresh water and seasoning, and cook 30 minutes or until tender. Don't "drown" your greens in water, but use just enough water to cover top of greens. (Although a piece of fatback is traditional seasoning, today's health-conscious cooks often use flavor substitutes.) Many people enjoy freshly chopped onion on their collards, along with just a drop or two of vinegar. Eat with cornbread, or try the cornmeal dumplings recipe that follows.

Cornmeal Dumplings. Combine 2 cups cornmeal, 1/2 teaspoon sugar, 1/4 teaspoon pepper, 1/2 teaspoon celery seed, and 1 teaspoon dry mustard. Stir in 2 tablespoons melted shortening. Add enough boiling water to make a medium stiff mixture. Cover and let set for 5 minutes. Then shape into small, flat dumplings and drop on top of cooked greens. Cover pan and allow to cook 20 to 30 minutes. (If desired, before cooking, add 3 grated green onions to cornmeal mixture.)

Old-Fashioned Banana Pudding. Many of today's banana puddings are made with pudding mixes. If you want to taste the way banana pudding is supposed to be, try this old recipe.

Mix together 4 egg yolks, 1 cup milk, 2 cups sugar, 1 tablespoon butter, 1 tablespoon flour, and a pinch of salt. Cook in a double boiler and stir while boiling. Cook until it ropes (begins to get thick). Let this filling cool. In a flat dish, put a layer of vanilla wafers, then a layer of sliced bananas. Pour filling over all. Repeat until all the filling is used. Beat the egg whites until stiff and ice the pudding (put over pudding). Put in oven long enough for the icing to brown. Let cool and then it is ready to serve. (This recipe suggests serving the pudding over cake!)

Where to Eat

Beall's 1860 Restaurant and Lounge, ** Macon. On the National Register of Historic Places. Magnificent home built in 1860 by wealthy planter Nathan Beall. The surroundings and food seek to provide the flavor of the Old South. Dinner Mon.–Sat. 5 p.m. 315 College St. 912-745-3663.

Damon's, the Place for Ribs,* Augusta. Ribs and prime rib are the specialties. Sun.–Thu. 11 a.m.–10 p.m.; Fri.–Sat. 11 a.m.–11 p.m. 3064 Washington Rd. 706-860-7427.

King George Pub,* Augusta. You can order English specialties or classic American fare. On the plaza at 2 8th St. 706-724-4755.

LaMaison,** Augusta. Offers game dishes and on-the-premise prepared desserts. Mon.–Sat. 6–10:30 p.m. 404 Telfair St. 706-722-4805.

Len Berg's,* Macon. Casual dress; carryout; good food. Mon.–Sat. 11:15 a.m.–2:30 p.m. Closed Sun. and holidays. Old Post Office Alley. 912-742-9255.

Natalia's,** Macon. Italian cuisine, upscale. Mon.–Sat. 6–11 p.m. 2720 Riverside Plaza. 912-741-1380.

Pomos House of Barbecue,* Warner Robins. Barbecue and side dishes. Mon.–Wed. 11 a.m.–9:40 p.m.; Thu.–Sat. 11 a.m.–10 p.m. 2766 Watson Blvd. 912-953-2060.

Sconyer's Barbecue,* Augusta. Specializes in hickory-flavored barbecue, including a low-cholesterol low-sodium version. 2250 Sconyers Way. Exit 6 off I-520. 706-790-5411.

Whistle Stop Cafe,* Juliette. This was the movie set for the film version of Fannie Flagg's novel, *Fried Green Tomatoes at the Whistle Stop Cafe.* Sample the fried green tomatoes at the cafe located on the banks of the Ocmulgee River. Southern specialties at breakfast and lunch daily year-round. Mon.–Sat. 8 a.m.–2 p.m.; Sun. noon–7 p.m. It's 18 miles east of Forsyth. Take exit 61 off I-75 S, or exit 62 off I-75 N. 912-994-3670.

Word of Mouth Cafe,* Augusta. Serves dinner. Live jazz. Tue.–Sun. 6 p.m. 724 Broad St. 706-722-3477.

SLEEPING

Crockett House, Eatonton. A stately and gracious turn-of-the-century antebellum home offers year-round accommodations.

Includes continental breakfast. 671 Madison Rd. US 441. 706-485-2248.

1842 Inn, Macon. An 18-column Greek Revival mansion with 21 rooms. Evening cocktails and appetizers. Historic District, walk to restaurants and museum houses. 353 College St. Junction of I-75 and I-16. 912-741-1842; 800-336-1842.

1810 West Inn, Thomson. This restored farmhouse dates from about 1810 along with other renovated country houses on 12 landscaped acres. All rooms with private baths, central heat and AC, antique furnishings, and fireplaces. Country kitchen, screened veranda, peacocks, and nature trails. Continental breakfast served. 254 N. Seymour Dr. 706-595-3156.

Four Chimneys Bed & Breakfast, Thomson. Early 1800s plantation house with original hand-planed pine board interior. Antiques and reproductions, four-posters and fireplaces. Rocking chair front porch; colonial style herb and flower gardens. Equestrian events, golf, and antique shops nearby. German spoken. 2316 Wire Rd. (easy access to I-20). 706-597-0220.

Holmes Hotel, Culloden. Bed-and-breakfast in 100-year-old Victorian home. Private baths and cable TV. Continental breakfast buffet. 192 Main St. (30 minutes from Macon), one mile from US 341 and GA 74 intersection. 800-484-8580, ext. 1894.

Inn Scarlett's Footsteps, Concord. A southern antebellum mansion. Five rooms with private baths. You can also visit the owner's private *Gone with the Wind* collection in the museum and gift shop. From the screened porch, you can enjoy the grounds and horses. 138 Hill St. 770-495-9012; reservations: 800-886-7355.

Partridge Inn, Augusta. A landmark beloved by residents, it was built around 1890 and offers 105 fully restored, oversized suites. Most have open or private verandas once walked on by John D. Rockefeller and Alexander Graham Bell. It is only one of two hotels in Georgia chosen by the National Trust for Historic Preservation. (The Windsor in Americus is the other.) Complimentary hot buffet and complimentary beverage on arrival. Restaurant on premises. 2110 Walton Way. 706-737-8888; 800-476-6888.

Rosewood, Eatonton. In the historic district, this restored Victorian house was built around 1888. Large rooms, wraparound porch, original hand-carved mantels, and heart-pine floors. Afternoon refreshments. Rose garden, antiques, angel collection, and a *Gone with the Wind* bedroom. 301 N. Madison. 706-485-9009.

Statesboro Inn, Statesboro. This Victorian-style National Historic Register home has 15 rooms. Complimentary country breakfast. Public restaurant. 106 S. Main St. 912-489-8628; 800-846-9466.

Telfair Inn, Augusta. The Clarion Telfair Inn has transformed a block of turn-of-the-century Victorian homes into a historic inn complex with a pool. Rooms are furnished in period detail. Restaurant. Tue.–Sat. 6–10:30 p.m. 326 Greene St. 706-724-3315; 800-241-2407.

SHOPPING

Augusta Mall, Augusta. Wrightsboro Rd. off I-520. 706-733-1001.

Burlington Coat Factory Warehouse, Augusta. 1329 West Parkway. 706-650-0544.

Juddy's Country Store, Jonesboro. Built in 1894, it is located on the grounds of Stately Oaks Plantation (see *Where to Go and What to See*). Mementos and many *Gone with the Wind* gift items. Exit 76 on I-75 south of Atlanta.

Macon Mall, Macon. Mon.–Sat. 9:30 a.m.–9:30 p.m.; Sun. 1–6 p.m. 3661 Eisenhower Parkway east of I-475. 912-477-7328.

Peach Festival Outlet Mall, Byron. Mon.–Sat. 9 a.m.–9 p.m.; Sun. 9 a.m.–6 p.m. Exit 46 on I-75 and GA 49. 912-956-1855.

Southlake Mall, Morrow. Hundreds of retail establishments offer exceptional value in everything from athletic shoes to evening wear. Mon.–Sat. 8 a.m.–9 p.m.; Sun. 10 a.m.–5:30 p.m. GA 54 at I-85.

ANTIQUES AND CRAFTS

A-Ok Antiques and Etc., Macon. Exit 55 off I-75, go one mile north on GA 87. Thu.–Sat. 10 a.m.–5 p.m. 912-477-1422.

Big Peach Antiques and Collectibles, Byron. Antiques and collectibles in 50,000 square feet. Exit 46 off I-75 at GA 49. Mon.–Sat. 10 a.m.–7 p.m.; Sun. 1–6 p.m. 912-956-6256.

Broad Street Downtown Augusta, Augusta. Antique shops; also galleries and studio artists at work. 706-724-0436.

Fox Hunt Antiques, Eatonton. 109 N. Jefferson Ave. 706-485-6402.

Hav-A-Jar, Meansville. Cookie jars, books, antique collectibles, arts, and crafts. Mon.–Tue. 10 a.m.–4 p.m.; Wed. noon–4 p.m.; Thu.–Sat. 10 a.m.–4 p.m. Closed Sun. 1089 Hwy. 19 S. 706-647-5679.

Juliette Mill, Juliette. World's largest water-powered gristmill. Specialty shops and antique mall. Mon.–Sat. 10 a.m.–5 p.m.; Sun. 1–5 p.m. Exit 61 off I-75 S, then go eight miles east to Juliette. 912-994-0084.

Lion's Share, Warner Robins. Antiques and art in more than 25,000 square feet. Mon.–Sat. 10 a.m.–6 p.m.; Sun. 1–5 p.m. Closed Tue. 2069 Watson Blvd. Exit 45 off I-75; east on Watson Blvd. 912-922-1973.

Lord Byron Antiques, Byron. Antiques and collectibles. Mon.–Sat. 10 a.m.–7 p.m.;

Sun. 1:30–5:30 p.m. Main St. and E. Heritage Blvd. 912-956-2789.

Muzik's Antique Gift Shop, Concord. Furniture; glassware—primitive to the 1920s and depression-era glass. Tue.–Sat. 9:30 a.m.–4 p.m. GA 18. 706-495-5555.

My Favorite Things, Palmetto. Antiques and the unique, porcelains, linens, gifts, and especially early furniture. 503 Toombs St. 770-463-3302.

Payne Mill Village, Macon. Antiques and collectibles. Mon.–Thu. 10 a.m.–5 p.m.; Fri.–Sat. 10 a.m.–6 p.m.; Sun. 1–6 p.m. Flea market: Fri. 12–5 p.m.; Sat.–Sun. 9 a.m.–5

p.m. Rose Ave. (One block off Vineville Ave. close to I-75 in historic mill village.) 912-741-3821.

Uncle Remus Attic, Eatonton. Antiques. 101 S. Jefferson St. 706-485-2263.

Entrance to Augusta Golf Club

MASTERS GOLF TOURNAMENT

The Augusta National Golf Course was built by Bobby Jones after he retired from competition. Instead of building his dream course in his native Atlanta, Jones chose Augusta as the home of what he then called the Augusta Invitational Tournament (now the Masters). The land was once one of the largest indigo plantations in the South, with 40 varieties of azaleas and flowers imported from around the world. A long double row of magnolia trees set out before the Civil War is part of the impressive entrance to the old manor house now used as the main clubhouse building. When Jones and the architect Dr. Alister MacKenzie developed the Augusta National, they named each hole for one of the shrubs or flowers on the old plantation. Order tickets well in advance. Don't expect to buy tickets after you get there. 706-667-6000.

The national shrine of golf is in Augusta. The private Augusta National Golf Course at 2604 Washington Rd. hosts the Masters Golf Tournament each April. 706-738-7761.

American Wilderness Outfitters Ltd., Augusta. You can rent canoes, kayaks, and camping equipment. They run shuttles. They also organize paddling trips. 522 Shartom Dr. Washington Rd. exit off I-20. 706-860-0278.

Atlanta Beach Sports and Entertainment Park, Jonesboro. Family fun at a 100-acre water and recreation park. Spring-fed lake with sandy beach, kiddie pool, and entertainment. Daily 10 a.m.–8 p.m. Seasonal. 2474 Walt Stephens Rd. 770-478-1932.

Augusta Canal, Augusta. This canal stretches across two counties from downtown Augusta to Evans-to-Locks Rd. in Columbia Co. Opportunities for bicycling, canoeing, hiking, fishing, and leisure walking. Easy access to visit Savannah Rapids Park. 706-868-3349. Information: 706-722-1071.

Lake Oconee and Lake Sinclair. They cover more than 36,000 acres. If you're looking for fishing, camping, skiing, golf, tennis, croquet, or polo resorts, you'll find it. Georgia Power Company has built and staffs three 85-acre parks that offer boating facilities, beaches, and campgrounds. Open to the public. 706-485-8704.

Lake Tobesofkee, Milledgeville. Three parks and 1,800 acres of fresh water. Tennis, fishing, boating, skiing, picnicking, and sunbathing available. Located four miles from major shopping, dining, and lodging accommodations. Open daily. Admission charged. Limited accessibility for persons with disabilities. 6600 Mosley Dixon Rd. 912-474-8770.

Reynolds Nature Preserve, Morrow. A green getaway with miles of leafy trails to walk and a kid-friendly nature center with environmental exhibits. In the spring, you'll see an amazing number of azaleas and dogwoods in bloom. Mon.–Fri. 8:30 a.m.–5:30 p.m. 5665 Reynolds Rd. Just north of exit 76 off I-75 south of Atlanta. 770-961-9257.

Riverfront Marina, Augusta. Downtown's Riverfront Marina at Prep Phillips Dr. centralizes water recreation on the Savannah River, the focal point of frequent river races.

Golf

Augusta GC, Augusta. 706-733-9177.

Barrington Hall GC, Macon. 912-757-8358.

Belle Meade CC, Thomson. 706-595-4511.

Bowden GC, Macon. 912-742-1610.

Cedars GC, Zebulon. 706-567-8808.

Cotton Fields, McDonough. 770-914-1442.

Forest Hills GC, Augusta. 706-733-0001.

Forsyth CC, Forsyth. 912-994-5328.

Four Seasons CC, Wrens. 706-547-2816.

Georgia National GC, McDonough. 770-914-9994.

Goshen Plantation CC, Augusta. 706-793-1168.

Green Valley GC, McDonough. 770-957-2800.

Griffin GC, Griffin. 770-229-6615.

Hickory Hill GC, Jackson. 770-775-2433.

Hunter Pope CC, Monticello. 706-468-6222.

International City Mun. GC, Warner Robins. 912-922-3892.

Jonesco GC, Gray. 912-986-3206.

Lake Spivey GC, Jonesboro. 770-477-9836.

The Links GC, Jonesboro. 770-461-5100.

Little Fishing Creek GC, Milledgeville. 912-452-9072.

Little Mountain GC, Ellenwood. 770-981-7921.

The Oaks Course, Covington. 404-221-0200.

Pebble Creek GC, Jonesboro. 770-471-5455.

The Pines GC, Williamson. 706-229-4107.

Reynolds GC, Reynolds. 912-847-4548.

Reynolds Plantation-Great Waters, Eatonton. 706-485-0235.

Reynolds Plantation-Plantation, Greensboro. 706-467-3159.

River's Edge GC, Fayetteville. 770-460-1098.

Riverview GC, Dublin. 912-275-4064.

Southerness GC, Stockbridge. 770-808-6000.

Southern Links, Statesboro. 912-839-3191.

Stathams Landing GC, Warner Robins. 912-923-5222.

Swainsboro CC, Swainsboro. 912-237-6116.

Thomson CC, Thomson. 706-595-2727.

Twin Lakes GC, Fairburn. 770-964-4824.

Uncle Remus GC, Eatonton. 706-485-6850.

Whispering Pines CC, Warrenton. 706-465-2577.

Whitewater Creek GC, Fayetteville. 770-461-6545.

Willow Lakes CC, Metter. 912-685-2724.

Willowpeg Creek GC, Rincon. 912-826-2092.

ENTERTAINMENT

Atlanta Beach Sports and Entertainment Park, Jonesboro. Visit a 100-acre park with lake, kiddie pool, raceway, and video arcade. Daily 10 a.m.–8 p.m. Seasonal. 2474 Walt Stephens Rd. 770-478-1932.

Atlanta Motor Speedway, Hampton. This is the site of some of the Winston Cup racing's big events. You can get a behind-the-scenes view of one of the top motor sports facilities in the country. Visit pit road and the NASCAR garage where million-dollar machinery makes or breaks the winners. Experience the feel of the 24-degree bank on the world's fastest 1.522-mile true oval. Then swoop down onto the nine-turn road-racing course. You can stand in victory lane where legends A. J. Foyt, Fireball Roberts, Dale Earnhardt, and Bill Elliott have stood. You can see the video of the speedway's past in one of the VIP suites high above the grandstand. No tours during race weeks. Tour schedule: Mon.–Sat. 9 a.m.–4:30 p.m.; Sun. 1–4:30 p.m. For groups, make advance reservations. Admission: $3. Approximately 30 miles south of downtown Atlanta. Take exit 77 on I-75 S to US 19/41 and continue for 15 miles. 770-707-7970.

Belle Meade Fox Hunt, Thomson. Season opens with a blessing of the hounds the first Sat. in November and runs every Sat. and Wed. through March. Contact Chamber of Commerce: 706-595-5584.

Guideo Gardens, Metter. The gardens, which are the production home of the Sower's Telecasts, are open daily. Enjoy the sparkling waterfalls, fountains, and gazebos, accompanied by music. Stop for a moment in the prayer chapel. See the Sower Topiary and the colorful gardens. Conducted tours of the Sower Studio Mon.–Fri. 8 a.m.–12 p.m. and 1–5 p.m. 600 N. Lewis St. (on GA 121, three miles north of I-16 exit 23). 912-685-2222.

Princess Augusta Riverboat, Augusta. Dinner cruises Tue.–Sat. evenings. Board at 10th St. dock. 706-722-5020.

Riverwalk, Augusta. Riverwalk promenade, the city's central attraction, is a walkable plaza along the river, atop the high levee and around modern and historic buildings that include hotels, a mall, an art museum, many restaurants, sidewalk cafes, and craft shops. Riverwalk entrance plaza is at 8th and Reynolds Streets.

Six Flags Over Georgia, west of Atlanta. Theme park off I-20 W (outside I-285). This is one of the state's major family attractions and offers a great day's entertainment. Six Flags Park has eight themed areas that reflect the state's heritage. More than 100 rides, attractions, and shows, including roller coasters and free fall. Musical revues; top name entertainment. Home to the Looney Tunes characters. (Actor-singer

John Schneider of *Dukes of Hazzard* got his start here.) Restaurants and snack bars throughout park. Weekends only March–mid-May. Daily Memorial Day–Labor Day 10 a.m. Closing times vary. Admission: adults $27; children 3–9 $19; 55 and over $14; under 3 free. Take Six Flags exit off I-20 W (about 12 miles from downtown). 770-739-3400.

Spivey Hall, Morrow. Classical and jazz performances in 400-seat performance hall on the grounds of Clayton State College. 770-961-3683.

Word of Mouth Cafe, Augusta. Live local jazz. 724 Broad St. 706-722-3477.

FESTIVALS

March

Cherry Trees in Bloom

Cherry Blossom Festival, Macon. Lasts 10 days. Enjoy one of the most scenic festivals when 170,000 cherry trees bloom with the light pink blossoms. Activities range from bed races, hog-calling contests, storytelling, floats, and parades to hot-air balloons and many cultural art performances. 912-743-3401.

Saint Patrick's Festival, Dublin. Month-long festival. Special feature is world's largest pot of Irish stew. 912-272-5546.

April

Forsythia Festival, Forsyth. Arts, crafts, 5K run, fishing, golf, games, entertainment, and parade. 912-994-9239.

Jones Co. Wildlife Cook-off and Crafts Festival, Gray. 912-986-1433.

May

Spring Fling, Juliette. Arts, crafts, and entertainment on Main St. Juliette River Club, P.O. Box 84, Juliette, 31046.

June

Georgia Peach Festival, Byron and Fort Valley. Mid-June. Weeklong event of parades, street dances, peach pie cook-off, peach eating contests, and election of a king and queen. 912-825-4002.

August

Brooklet Peanut Festival, Statesboro. 800-LOVE-301.

September

Arts in the Heart of Augusta, Augusta. The Riverwalk. 706-826-4702.

Barnesville Buggy Days, Barnesville. Arts, crafts, parade, fireworks, and antique car display. 404-358-2732.

Blind Willie Blues Festival, Thomson. Celebration of legend of blues great Blind Willie McTell. Live performances by blues singers. 706-595-5584.

Cat Face Turpentine Festival, Statesboro. 800-LOVE-301.

Native American Festival, Indian Springs. 770-775-6735.

Oconee Riverfest, Lake Oconee. Children's activities, boat rides, arts, crafts, barbecue, and entertainment. Parks Ferry Recreational Area. 706-453-7592.

Peachtree Crossings Country Fair, Fairburn. 770-434-3661.

Southern Crescent Celebration, Morrow. Artistic demonstrations, business exhibits, and children's activities. Clayton State College. 770-961-3580.

Southern Jubilee, Macon. Two-week-long event. Home tours, a folk art festival, and a music weekend outdoors. 912-741-8000.

Sylvania Air Show and Fly-In, Sylvania. Wing walkers, crop dusters, helicopters, flying shows, arts, and crafts. Plantation Air Park. 800-972-7887.

Taste of Thomaston, Thomaston. Courthouse square. 706-647-8311.

October

Arrowhead Arts and Crafts Festival, Macon. Native American encampment. Lake Tobesofkee at Arrowhead Park. 912-474-8770.

Brown's Crossing Fair, Milledgeville. Third weekend of October. Major regional exhibition of handmade arts and crafts. Held at an extinct cotton-ginning town, nine miles west of town. 400 Browns Crossing Rd. NW. 912-452-9327.

Georgia State Fair, Macon. Third week of October. Carnival games, livestock shows, arts, and crafts. 912-746-7184.

Jonesboro Fall Festival and Battle Reenactment, Jonesboro. Stately Oaks Plantation. 770-473-0197.

Olde Gristmill Festival, Juliette. 912-994-5189.

December

An Old South Christmas Festival, Macon. Dressed-up historic homes with period decorations and costumed guides. 912-743-3401.

AN EXTRA TOUCH OF MIDDLE GEORGIA: THE GOODALL HOUSE

The town of Jacksonboro was established as the county seat of Screven Co. in 1797, and it became a thriving business center in rural Georgia. In 1821, an itinerant preacher, Lorenzo Dow, was attacked by the rowdies of the town, whom he angered because he denounced their immorality.

Goodall House

Dow took refuge in the home of Seaborn Goodall (built 1815), described as "a godly man." Dow stood on the bridge over a nearby creek and cursed the town of Jacksonboro, but he asked that God bless the home of Goodall.

Goodall House

In 1847, the county seat moved to nearby Sylvania, and Jacksonboro became a ghost town. Today, nothing remains of the town of Jacksonboro except the Goodall House. On US 302, about five miles north of Sylvania in Screven Co.

CHAMBERS OF COMMERCE

(Italics indicate a county name.)

Augusta	706-821-1300
Barnesville-*Lamar*	770-358-2732
Burke	706-554-5451
Butts	770-775-4839
Clayton	770-478-6549
Dublin-*Laurens*	912-272-5546
Eatonton-*Putnam*	706-485-7701
Effingham	912-754-3301
Fayette	770-461-9983
Greene	706-453-7592
Griffin/*Spalding*	770-228-8200
Henry	770-957-5786
Jefferson	912-625-8134
Jenkins	912-982-5595
Macon, Greater	912-741-8000
Metter-*Candler*	912-685-2159
Milledgeville-*Baldwin*	912-453-9311
Monroe	912-994-9239
Monticello-*Jasper*	706-468-8994
Newton	770-786-7510
Peach	912-825-3733
Pike	706-567-0616
Roberta-*Crawford*	912-836-3825
Screven	912-564-7878
South *Fulton*	770-964-1984
Statesboro-*Bulloch*	912-764-6111
Swainsboro-*Emanuel*	912-237-6426

| Thomaston-*Upson* | 706-647-9868 | *Warren* | 706-465-9604 |
| Warner-Robins | 912-922-8585 | Wrightsville-*Johnson* | 912-864-2501 |

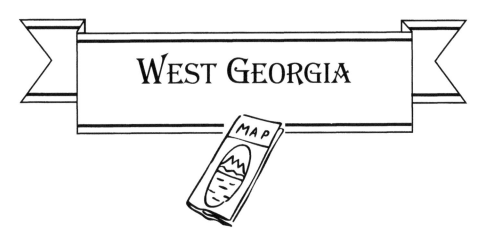

WEST GEORGIA

Cities of West Georgia

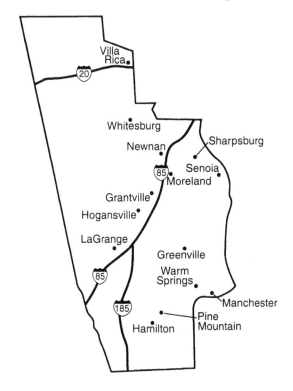

LOCATION	TO SEE/DO	EATING	SLEEPING	OTHER
	WEST GEORGIA AT A GLANCE			
Grantville	Driving tour Meadows Log Cabin		Bonnie Castle	
Greenville	Historical District			
Hamilton		Oak Tree Victorian Restaurant	Wedgwood B&B	
Hogansville	Driving tour	Grand Hotel Hogan's Heroes	Fair Oaks Inn Grand Hotel	Antique shops
LaGrange	Bellevue Mansion Chattahoochee Valley Art Museum	Taste of Lemon	Thyme Away B&B	Antique mall
Manchester			Sweet Dreams B&B	
Moreland	Lewis Grizzard Museum Little Manse (Erskine Caldwell Museum) Old Mill Building			
Newnan	Catalpa Plantation Male Academy Museum Driving tour	Gen. Wheeler's Mess Tent Redneck Gourmet Something Special Tea Room Sprayberry's Barbecue	Old Garden Inn Southern Comfort	Antiques
Pine Mountain	Callaway Gardens	Bon Cuisine Callaway Country Store	Callaway Gardens Storms	Wild Animal Safari
Senoia	Baggarly Buggy Shop Driving tour Starr's Mill Senoia Historical Society House	Culpepper B&B Veranda		Antiques
Sharpsburg			Homeplace	Antiques
Villa Rica		Twin Oaks B&B		
Warm Springs	Little White House	Bulloch House Victorian Tea Room	Hotel Warm Springs	Crafts Antiques

WEST GEORGIA AT A GLANCE				
LOCATION	**TO SEE/DO**	**EATING**	**SLEEPING**	**OTHER**
Whitesburg	McIntosh Reserve			
Special Mention:	Red Oak Covered Bridge (Meriwether County) West Point Lake			

West Georgia has come to represent history and scenery. Most Georgians immediately think of two outstanding attractions (both are on our don't-miss-it list): Callaway Gardens at Pine Mountain and the Little White House near Warm Springs.

This section of the state includes the counties of Haralson, Carroll, Coweta, Heard, Meriwether, Troup, and Harris. Major highways through West Georgia include I-20 west from Atlanta, and I-85 south from Atlanta that continues to the Alabama border. I-185 exits from I-85 near LaGrange and continues south. US 27 and GA 85 are also frequently traveled roads.

You can visit almost anyplace in this area in less than a two-hour drive from midtown Atlanta. You'll find a range of B&Bs for overnight lodging. Just driving through the historic towns such as Newnan and Greenville is a pleasure. Allow yourself time to stop and browse through the antique and collectible shops.

An interesting feature of this area is the number of churches, large and small, that fill the countryside. Riding along some of the back roads, occasionally you can still spot a two-door church. The churches were built in the days when men were separated from women, and each gender came in through its own door. Most of them have long been converted into one-door churches when times changed and congregations renovated their buildings.

Two-door Church in Corinth

AN EXTRA TOUCH OF WEST GEORGIA: MCINTOSH RESERVE, WHITESBURG (ALSO KNOWN AS LOCHCHAU TALAFAU)

In 1825, Chief William McIntosh, Jr., son of a Scottish father and a Creek Indian mother, and other Lower Creek chiefs deeded all their lands in Georgia west of the Flint River to the white settlers. Angered over this treaty, a party of Upper Creek Indians attacked his house. They spared the women, children, and all whites, but killed McIntosh. They devastated a mile-square area around his home. Legend says that McIntosh buried gold on the plantation before his death, and the gold was never found. This site, burial place of William McIntosh, is about five miles south of Whitesburg.

WHERE TO GO AND WHAT TO SEE

 Architectural Walking Tour, LaGrange. Pick up a brochure for a self-guided walk through downtown LaGrange. Among places you'll want to see are the Chattahoochee Valley Art Museum, LaFayette Square, Davis Pharmacy, and the Troup Co. Courthouse. For information and brochure, call LaGrange-Troup Co. Chamber of Commerce: 706-884-8671; or Troup Co. Archives and Historical Society: 706-884-1828.

Baggarly Buggy Shop, Senoia. Built about 1905, the large building next to the post office was formerly a Coca-Cola bottling plant. It's now filled with antique cars and farm tool equipment related to horse-and-buggy days and rural homemaking. Open by appointment. W. R. Baggarly: 770-253-1018; Janet Baggarly: 770-254-2894.

Bellevue Mansion, LaGrange. A National Historic Landmark. This beautiful home of the late U.S. Senator Benjamin Harvey Hill was built in 1854–55 and typifies the Greek Revival architecture popular in the Old South. Daily (except Mon.) 10 a.m.–noon and 2–5 p.m. Closed Christmas and New Year's Day. 204 Ben Hill St. Exit 4 off I-85. 706-884-1832.

Square in LaGrange

Callaway Gardens, Pine Mountain. **Don't Miss.** This privately owned area of 14,000 acres with its family-style golf and tennis resort is best known for its impressive gardens. Callaway Gardens opened in the 1930s to bring new life to the abandoned cotton fields. At the Visitors Center, see the introductory film—a treat in itself. Go to the Day Butterfly Center, a glass atrium filled with tropical plants, where you can see more than a thousand varieties of butterflies flying free.

Daily 7 a.m.–6 p.m. Admission: adults $7.50; children 6–11 $1.50; under 6 free. (Some events require additional fees.) US 27. 706-663-2281; 800-282-8181.

Tree at Catalpa Plantation

Catalpa Plantation and Herb Farm, Newnan. National Register of Historic Places. This Federal-Vernacular residence was built by architect William Yarbrough between 1835 and 1840 for the widow Ann Dance Goodwyn and her son Thomas of Dinwiddie Co., Virginia. Descendants of colonial legislators, jurors, educators, and soldiers, the Goodwyns and the Baileys— neighbors whose children married each other—prospered in cotton and farming. The present owner's authentic restoration of Catalpa Plantation has won praise from

architectural historians. The summer kitchen in Catalpa's main house is one of three known to exist in the area. House and grounds open for tours by appointment. Children must be supervised by adults at all times. No smoking inside buildings. Donations accepted to support growth and operation (privately funded project). It's a 45-minute trip south of Atlanta. 2295 Old Poplar Rd. 800-697-1835; 770-253-9745.

Chattahoochee Valley Art Museum, LaGrange. The building was constructed in 1892 and used for the Troup Co. jail until 1946. This distinctive Victorian building is a fine example of a renovation project that has maintained the building's original architecture. Contains art collections and a shop of arts and crafts. Mon. 9 a.m.–5 p.m.; Tue.–Sun. 1–5 p.m. 112 Hines St. Exit 4 off I-85 S. 706-882-3267.

Driving Tour of Newnan. Newnan, the county seat of Coweta Co., is known as the city of homes. Legend reports that Newnan was spared the ravages of the Civil War because Confederate and Union hospitals were located there. You can still view lovely southern town architecture from the earliest settlement days through the 20th century. Pick up a map of the driving tour of Newnan homes at the Male Academy Museum (see listing).

Erskine Caldwell Home. See *Little Manse.*

Grantville Historical Driving Tour. Located 50 minutes south of Atlanta and 15 minutes from Newnan, Grantville is situated on land purchased from Native Americans by William Bundy Smith around 1821. By 1849, it had become a small community known simply as Calico Corner. When the railroad arrived in 1852, the residents changed the name to Grantville to honor L. P. Grant, the first chief construction engineer and superintendent of the Atlanta–LaGrange Railroad. You can still see many of the beautiful homes built during that era. Pick up a brochure with pictures and descriptions of the homes at Grantville City Hall, 1 Main St. Exit 7 off I-85 S; follow signs to Grantville.

Greenville Historical District. Includes more than 200 structures and three historic African-American neighborhoods: Baptist Hill, Baldwin Hill, and Methodist Hill. The communities reflect African-American residential patterns in the South, and today few such well-preserved areas remain. Boundaries: Gresham Street, Greenville Cemetery, Talbotton, Gaston, Baldwin, and Bottom Streets, and Martin Road. Self-guided tours.

Hogansville. Driving tour of historic homes. On the self-guided tour, you will see 24 homes built from 1840 to 1940 in various architectural styles. Tour brochure available at Fair Oaks B&B on Main St., City Hall, and Troup Co. Chamber of Commerce in LaGrange.

LaGrange. The city has nicely preserved its historic square with several 19th-century buildings. Bellevue is a stately 1850 Greek Revival mansion. 204 Ben Hill St. Tue.–Sat. afternoons.

LaGrange College, founded in 1831 as LaGrange Female Academy, is the state's oldest independent college. In 1836, the name changed to LaGrange Female Institute. Twenty years later, the Methodists bought it and changed it to the present name, and it is coed. On campus is the Lamar Dodd Art Center, where you can see a collection of works by this well-known Georgia artist. 706-882-2911.

Lewis Grizzard Museum, Moreland. For fans of the humor of Lewis Grizzard (1946–93), this is a must-stop place. You'll see a collection of personal items and memorabilia of this well-known and much-loved southern columnist and writer. Sat. 10 a.m.–4:30 p.m.; Sun. 1–4:30 p.m.; and by appointment. 27 Main St. Exit 8 off I-85 S, then go south on US 29 about two miles. 770-304-1490.

Lewis Grizzard Museum

Little Manse, Moreland. The town of Moreland (pop. 470) is currently restoring the birthplace of writer Erskine Caldwell (1903–87) to its 1903 appearance. The intent is to preserve the sense of place portrayed by Caldwell in his books about the rural South, such as *Tobacco Road.*

The house includes a display of the life and literary significance of Caldwell, who wrote more than 50 other books. Sat.–Sun. 1–4 p.m. and by appointment. Admission charged. Take I-85 S to exit 8; travel south on US 29 about two miles. One block west of US 29 adjacent to the Old Mill complex. 770-251-4438. (Note: The Little Manse, Lewis Grizzard Museum, and Moreland Museum–Old Mill Building are all located at one site.)

Little White House, Warm Springs. **Don't Miss.** State historic site. Franklin Delano Roosevelt built the Little White House in 1932 when he was still governor of New York, prior to being inaugurated as president in 1933. It was the only home he ever owned, and it cost him the then magnificent sum of $7,734 to build. He died in the living room of the cottage. The house and furnishings have been preserved as Roosevelt left them in 1945.

The adjacent museum displays memorabilia collected in honor of this world statesman and presents a brief introductory film containing historic footage of Roosevelt and his contemporaries during their activities at Warm Springs. (See *An Extra Touch of West Georgia: The Little White House.*)

Open year-round. Daily 9 a.m.–5 p.m. Last full tour at 4 p.m. Closed major holidays. Admission charged. Primary buildings accessible for persons with disabilities. Located one-fourth mile south of Warm Springs on GA 85 W. 706-655-5870.

Male Academy Museum, Newnan. Now a museum, Newnan's first male academy opened in 1883 with 60 pupils. The city of Newnan authentically renovated the building in 1976. Permanent displays include the Ellis Smith collection of early Coweta Co. furniture, tools, pottery, toys, and Native American and Civil War artifacts. The museum also boasts of having one of the finest collections of period clothing in the South.

The museum offers a driving-tour-of-homes brochure with a map that identifies many architectural masterpieces. The gift shop sells history-related items, jewelry, paper dolls, and local history books. Pause to skim through the Coweta Co. marriage and cemetery records. Tue.–Thu. 10 a.m.–noon and 1–3 p.m.; Sat.–Sun. 2–5 p.m.; and by appointment. Corner of College St. and Temple Ave. Take exit 8 or 9 off I-85 S, then go west into Newnan. 770-251-0207.

Meadows Log Cabin, Grantville. The log cabin was built about 1828 by John and Julia Meadows and was originally part of the Meadows Plantation near I-85. It was moved to Grantville in 1971 and is now at the Coweta Co. Recreation Field. Shown by appointment. Exit 7 off I-85 S. Grantville City Hall, 1 Main St. 770-583-2289.

Moreland Museum—Old Mill Building, Moreland. National Register of Historic Places. You'll see a variety of farm implements and household items from local farm life in the Moreland area before 1940. Housed in the former W. A. Brannon Store (built in 1894) and 1920s Moreland Knitting Mill. Exit 8 off I-85 S. Approximately two miles south from exit on US 29. By appointment. 770-253-1963.

Red Oak Creek Covered Bridge, Meriwether Co. (See **Covered Bridges and Gristmills of Georgia**.) Between Gay and Woodbury, on an unpaved road, east of GA 85.

Senoia Historical Society House. Built about 1870, this is a structure of blended architectural characteristics that is being restored and expanded as a place to display local collections. 770-599-3679.

Senoia Historic District Driving Tour. Senoia was named for the wife of William McIntosh and the mother of William McIntosh, Jr., who was chief of the Lower Creek Indians. The McIntosh family settled around 1830 because of a land grant. Senoia was officially founded as a town in 1860. You can pick up a map of the driving tour with a brief history of each of the 24 houses at city hall or the library. GA 16 near GA 85.

Starr's Mill, Senoia. This is one of Georgia's most photographed landmarks. The 200-year-old red frame mill has a pond and

waterfall for background. Junction of GA 85 and GA 74.

Starr's Mill

West Point. This is the heart of the textile industry in Georgia. The original settlement began with the building of a store in 1829, and it was called Franklin. In 1832, it received its present name because it was the westernmost community on the Chattahoochee River in Georgia. Later, the city became the terminal of the Atlanta & West Point Railroad.

West Point Stevens Corporation, a Fortune 500 company, is headquartered here.

At West Point Lake, you can roam 25,900 acres, with miles of forested shoreline for campers. For hunters and naturalists, there is a wildlife management area in the upstream part of the lake near Franklin.

West Point also has a Civil War story. In the summer of 1865, Union General James Wilson sent 3,000 troops to take West Point, which was being defended by 265 men (125 from West Point and 140 from nearby LaGrange). The defense held off two attacks, but a third assault overwhelmed them. The Yankee troops, under the command of Colonel Oscar LaGrange, imprisoned the survivors and destroyed trains, bridges, and buildings. He did parole 16 prisoners to care for the Confederate wounded. When his troops moved out, the colonel left a supply of food for the civilians.

AN EXTRA TOUCH OF WEST GEORGIA: THE LITTLE WHITE HOUSE

Franklin Delano Roosevelt first visited Warm Springs in 1924, searching for relief in the famous warm springs from polio, which had struck him three years earlier. He swam in the spring waters but found no cure, although he insisted they improved his condition.

He bought a beautiful site on the north slope of Pine Mountain that overlooked a deeply wooded ravine. He had plans drawn to build what became known as the Little White House. Roosevelt ordered the natural setting to be preserved. In 1932, the house was completed at a cost of less than $8,000—a large sum in those days. The house and furnishings reflect Roosevelt's desire for simple comfort. The Little White House is impressive for its utility.

Elected four consecutive times as president of the United States, Roosevelt took office when the Great Depression in America was at its height. He led the nation from the depression and through the dark days of World War II (1941–45). He died April 12, 1945, a few months before the end of the war.

During his 41st trip to the rural community of 500, he suffered a massive stroke. He had been posing for a portrait and died before it was finished. The unfinished portrait is a focal point of the Little White House tour. Roosevelt's six-room house has been maintained as it was when he lived there, furnished with mementos, paintings, and personal items.

Little White House Sign

Here are a few special things to look for:

- The Memorial Fountain, called the hub of the Little White House, is fed from the famous nearby springs.
- Walk of the States is an ornamental walkway that leads to the museum and is flanked by native stones and flags from each of the 50 states and the District of Columbia.
- The unusual bump gate was designed

to open when touched by an automobile bumper, and it is the entrance to the original Little White House grounds.

- Two of FDR's 1938 convertible roadsters are on display, equipped with custom-built hand controls that allowed the president to drive himself.
- The Little White House Museum shows the treasures of the man and the exhibits that characterized his life, including gifts from foreign embassies, and especially his walking cane collection.
- *A Warm Springs Memoir of Franklin Delano Roosevelt* is a 12-minute film that shows continuously in the museum's auditorium at no additional charge.

EATING

Recipes

French Honey Bread. Thanks to Anita Styanoff, mess sergeant for General Wheeler's Mess Tent in Newnan, who shared this recipe with us.

Place in large bowl 1 cup lukewarm water, 1 package yeast, and 1 tablespoon honey. Let stand for 5 minutes. Then add 1 tablespoon honey, 1-1/2 teaspoons salt, and 2 tablespoons oil. Stir well, and add 1 cup all-purpose flour. Add an additional 2 cups all-purpose flour a little at a time until you make a stiff dough. Let dough rest for 10 minutes. Then divide dough into 2 parts. Flatten dough with rolling pin until about 3/4-inch thick. Roll up tightly to make a slender loaf. Press firmly at edges to seal. (Dough may also be placed in regular bread pan. Anita prefers to bake it this way because it is a great bread for sandwiches.) Sprinkle cookie sheet with cornmeal and place loaves on sheets. Let rise until double in size and bake at 325° for about 25 minutes.

Rhubarb Custard Pie. Occasionally someone unfamiliar with rhubarb pie will, upon first glance, mistake it for a strawberry pie because of its reddish color. But there's no mistaking the taste of this tangy-sweet dessert.

Pour 2 cups finely chopped rhubarb into an unbaked pie shell. Over this pour a mixture of 2 eggs, slightly beaten; 1 cup sugar; 2 tablespoons flour; 2 tablespoons lemon juice; and 2 tablespoons water. Dot with butter and sprinkle with nutmeg. Bake as you would a custard pie. (This means bake in a very hot oven, 450°, for 10 minutes; then lower temperature to 350°, and bake 30 to 40 minutes longer.) If a meringue is desired, use 2 egg whites beaten until frothy, then gradually add 4 tablespoons sugar. Beat until stiff. Spread over baked pie, taking it all the way to the edge, then bake in 325° oven 15 to 18 minutes until lightly browned. (Warning: Too much sugar will make the meringue "weep" and a too-hot oven will cause the meringue to be tough. Dipping the knife in hot water before you slice the pie will give you a smoother cut on the meringue.)

Spoonbread. This bread is moist and soft and served with a large spoon, hence its name. It's great as a side dish with almost anything.

Combine 2 cups yellow cornmeal, 1-1/2 teaspoons salt, 1 teaspoon soda, and 3 egg yolks. Pour into this 2 cups boiling water. Mix well. Add 2 cups sour milk (buttermilk is okay) and 1 tablespoon melted shortening (or oil). Then fold into the mixture the egg whites, well beaten. Bake in buttered baking dish at 425° for 30 to 35 minutes.

Where to Eat

*Bon Cuisine,*** Pine Mountain. Where else can you order alligator steak and wild game for dinner? Reservations. Mon.–Sat. from 5:30 p.m. 113 Chipley Square downtown. 706-663-2019.

*Bulloch House Restaurant,** Warm Springs. The Bulloch House was built around 1892 and sold to its present owners in 1990. They have expanded the original home to include a large banquet room. Among the truly Georgian food items, you'll find fried green tomatoes and pulley bones. Dress casual (shirt and shoes required). Lunch daily 11 a.m.–2:30 p.m.; dinner Fri.–Sat. 5:30–8:30 p.m. 706-655-9068.

*Callaway Country Store,** Pine Mountain. You can get a cross section of southern cooking. How about speckled grits? Maybe muscadine sauce? If you like what you eat, you can buy the ingredients and recipe to make it yourself at home. US 27 at GA 190. 706-633-8136.

Gen. Wheeler's Mess Tent

*General Wheeler's Mess Tent,** Newnan. **Don't Miss.** Just look for the military tent and Confederate flag in the front yard. The mansion dates to 1863. The dining rooms are decorated to reflect the "glory of our arms" (the Confederacy). Live music and entertainment (political satire) by the Politically Incorrect Players Fri.–Sat. nights. Reservations recommended for dinner shows. Mon.–Sat. 11 a.m.–9 p.m. 9 Perry St. Exit 9 or 8 off I-85 S. 770-253-8874.

*Grand Hotel,** Hogansville. Dine in an 1898 restored hotel and restaurant. French cuisine available. On Main St. Exit 6 off I-85. 706-637-5100.

Hogan's Heroes,* Hogansville. Italian restaurant in casual building. Dinner reservations necessary. No credit cards. Lunch Tue.–Sat. 11 a.m.–2 p.m.; Dinner Tue.–Thu. 5–9:30 p.m.; Fri.–Sat. 5–10 p.m. 235 Hwy. 29. 706-637-4953.

Oak Tree Victorian Restaurant,** Hamilton. Eat dinner in an 1871 yellow two-story Victorian building. GA 190 near FDR State Park. 706-628-4218.

Redneck Gourmet,* Newnan. Specialty foods, custom gift baskets, deli, and cafe. 11 N. Court Square. Exit 8 or 9 off I-85. 770-251-0092.

Something Special Tea Room,* Newnan. The "something special" comes out as quiche, strawberry desserts, and more. Lunch Mon.–Tue. and Thu.–Sat. 11 a.m.–2 p.m. 83 Greenville St. Exit 8 or 9 off I-85 S. 770-253-5513.

Sprayberry's Barbecue,* Newnan. At this well-known local barbecue restaurant, you might want to try the pineapple sandwich. Mon.–Sat. 7 a.m.–9 p.m. 229 Jackson St. Exit 9 on I-85 S. 770-253-4421.

Taste of Lemon,* LaGrange. St. John's Church and neighboring houses, built in the 1890s, were originally located on Hines Street just east of downtown. In the early 1980s, they were moved to the corner of Broome and Morgan Streets. Church and houses are now operated as a restaurant and antique shops. Lunch Mon.–Sat. 11 a.m.–2:30 p.m. One block south of La Fayette Parkway on Morgan St. Parkway. Use exit 4 off I-85 S, and go west into LaGrange. 706-882-5382.

Victorian Tea Room,* Warm Springs. The building was constructed in 1906 as a general merchandise store called the Talbott Building, owned and operated by the Talbott family. Notice the original 20-foot-high ceiling that still has the original tongue-and-groove construction. Lunch Sun.–Fri. 11:30 a.m.–3:00 p.m.; extended hours on Sat. On Broad St. in the heart of Warm Springs Village. Take I-85 south from Atlanta, pick up US 27 to Warm Springs. 706-655-2319.

Victorian Tea Room

Warm Springs Village, Warm Springs. You'll find several restaurants with a range of southern traditional to barbecue to seafood. US 27 about 65 miles south of Atlanta.

See **Georgia's Gorgeous Outdoors** for list of state parks with campsites, lodges, or cottages.

Bonnie Castle, Grantville. National Register of Historic Places. This is an 1896 two-story, 20-room mansion. It has four guest rooms. Begin your tour on the front veranda where you can relax. Breakfast served with silver, china, and crystal each morning, and refreshments in the evenings. Enjoy the antique furniture and art collection. 2 Post St. One and a half miles west of I-85 S at exit 7. 770-583-3090; 800-261-3090.

Bonnie Castle

Callaway Gardens and Resort, Pine Mountain. (See more information under *Entertainment.*) 800-282-8181.

Culpepper House Bed & Breakfast, Senoia. You'll easily recognize this restored two-story clapboard because it's yellow. One mile west on GA 85. 770-599-8182.

Fair Oaks Inn, Hogansville. This 1901 Victorian house has been restored to its original elegance and furnished with antiques. Breakfast. Less than 30 minutes from Atlanta. Take exit 6 off I-85 S. About three miles into Hogansville. 703 E. Main St. 706-637-8828.

Grand Hotel

Grand Hotel, Hogansville. In this restored 1898 hotel, rooms have private baths and look out to a wraparound balcony. Furnished with period antiques. Main St. at Oak. Exit 6 off I-85 S. 706-637-5100.

Grand Hotel

Homeplace, Sharpsburg. This plantation house was built in the 1820s. 1262 Bob Smith Rd. Exit 10 off I-85. 770-253-9745.

Hotel Warm Springs, Bed & Breakfast Inn, Warm Springs. Decorated in collectible President Franklin Delano Roosevelt furniture and family antiques of the 1930s and 1940s. The hotel dates to 1907. 17 Broad St. 706-655-2114.

Old Garden Inn, Newnan. B&B, four guest rooms with private baths. 51 Temple Ave. 770-304-0594.

Southern Comfort, Newnan. B&B in Greek Revival architecture. 66 LaGrange St. 770-254-9266; 800-818-0066.

Storms, Pine Mountain. B&B. This Victorian inn was built in the late 1890s. 706-663-9100.

Sweet Dreams, Manchester. B&B. One to three spacious suites available in a downtown building. Furnished in antiques. Large bath accessible for persons with disabilities. Full breakfast at your convenience. Five minutes to Warm Springs; 20 minutes to Callaway Gardens. Affiliated with Bulloch House Restaurant. 12 E. Main St. 706-655-9068.

Thyme Away Bed & Breakfast, LaGrange. Relax in a gracious old mansion. 508 Greenville St. 706-885-9625.

Twin Oaks B&B and Farm Vacations, Villa Rica. Private Victorian cottage on 23 acres in country atmosphere. About 35 minutes

from downtown Atlanta. Lots of animals for viewing. Picnic area, walking trails, swimming pool, and hot tub. 9565 E. Liberty Rd. Off I-20 W. 770-459-4374.

Veranda, Senoia. This restored turn-of-the-century inn on the National Register is furnished in antiques. Nine rooms with private baths decorated according to a theme. One whirlpool. Children accepted. 252 Seavy St. 770-599-3905.

Wedgwood Bed & Breakfast, Hamilton. This 1850 two-story white-columned private home has antique furnishings. No smoking. No pets. Located five and one-half miles south of Callaway Gardens. 706-628-5659.

SHOPPING

The Alamo, Newnan. Gifts, collectibles, jewelry, and Georgia products. More than 3,000 square feet in a restored theater building that dates back to 1898. Mon.–Sat. 9:30 a.m.–6 p.m. 19 W. Court Square. Exit 8 or 9 off I-85 S. 770-254-1474.

Euro Collections, Newnan. Factory store for Bleyle and Fashion Star. Mon.–Sat. 10 a.m.–6 p.m. Eastgate Shopping Center, Bullsboro Dr. Exit 9 off I-85 S. 770-251-5310.

Mansour's Department Store, LaGrange. Known for legendary sales with reductions so sharp, the lines wind all the way down the block. Mon.–Sat. 9:30 a.m.–6 p.m.; Sun. 1–6 p.m. On W. La Fayette Square. 706-884-7305.

Peachtree Factory Stores, Newnan. Exit 9, off I-85 S.

Warm Springs Village, Warm Springs. (See *Antiques and Crafts.*) Contact Warm Springs Merchant Association: 706-655-2609 or 655-9093; or Chamber of Commerce: 706-655-2558. Ask for the Warm Springs Village brochure.

West Georgia Commons Mall, LaGrange. Daily. 1501 La Fayette Parkway. Exit 4 off I-85 S. 706-882-5589.

ANTIQUES AND CRAFTS

Antiques and Crafts Unlimited Mall, Warm Springs. Antiques, collectibles, arts, and crafts in 114 shops. Daily 9:30 a.m.–7 p.m. April–October; 9:30 a.m.–6 p.m. November–March. Tour buses welcome. Home of Green Grass Fair (see *Festivals*). Festival of Lights last week November–December. Open Fri.–Sat. until 9 p.m. for Christmas shopping. Two miles north of Warm Springs, GA 41 and US 27 Alt. 706-655-2468.

Carriage House Antiques, Senoia. Country antiques, primitives, handcrafted accessories, art, and limited edition prints. 7412 E. Hwy. 16 (one mile west of GA 85). 770-599-6321.

Hen Pen, Warm Springs. Dollhouses and miniatures, Jan Hargare collectibles, Cat's Meow, Mary Engelbright, Louisville Stoneware, Valorie, Ginny, Lee Middleton, Jerri and the Doll Maker, and linens. Broad St. 706-655-9003.

Jefferson House, Newnan. Antiques, gifts, and home accessories. Mon.–Sat. 10 a.m.–5 p.m. 51 Jefferson St. 770-253-6171.

Liberty Hill Antiques, Hogansville. Period and country furniture, estate jewelry, silver, porcelain, earthenware, decorative arts, and folk art. Tue.–Sat. 11 a.m.–7 p.m. A monthly auction, call for date. 301 Hwy. 29 S. 706-637-5522.

Lithia Antique and Accessories Mall, Tallapoosa. Antiques, gifts, primitives, glassware, dolls, collectibles, hand-painted furniture, and items for the garden and Christmas in 18 shops. Annual Christmas Open House Thanksgiving afternoon. Tue.–Sat. 10 a.m.–5 p.m.; Sun. 1–5 p.m. 108 Head Ave. Four miles north of I-20 W at exit 1. 770-574-5670.

Main Street Antique Mall, LaGrange. Fine glassware, furniture, records, collectibles, dishes, primitives, pottery, jewelry, and linens offered by 25 dealers. Mon.–Sat. 10 a.m.–5 p.m.; Sun. noon–5 p.m. 130 Main St. 706-884-1972.

Maxwell-Rowe Enterprises, Hogansville. Antiques, crafty uniques, birdhouses, wood carvings, glassware, and brass. Mon.–Sat. 9

a.m.–5 p.m. Exit 6 off I-85. 404 E. Main St. 706-637-5540.

Nana's Porch, Warm Springs. Antiques, fine art, gifts, collectibles, and crafts. Across from Bulloch House Restaurant. 706-655-2707.

Old Town Sharpsburg, Sharpsburg. Antiques, quilts, wicker furniture, brass, dolls, trains, and pottery in 10 shops. Exit 10 off I-85 S, then go east on GA 154 to sign. Or exit 8, then east on GA 16. 770-251-8440.

Newnan Old Mill Antiques, Newnan. Antiques, collectibles, and fine furniture. Mon.–Sat. 10 a.m.–6 p.m.; Sun. 1–6 p.m. Market Place, 17 Augusta Dr. Exit 8 or 9 off I-85 S. 770-251-0999.

Pine Mountain Antique Mall and Auction Center, Pine Mountain. Antiques and collectibles offered by 75 dealers. Mon.–Sat. 10 a.m.–6 p.m.; Sun. 1–6 p.m. Fifteen miles from LaGrange on US 27 S, just past Pine Mountain. 230 Main St. 706-663-8165.

Potpourri, Hogansville. Antiques, gifts, and boutique items. 302 E. Main. Exit 6 off I-85 S, then west into Hogansville (about three miles). 706-637-5564.

Ray Cheatham Collectibles, Hogansville. Antiques, collectibles, and good used furniture. Mon.–Sat. 9 a.m.–6 p.m. Closed Wed. and Sun. 304 E. Main St. Exit 6 off I-85. 706-637-6227.

St. John's Place, LaGrange. The Lemon Tree Shoppes, one block south of La Fayette Parkway on Morgan St. Includes Taste of Lemon Restaurant. Gifts, antiques, and floral arrangements. 706-882-5382.

Santa Fe Art Gallery, Warm Springs. Functional art. Inside Antiques and Crafts Unlimited Mall (see listing for location).

Three Crowns Antiques, Ltd., Newnan. Furniture and accessories. More than 15,000 square feet. Daily. 733 Bullsboro Dr. Exit 9 off I-85 S. 770-253-4815.

Treasure Chest, Hogansville. Antiques, collectibles, and books. Tue.–Thu. 10 a.m.–5 p.m.; Fri. 10 a.m.–6 p.m.; Sat. 10 a.m.–5 p.m. 307 Hwy. 29 S. Exit 6 off I-85. 706-637-9999.

Warm Springs Village, Warm Springs. Antiques, crafts, and collectibles in 65 shops. Candlelight tour of village the weekend before Thanksgiving each year. Mon.–Sat. 11 a.m.–5 p.m.; Sun. 1–5 p.m. (Some shops closed Mon.) On US 27 65 miles south of Atlanta. Chamber of Commerce: 800-532-1690.

OUTDOORS

Blanton Creek Park. The Georgia Power Company recreation area on 5,800-acre Lake Harding features 51 RV and tent camping sites ($10 a night). All have electric and water hookups. The park also has boat ramps, picnic pavilions, and playgrounds. Exit 11 on I-185. 770-643-4338.

Callaway Gardens, Pine Mountain. All outdoor sports; four nationally recognized golf courses, 17 tennis courts, bicycling trails, and a lakefront beach. At Mountain Creek Lake you can fish for large-mouth bass and bream. (See complete information under listing in *Entertainment.*)

Dunaway Gardens, Roscoe. In the early 20th century, Dunaway Gardens was a 64-acre complex of landscaped "garden rooms." Many famous people, including Minnie Pearl, performed at one of the three amphitheaters. Visit by appointment. Eight miles north of Newnan on GA 70. 770-251-2109.

Earl Cook Recreational Area, LaGrange. Day-use beach with bathhouse and nature trails. US 29 south of LaGrange about five miles, north on Lower Glass Bridge Rd. to the water.

Flat Creek Ranch Campground and Stables, Hogansville. This campground for horsemen and horsewomen holds several annual equestrian events. Exit 6 off I-85 S. 706-637-4862.

Highland Marina, LaGrange. Boat, water ski, and inner tube rentals, as well as lodging and full-service marina. On Whitaker Rd., off GA 109 west of LaGrange. 706-882-3437.

Oak Grove Plantation, Gardens, and Shops, Newnan. This 1830s plantation home's gardens have been the subject of numerous magazine articles. Visit by appointment. 4537 N. Hwy. 29. 770-463-3010.

Pine Mountain Trail, Pine Mountain. Starting at the Callaway Gardens Country Store on US 27, the trail winds past rock formations, waterfalls, big stands of trees, and lush vegetation on its way to its terminus at the TV tower on GA 85 W near Warm Springs. One of the country's southernmost mountain trails with 12 access points, so you can get on and off with ease. Pick up a trail map at the FDR Park office.

Shenandoah Environment and Education Center, Newnan. A hands-on learning and research center, it serves as a satellite campus for area colleges. Call for nature trail hours. 7 Solar Circle, Shenandoah Industrial Park. 800-342-6547.

Warm Springs Regional Fisheries Center, Warm Springs. This was built in 1990 as the final step in developing a field station in the Southeast region's fishery program to incorporate a centralized fish health laboratory, a national fish hatchery, a fish technology center, and an environmental education unit into a single complex. Daily 7:30 a.m.–4 p.m. Closed major holidays. GA 85 between Warm Springs and Manchester. 706-655-3382.

West Point Lake, West Point. This U.S. Army Corps of Engineers lake extends 35 miles along the Chattahoochee River, just north of West Point. It's surrounded by forests and fields on the Alabama-Georgia state line. You can fish and camp. Off GA 29 near LaGrange. Resource Management

Office near the southeast end of the dam, 500 Resource Management Dr. 706-645-2937.

West Point Lake

Golf

American Legion, LaGrange. 706-884-4379.

Beaver Lake, Gay. 706-538-6994.

Bowden, Bowden. 770-258-3877.

Callaway Gardens, Pine Mountain. Mountain View, Garden View, Lake View, and Sky View. 800-282-8181.

The Fields, LaGrange. 706-845-7425.

Goldmine, Carrollton. 770-854-5940.

Maple Creek, Bremen. 770-537-4172.

Orchard Hills, Newnan. 770-251-5683.

Pebble Brook, Woodbury. 706-846-3809.

Roosevelt Memorial, Warm Springs. 706-655-5230.

Tallapoosa Municipal, Tallapoosa. 770-574-3122.

ENTERTAINMENT

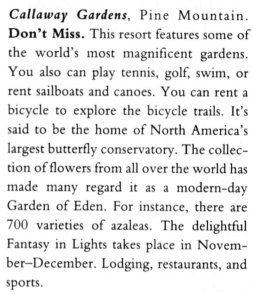

Callaway Gardens, Pine Mountain. **Don't Miss.** This resort features some of the world's most magnificent gardens. You also can play tennis, golf, swim, or rent sailboats and canoes. You can rent a bicycle to explore the bicycle trails. It's said to be the home of North America's largest butterfly conservatory. The collection of flowers from all over the world has made many regard it as a modern-day Garden of Eden. For instance, there are 700 varieties of azaleas. The delightful Fantasy in Lights takes place in November–December. Lodging, restaurants, and sports.

Callaway golf courses are ranked among the top U.S. courses by *Golf Digest* and *Golf* magazines. The PGA Tour's Buick Southern Open tees off each fall. There is a fee to drive through the gardens. Take I-85 south from Atlanta to I-185; continue south to exit 14. Turn left on US 27 and drive 11 miles to Callaway Gardens. 800-282-8181; 706-663-2281.

Manget-Brannon Alliance for the Arts, Newnan. The 1909 Warehouse Gallery and Theater feature art exhibits, theatrical events, and workshops throughout the year. First Ave. and Long Place. Exit 8 or 9 off I-85 S. 770-251-1276.

Shenandoah Environment and Education Center, Newnan. Environmental education center operated by Georgia Power for anyone interested in environmental science. Admission: free. Open year-round. 7 Solar Circle. 770-506-2460.

Wild Animal Safari, Pine Mountain. Included in this 500-acre park is a drive-through wilderness area where hundreds of animals represent every continent. Stop at an Old McDonald walk-through section, petting zoo, monkey house, bird house, and alligator pit. Restaurant, gift shop, and picnic area. Summer season includes guided tour buses, educational shows, and hands-on animal experiences. Daily 10 a.m. except Christmas. Closing time varies with season: winter 5:30 p.m.; spring and fall 6:30 p.m.; summer 7:30 p.m. Last ticket sold one hour before closing. No pets allowed, but if you are traveling with your pet, there is a place for it to stay during your visit. Admission: adults $11.95; senior citizens $10.95; children 3–9 $7.95; children under 3 free. 1300 Oak Grove Rd. From Atlanta take I-85 S to exit 5 (I-185). Continue straight to exit 14 (US 27). Turn left and go 6.8 miles to Oak Grove Rd. Turn right and park is two miles on left. 706-663-8744; 800-367-2751.

FESTIVALS

March

Azalea Festival (Callaway Gardens), Pine Mountain. March or April (depends on blooming). 800-282-8181; 706-663-2281.

April

Green Grass Fair, Warm Springs. First weekend in April (and November). Antiques, collectibles, arts, and crafts. Two miles north of Warm Springs on GA 41/US Alt. 27. 706-655-2468.

Old Town Sharpsburg Spring Festival, Sharpsburg. Usually third weekend. Booths with arts, crafts, antiques, and collectibles. Entertainment and barbecue. Exit 10 off I-85 S, east on GA 154 to sign. 770-251-8440.

June

Magnolia Blossom Festival, Newnan. Local artisans and craft makers. 770-254-3703.

July

Puckett Station Arts and Crafts Fair, Moreland. July 4th weekend. Exhibits and entertainment. 770-253-0567.

September

Coweta Co. Fair, Newnan. Sponsored by Newnan Kiwanis Club. Arts, handiwork, food, poultry, livestock, midway rides, and live entertainment. 770-253-2413.

Down by the Riverside Arts and Crafts Festival, West Point. Entertainment, rides, crafts, and arts. 770-429-0239.

Gold Rush Festival, Villa Rica. 770-459-3885.

Old Town Sharpsburg Fall Festival,

Sharpsburg. Third weekend. (See April listing.)

Powers Crossroads Country Fair and Art Festival, Newnan. Labor Day weekend. Learn about southern traditions and visit a country store. See work of artists and craft makers. Live entertainment. 770-253-2270.

October

Burwell Arts and Crafts Festival, Carrollton. 770-258-2469.

Cotton Pickin' Country Fair, Gay. 706-538-6814.

Halloween Festival, Villa Rica. Gold Dust Park. 770-459-7011.

McIntosh Reserve Fall Festival, Whitesburg. 770-830-5879.

Pine Mountain Heritage Festival, Pine Mountain. Arts, crafts, and entertainment. Pine Mountain Heritage Festival, P.O. Box 177, Pine Mountain, GA 31822.

November

Fantasy in Lights, Pine Mountain. November–January 1. Callaway Gardens. Must purchase tickets in advance. 800-282-8181; 706-663-2281.

Green Grass Fair, Warm Springs. (See *April* listing.)

Old Town Sharpsburg Christmas Open House, Sharpsburg. First full weekend in November. Exit 10 off I-85 S and follow GA 154 to sign. 770-251-8440.

CHAMBERS OF COMMERCE

(Italics indicate a county name.)

Carroll	770-832-2446
Haralson	770-537-5594
Harris	706-628-4381
Heard	706-675-6507
Meriwether	706-655-2558
Newnan–*Coweta*	706-253-2270
Pine Mountain	706-663-4000
Troup	706-884-8671
Valley, Greater	706-645-8877

CHAPTER THIRTEEN

SOUTH GEORGIA

Cities of South Georgia

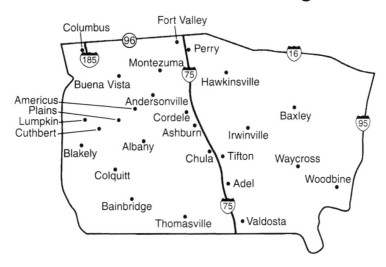

LOCATION	TO SEE/DO	EATING	SLEEPING	OTHER
	SOUTH GEORGIA AT A GLANCE			
Adel		King Frog Restaurant		Outlet stores
Albany		Carter's Grill Radium Springs Restaurant		Chehaw Wild Animal Park
Americus	Koinonia Windsor Hotel	Windsor Hotel	Pathways Inn Windsor Hotel	
Andersonville	Civil War Village Civil War Prison National Cemetery			
Ashburn	World's largest peanut			
Bainbridge			White House B&B	
Baxley	Edwin L. Hatch Visitors Center			
Blakely	Kolomoki Mounds Peanut Monument			
Buena Vista	Pasaquan	Morgan Towne House	Morgan Towne House Yesteryear Inn	
Chula			Hummingbird's Perch	
Colquitt			Country Inn Tarrer Inn	
Columbus	Blind Tom's Grave Columbus Museum Confederate Naval Museum Isaac Maund House Liberty Theater National Infantry Museum Patterson Planetarium Rainey House Spencer Opera House W. H. Spencer House	Ezell's Catfish Goetchius House		Shopping mall
Cordele	Georgia Veterans Memorial Park			
Cuthbert	Fletcher Henderson House			
Hawkinsville			Black Swan Inn	

SOUTH GEORGIA AT A GLANCE				
LOCATION	TO SEE/DO	EATING	SLEEPING	OTHER
Ft. Valley			Evans-Cantrell House	Massey Lane Gardens
Hawkinsville			Black Swan Inn	
Irwinville	Jefferson Davis Memorial			
Lumpkin	Westville			Providence Canyon
Montezuma		Yoder's Deitsch Haus		
Perry			Swift Street Inn	
Plains	Jimmy Carter Historic District and Museum		Plains B&B	
Thomasville	Lapham-Patterson House Lt. H. O. Flipper's Grave		Deer Creek B&B 1884 Paxton House Evans House Grand Victoria Inn Our Cottage on the Park	Parrish Livery & Carriage
Tifton	Agrirama			
Valdosta	Lowndes County History Museum The Crescent	Fiddlers Green		
Waycross	Obediah's Okefenok Okefenokee Swamp			
Woodbine		Angelo's at Harriet's Bluff		

When you go into South Georgia, you'll see the state's major agricultural area. It may surprise you to know that peaches aren't the prime crop. It's peanuts. There's even a monument to the peanut in Blakely.

Particularly, you'll want to visit Jimmy Carter country in and around Plains. At Americus is Habitat for Humanity, the non-profit organization that the Carters have been heavily involved with since he left office in 1980. (See Koinonia in *Where to Go and What to See.*)

While you're in this part of the state, you'll want to visit Koinonia Farm—established by Clarence Jordan in the 1940s as an integrated communal farm. There is also the "plantation trace" region centered on

Thomasville. And at Andersonville is the Civil War prisoner-of-war camp.

In the very southernmost part of the state, you'll find the beautiful Okefenokee Swamp beckoning you to explore.

All over South Georgia, you'll find small towns with something special to offer you as a visitor. Get ready to enjoy yourself!

WHERE TO GO AND WHAT TO SEE

Blind Tom's Grave Marker

AN EXTRA TOUCH OF SOUTH GEORGIA: BLIND TOM'S GRAVE

Blind Thomas Wiggins was born into slavery in 1834. His owners discovered the boy's musical talent when they returned to their home in Columbus and heard him playing their piano. Years later, Wiggins thrilled audiences in America and Europe with his remarkable talent. He could perfectly produce on the piano any sound he heard, from classical compositions to the

songs of birds. On European tours, he played before royalty. Thomas's grave site is at US 27A about six miles north of Columbus, Muscogee Co.

◆◆

Agrirama, Tifton. Georgia Agrirama, the state's living history museum, opened July 1, 1976. You'll see a traditional farm community of the 1870s, a progressive farmstead of the 1890s, an industrial site complex, and a rural town. More than 35 structures have been relocated to the 95-acre site and preserved or restored. Costumed interpreters are present to explain and demonstrate the lifestyle and activities of the period. Tue.– Sat. 9 a.m.–5 p.m.; Sun. 12:30–5 p.m. Closed Mon. Closed Thanksgiving Day, three days prior to Christmas, and Christmas Day. Admission charged. Exit 20 on I-75 S. 912-386-3344.

Andersonville: Civil War Village, Civil War Prison, National Cemetery, Andersonville. **Don't Miss.** During the Civil War, the village of Andersonville, located near the end of the Southwestern Railroad, became the terminal where 45,000 Federal prisoners of war arrived by rail during 1864 and 1865. This prison has a notorious history. In the 14 months of its existence, 13,000 prisoners died from overcrowding, disease, malnutrition, poor sanitation, and exposure.

After the war, when this information became public, the outcry brought about the eventual hanging of the camp's commandant in Washington, DC, in 1865. You can visit the cemetery and see the rows of white markers spreading across the hillside. Also, see where the stockade housed the prisoners.

The town of Andersonville has a farm area complete with log cabin, barn, farm animals, a sugarcane mill, and syrup kettle. Visit Andersonville's beautiful log church, Pennington St. James, which is an architectural gem designed by Cramm and Ferguson—who designed the Cathedral of St. John the Divine in New York City. Open daily. It was built in 1927 of cypress logs and native fieldstone by Dr. James Bolan Lawrence, a much-loved Episcopal minister. Go to the Welcome Station and Museum, which are housed in a quaint 19th-century railroad depot. 9 a.m.–5 p.m. October 1–April 30; 9 a.m.–5:30 p.m. May 1–September 30. Fifty miles south of Macon on GA 49. 912-924-2778.

Buena Vista

Buena Vista. This small town has added interesting attractions (see *Pasaquan* listing). Southeast of Columbus on GA 41, it offers

an Elvis Presley museum (800-337-6072), Silver Moon Music Barn (800-531-0677), and National Country Music Museum (800-531-0677). Call to confirm hours of operation. All are located around the square.

Coheelee Creek Covered Bridge, Early Co. (See **Covered Bridges and Gristmills of Georgia**.) Old River Rd. Two miles north of Hilton on GA 62.

Columbus Museum, Columbus. This is the major arts center for the region with historical, cultural, and visual-arts exhibits. Watch the impressive film *Chattahoochee Legacy* shown throughout the day, and see the historical exhibit surrounding the theater. Tue.–Sat. 10 a.m.–5 p.m.; Sun. 1–5 p.m. Admission: free. 1251 Wynnton Rd. 706-649-0713.

Confederate Naval Museum, Columbus. On display are the salvaged remains of two Confederate gunboats, ship models, and blockade-running mementos. Tue.–Fri. 10 a.m.–5 p.m; Sat.–Sun. 1–5 p.m. 202 4th St. 706-327-9798.

The Crescent, Valdosta. Built in 1898, the house has a crescent-shaped porch and 13 columns to represent the 13 original colonies of America. Today it is the home of the Valdosta Garden Center. Open for tours Mon.–Fri. 2–5 p.m. and by appointment. 904 N. Patterson St. 912-242-2196.

Edwin L. Hatch Visitors Center, Baxley. Did you ever wonder what happens inside a nuclear power plant? For the answer and other information on energy and electricity, visit this center. Mon.–Fri. 8:30 a.m.–5 p.m. Twelve miles north of Baxley on US 1. 912-367-3668 or 537-0500; 800-722-7774.

Fletcher Henderson House, Cuthbert. Built in 1888 for Fletcher Henderson, who was a leading educator in Cuthbert for 64 years. His son, Fletcher Henderson, Jr., became one of America's jazz greats on the piano. *Not open to the public.* 1016 Andrew St.

Georgia Veterans Memorial State Park, Cordele. The park with its two museums is a memorial to all U.S. veterans. An indoor museum has exhibits about wars and famous battles from the French and Indian Wars of the 18th century through the Vietnam War. In the outside museum, you'll find war machines (planes, cannons, and tanks) beginning with World War I (1917–18) through Vietnam. 9 a.m.–5 p.m. Three miles west of I-75 (exit 33), near Cordele on US 280. 912-276-2371.

Isaac Maund House, Columbus. Maund, African-American mill worker and carpenter, built this house himself in 1896. It stands as a testimony that affluent whites and African-Americans could live together in an integrated neighborhood in the late 19th and early 20th centuries. *Not open to the public.* 1608 3rd Ave.

Jefferson Davis Memorial Museum and Park, Irwinville. Listed on the National Register of Historic Places, this is the site where Jefferson Davis, president of the Confederate States during the Civil War, was captured. Enjoy the museum and visit the monument in the park. Tue.–Sat. 9 a.m.–5 p.m.; Sun. 1–5 p.m. Closed Mon. Admission charged. North of Tifton. 912-831-2335.

Jefferson Davis Museum

Jimmy Carter Historic District, Plains. Start at the railroad depot from which Carter ran his presidential campaign because it's now the Visitors Center for a 77-acre historic district. Ask for the audiotape tour. You'll learn about President Carter's birthplace, the family, and his school. You'll probably see a flyer inviting you to join Mr. Carter at the Maranatha Baptist Church, where he still teaches Sunday school.

Look for the High School Museum, where both the former president and his wife, Rosalynn, went to school. The long-time empty school should be open for the 1996 Olympics as part of the Jimmy Carter

National Historic Site operated by the National Parks Service. Plans are to have at least one classroom set up as it was during the Carters' high school years. Visitors Center 9 a.m.–5 p.m. 912-824-3413.

Town of Plains

Jimmy Carter Campaign Headquarters in Plains

Koinonia, Americus. Pronounced Koy-no-NEE-ah, the Greek word for *fellowship*. Koinonia was started 50 years ago by an idealistic Baptist preacher named Clarence Jordan. Local segregationists condemned him because of his policy of equality among races in an ecumenical setting. Those at Koinonia still live communally. They support themselves with a mail-order candy business that specializes in pecan and pea-

nut confections. Weekdays 8–11:45 a.m.; 12:45–5 p.m. Dawson Rd. (GA 49), south of Americus. 912-924-0391.

From Koinonia grew Habitat for Humanity, which was established in 1976 because of the vision of Millard and Linda Fuller. Their goal is to construct houses around the world for impoverished people. Their work depends on donations and volunteers who work alongside the new owners to build the homes. The new owners must give 500 hours of "sweat equity" on their homes, and then pay for it on a 20-year no-interest plan. The money is then used to build more Habitat homes. Visitors welcome. Habitat's international headquarters is in Americus at 121 Habitat St. 912-924-6935.

Kolomoki Mounds

Kolomoki Mounds, Blakely. State historic site. This important archaeological site includes Georgia's oldest great temple mound. Seven mounds were built in the 12th and 13th centuries by the Weeden Island and Swift Creek Indians. Museum Tue.–Sat. 9 a.m.–5 p.m.; Sun. 2–5 p.m.

Closed Mon. Six miles north of Blakely off US 27. 912-723-5296.

Lapham-Patterson House, Thomasville. State historic site. The Lapham-Patterson House is a monument to the imagination, creative engineering, and craftsmanship of the Victorian period. Built in 1884–85 as a winter cottage for a prosperous shoe merchant, C. W. Lapham of Chicago, the residence was equipped with its own gas lighting system, hot and cold running water, indoor plumbing, and modern closets. Like many other successful northerners, Lapham came to the bustling resort town of Thomasville for its mild climate and the supposed therapeutic value of the pine-scented air. The Laphams sold the winter house in 1894, and it was resold in 1905 to James G. Patterson. The Pattersons remained in possession until 1970.

The Lapham-Patterson House is a fine example of Thomasville's Victorian resort period. Fishscale shingles, Oriental-style porch decorations, long-leaf pine inlaid floors, a double-flue chimney, a walk-through stairway, and cantilevered balcony exemplify the quality and skill of its creators. Because of its outstanding architectural significance, the Lapham-Patterson House was named a National Historic Landmark in 1975. Open year-round. Tue.–Sat. 9 a.m.– 5 p.m.; Sun. 2–5:30 p.m. Closed Mon., Thanksgiving, and Christmas Day. Tours on the hour. Last tour at 4 p.m. Admission charged. 626 N. Dawson St. 912-225-4004.

Liberty Theater, Columbus. This was the major entertainment center for the African-American community of Columbus for more than half a century. Movies were shown during the week, and live performances were presented Saturday night. It was on the circuit for jazz and blues performances, with performances by "Ma" Rainey (often called the mother of the blues, who was a Columbus native), Marian Anderson, Ella Fitzgerald, Ethel Waters, Lena Horne, Duke Ellington, Cab Calloway, and Fletcher Henderson. Open by appointment only. 821 8th Ave. 706-322-1014.

Lt. Henry O. Flipper's Grave, Thomasville. In the Old Cemetery on Madison St. you can view Flipper's grave. A native of Thomasville, he was the first African-American graduate of West Point, class of 1877.

Lowndes Co. Historical Museum, Valdosta. Filled with memorabilia dating back to 1825. Mon.–Fri. 2–5 p.m. 305 W. Central Ave. 912-247-4780.

National Infantry Museum, Fort Benning, Columbus. Established on an old plantation site south of Columbus in 1918, the army's Fort Benning has since become the largest infantry training center in the world. You can visit the on-base three-story museum that traces American infantry history from the French and Indian War to the Persian Gulf. Admission: free. Tue.–Fri. 10 a.m.–

4:30 p.m.; Sat.–Sun. 12:30–4:30 p.m. 706-545-2958.

Obediah's Okefenok, Waycross. Historic site and 1800s homestead. In the early 1800s, Obediah Barber and his father, Isaac, were among the first white settlers to live on the northern border of the great Okefenokee Swamp. Obediah built a one-story cabin with wooden pegged walls and puncheon floors. Self-guided tour of homestead and historic cabin; walking trails; wildlife; entertainment as scheduled. Mon.–Sat. 10 a.m.–5 p.m.; Sun. 2–4 p.m. Closed major holidays. Admission charged. 500 Obediah Trail. Exit US 82 (S. GA Parkway/520) onto Gilmore St. 912-287-0090.

Pasaquan. Buena Vista. The home of the late Eddie Owens Martin, who called himself St. EOM, the Wizard of Pasaquan. Known as an eccentric, he left school after the sixth grade. His house reflects the vision he lived and died with: It is considered one of the most important folk art centers in America. Since the death of Martin, his work has gained a measure of acceptance, and his work hangs in museums and galleries. Sat. 10 a.m.–6 p.m.; Sun. 1–6 p.m. Weekday tours can be scheduled. Admission: $5. North of Buena Vista off GA 127. Go left, take County Rd. 78 (second paved road on right). 912-649-9444.

Patterson Planetarium, Columbus. Cosmic shows. Call for schedule. 2900 Woodruff Farm Rd. 706-568-1730.

Peanut Monument, Blakely. Honors local peanut production. Courthouse square. US 27. 912-723-3741.

Peanut Monument in Blakely

Plains. Stop by B. J.'s Pit Stop (once a service station owned by Billy Carter, the former president's brother) in Plains for guided tours past the president's current residence and the old railroad depot that he used as campaign headquarters in 1976. Georgia Welcome Center: 912-824-7477.

Rainey House (Gertrude Pridget "Ma" Rainey), Columbus. National Register of Historic Places. This was the last home of the woman credited with being the mother of the blues. She sang both blues and gospel and was a national recording artist in the 1920s. *Not open to public.* 805 5th Ave.

(William H.) Spencer House, Columbus. This two-story building is an excellent example of neoclassical revival architecture, which has been completely restored. Listed on the National Historic Register, it was the custom-built home of William Spencer, a member of the Columbus Public School System. The city named the high school in his honor. Visit by appointment. Corner of 4th Ave. and 8th St. 706-322-1014.

Springer Opera House, Columbus. A red plush-and-gilt jewel box officially designated the state theater of Georgia, the theater continues to hold performances. The small museum highlights performers who appeared on stage, such as Oscar Wilde,

---

■■   ■■

THE HOUSE THAT SHERMAN SPARED

In the spring of 1864, General William Tecumseh Sherman and his Northern troops made their famous (or in the South, infamous) march to the sea. The Union troops destroyed everything in their path and torched town after town. Yet at Manassas, they left one house untouched.

An oversight? A momentary lapse of policy? Or was it an affair of the heart? We like the story that says in the 1840s, 20 years before the Civil War, Sherman fell in love with Cecilia Stovall. She didn't love him and turned away his advances. But he never forgot his beloved Cecilia.

When his troops reached Manassas, he destroyed everything except one house—the residence of the former Cecilia Stovall.

Sherman tacked a note to the door of Cecilia Stovall's house (then Mrs. Shellman) that read:

Dear Madam,
You once said that you would pity the man who would ever become my enemy. My answer was that I would ever protect and shield you. That I have done. Forgive me all else. I am but a soldier.

Respectfully,
W. T. Sherman[*]

[*] In *Civil War Treasury* by B. A. Botkin as quoted in *A Treasury of Georgia Tales* by Webb Garrison (Nashville: Rutledge Hill Press, 1987), p. 80.

Ethel Barrymore, and John Philip Sousa. Guided tours available by appointment. 103 10th St. 706-327-3688.

Westville, Lumpkin. Westville is 57 acres of a living history village. Realistic depictions of Georgia's preindustrial life and culture of 1850. Mon.–Sat. 10 a.m.–5 p.m.; Sun. 1–5 p.m. Closed major holidays. Admission charged. Intersection of US 27 and GA 27 south of Columbus. 912-838-6310.

Windsor Hotel, Americus. Known as the crown jewel of South Georgia, it was built in 1892. After a $5 million restoration of Victorian decor, the Windsor reopened in 1991. Drink afternoon tea in the Ladies Tea Parlor or dine in the Southern Grand Dining Room. Tours and tea daily. 125 W. Lamar St. 912-924-1555.

World's Largest Peanut, Ashburn. Ten-foot-tall peanut set in a gold crown with words GEORGIA: 1ST IN PEANUTS. On I-75.

EATING

Recipes

Beaten Biscuits. Whether for breakfast or the evening meal, hot biscuits tempt everyone to indulge in just one more.

Sift 2 cups all-purpose flour with 1/2 teaspoon salt and 3 teaspoons baking powder and a pinch of baking soda. Add 4 tablespoons shortening (in "olden days" cooks used lard, which is still used by some southern cooks) and 1 cup of milk. Work with fingers or pastry blender into a stiff dough, then beat dough with hands on biscuit board until it is smooth. Roll dough about 1/2-inch thick, and cut out biscuits with biscuit cutter. Stick biscuit on top with tines of a small fork, then brush lightly with just a trace of milk. Bake in hot oven (450°) 12–15 minutes. Serve at once. Makes 10 to 12 biscuits.

Southern Fried Chicken. There's something special about the way chicken is fried in the South. The variations abound, but this is our favorite way of doing it.

In a paper bag, mix 1 cup flour, 2 teaspoons salt, and 1/2 teaspoon pepper. Drop pieces of chicken into bag and shake to coat chicken thoroughly. In large heavy skillet, heat 3 tablespoons shortening. Place coated pieces of chicken in skillet, cover; let brown on one side at medium heat, cooking slowly. Turn on other side; cover and cook until done. Drain on paper towels. Serve with milk gravy.

Milk Gravy. Most folk in the South like mashed potatoes and hot biscuits with their fried chicken, and milk gravy made from the chicken drippings is great on both of them.

After you remove the fried chicken from the skillet, pour off remaining grease, but leave drippings from chicken in the pan. Add 2 tablespoons flour, dash salt and pepper to drippings, and blend. Then add 1 cup water and 1 cup milk to skillet. Heat to boiling and cook several minutes until blended and thick. Stir constantly to prevent sticking.

Pecan Pie. Devotees of pecan pie differ in whether to use pecan halves or chopped pecans in the recipe. Cooks most often tend to use halves, but it's delicious either way.

Mix together 1 cup sugar, 1 cup Karo syrup (dark), 2 eggs, 2 tablespoons melted butter (margarine may be substituted), 1 cup milk, and 2 tablespoons flour. Pour over 1 cup pecan halves placed in prepared 9-inch pie shell. Bake 50 to 60 minutes in 350° oven until knife inserted halfway between center and edge comes out clean. Cool before cutting.

Where to Eat

Eating in South Georgia is a little different from eating in other areas of the state. You won't find as many specialty restaurants. Also, many restaurants are not open late at night or on Saturday (such as in the Columbus Historic District). There are still plenty of nice places to stop and eat, and we've listed a few you might want to try.

Angelo's at Harriett's Bluff, * Woodbine. Italian specialties; pizza. I-95 (exit 3). 912-729-1000 or 729-1006.

Carter's Grill and Restaurant, * Albany. Pit barbecue and home-style cooking. Reservations needed. 321 W. Highland Ave. 912-432-2098.

Ezell's Catfish Cabin, * Columbus. All-you-can-eat catfish, popcorn shrimp, and other seafood plates. Mon.–Thu. 4:30–9:30

p.m.; Fri.–Sun. 11:30 a.m.–10 p.m. 4001 Warm Springs Rd. 706-568-1149.

Fiddlers Green, * Valdosta. Rustic atmosphere offering relaxed, romantic dining. Black angus steaks and seafood. 4479 N. Valdosta Rd. I-75 (exit 6). 912-247-0366.

Goetchius House, ** Columbus. For an elegant meal, go to the historic district's antebellum Goetchius House (pronounced GET-chez). Order frog legs, bourguignonne, chateaubriand, swordfish, or lobster in the 1839 mansion's formal dining room, or meet for oysters in the speakeasy downstairs. Mon.–Thu. 5–10 p.m.; Fri.–Sat. 5–11 p.m. Closed Sun. 405 Broadway. 706-324-4863.

King Frog Restaurant, * Adel. Family dining: seafood, steaks, chicken. Daily 6 a.m.–10 p.m. I-75 (exit 10). 912-896-2244.

Morgan Towne House Restaurant/Bed & Breakfast, * Buena Vista. Dine and stay in an 1880s restoration house with southern-style buffet meals. Lunch Tue.–Sun. 11:30 a.m.–2 p.m.; dinner Fri.–Sat. 5:30–8:30

p.m. Restaurant accessible for persons with disabilities. 2 Church St. 912-649-3663.

Radium Springs Restaurant, Albany. Restaurant in turn-of-the-century resort. 2500 Radium Springs Rd. 912-883-3871.

Windsor Hotel, Americus. Dining room is open to other than overnight guests, so stop in for good southern cooking. 125 W. Lamar St. 912-924-1555.

Windsor Hotel

Yoder's Deitsch Haus,* Montezuma. Cafeteria-style buffet with freshly prepared foods. Reasonably priced. Tue.–Sat. 11:30 a.m.–2 p.m. and 5–8:30 p.m. except Wed. GA 26 about three miles east of Montezuma. 912-472-2024.

SLEEPING

Black Swan Inn, Country Inn and Restaurant, Hawkinsville. This southern colonial-style mansion features six rooms with private baths, TVs, and telephones. Conti-

nental cuisine in restaurant. 411 Progress Ave. 912-783-4466.

Country Inn, Colquitt. Large colonial-style country inn. Five bedrooms with private baths. Guest access to separate kitchen. Hunting and fishing reserves. US 27 south of Colquitt. 912-758-5417.

Deer Creek Bed & Breakfast, Thomasville. This B&B is advertised as a place of rustic luxury in city limits; you get a view of woods from a scenic private treetop deck. Certified contract bridge lessons available daily. Located next to South's second oldest golf course. Scenic walking area. 1304 Old Monticello Rd. 912-226-7294.

1884 Paxton House Bed & Breakfast Inn, Thomasville. Victorian landmark in historical district. There are four rooms and suites with private baths. Custom decorating, quilts, fireplaces, footed tubs, heart-pine floors, millwork, and antiques throughout. 445 Remington Ave. 912-226-5197.

Evans-Cantrell House, Fort Valley. Italian Renaissance–style inn, built around 1916. Once home to A. J. Evans, called the Peach King in the early days of this century. 300 College St. 912-825-0611.

Evans House Bed & Breakfast, Thomasville. This restored Victorian home was built in 1898. Country kitchen breakfast served. In the Parkfront Historical District, across from beautiful 27-acre Paradise Park. 725 S. Hansell St. 912-226-1343; 800-344-4717.

Grand Victoria Inn, Thomasville. This 1893 eclectic Victorian inn offers four guest rooms, afternoon tea, and a full breakfast. 817 S. Hansell St. 912-226-7460.

Hummingbird's Perch, Chula. Modern country living. Opportunity for bird-watching, fishing, or seeing a beautiful sunset while strolling around the lake. Children 12 and up permitted. Exit 23 on I-75 S. 912-382-5431.

Morgan Towne House Restaurant/Bed & Breakfast, Buena Vista. Eat and sleep in an 1880s restoration house. Restaurant open to public. Church St. 912-649-3663.

Our Cottage on the Park, Thomasville. Overlooking historic Paradise Park, Our Cottage provides complete breakfasts, private baths, spacious porches, and a gift emporium. 801 S. Hansell St. 912-227-0404.

Pathways Inn, Americus. Built around 1906. In the historic district. Private baths. Offers murder mystery weekends. 501 S. Lee St. 912-928-2078; 800-889-1466.

Plains Bed & Breakfast Inn, Plains. Former Carter family home. Two-story Victorian. US 280. 912-824-7252.

Swift Street Inn, Perry. This 135-year-old home is filled with antiques. Breakfast served. 1204 Swift St. 912-987-3428.

Tarrer Inn, Colquitt. This 1903 hotel on the square in Colquitt has reopened with 12 rooms, three banquet halls, and a restaurant. 155 S. Cuthbert St. 912-758-2888.

White House Bed & Breakfast, Bainbridge. Antebellum, built about 1840–50, this traditional dogtrot-style home is in the historical district. The three rooms are furnished with family antiques and heirloom needlework. Near historic homes, antique shops, restaurants, and Lake Seminola. Children 10 and over welcome. Smoke free. 320 S. Washington St. 912-248-1703.

Windsor Hotel, Americus. Historic (about 1892) hotel with restored Victorian decor. 125 W. Lamar St. 912-924-1555.

Yesteryear Inn, Buena Vista. A white-columned antebellum inn, built about 1855, with heart-pine floors, antiques, quilts, and four-poster feather beds. Desserts on the front porch. Southern breakfast. Golf packages, hunting, fishing, and nature walks. 229 S. Broad St. 912-649-7307; 800-836-YALL.

SHOPPING

Factory Stores of America, Lake Park. Browse through 24 factory outlet stores; brand-name quality. I-75 (exit 2). 912-559-6177.

Historic Remerton Mill Village, Remerton. Antiques, collectibles, fine gifts, handmade crafts, home decor, lamps, accessories, and gift baskets. Two streets of restored mill houses converted into unique specialty shops. 1802 Plum St. 912-241-7145.

King Frog Factory Direct Clothing, Adel. Large selection of brand-name clothing, including big-and-tall men's clothing. Daily 6 a.m.–10 p.m. I-75 S (exit 10). 912-896-2244.

Lake Park Mill Store Plaza, Lake Park. More than 100 factory outlets. Mon.–Sat. 9 a.m.–8 p.m.; Sun. 10 a.m.–6 p.m. I-75 S (exit 2). 912-559-6822.

Peachtree Mall, Columbus. Shop at 100 stores. Mon.–Sat. 10 a.m.–9 p.m.; Sun. 1–6 p.m. I-85 at Manchester Expressway. 706-327-1578.

Valdosta Mall, Valdosta. Shop at 80 stores. Mon.–Sat. 10 a.m.–9 p.m.; Sun. 1–6 p.m. I-75 (exit 5). 912-242-0457.

ANTIQUES AND CRAFTS

Antiques from the Shed, Perry. Early Americana. Mon.–Sat. 10 a.m.–5 p.m. 1139 Macon St. 912-987-2469.

Ashburn Antique Mini Mall, Ashburn. Antiques and collectibles. Mon.–Sat. 9:30 a.m.–5 p.m. Closed Sun. 101 E. College Ave. 912-567-0121.

Carousel House, Bainbridge. Mon.–Sat. noon–6 p.m. 709 Calhoun St. 912-246-7022.

Columbus Antique Mall, Columbus. Shop 20,000 square feet with 35 dealers. Mon.–Sat. 10 a.m.–6 p.m.; Sun. 1–5 p.m. 1601 1st Ave. 706-322-9550.

Country Wares, Soperton. Antiques, collectibles, and crafts. Thu.–Sat. 10 a.m.–5 p.m. GA 29 S. 912-529-3113.

Courthouse Square Antique Mall, Vienna. Mon.–Sat. 10 a.m.–5 p.m.; Sun. 1–5 p.m. 103 S. 3rd St. 912-268-1496.

Dusty Rose, Bainbridge. Crafters and peddlers minimall. Mon.–Sat. 10 a.m.–6 p.m.; Sun. 1:30–5:30 p.m. Closed Wed. 1314 Dothan Rd. 912-243-1777.

Eastman Flea and Antique Market, Eastman. Mon.–Sat. 9 a.m.–5:30 p.m.; Sun. 1–5 p.m. 1107 Herman Ave. 912-374-7868.

Lion's Share, Warner Robins. Mon.–Sat. 10 a.m.–6 p.m.; Sun. 1–5 p.m. Closed Tue. 2069 Watson Blvd. 912-922-1973.

Lord Byron Antiques, Byron. Antiques and collectibles. Mon.–Sat. 10 a.m.–7 p.m.; Sun. 1:30–5:30 p.m. Main St. and E. Heritage Blvd. 912-956-2789.

Perry Antiques and Collectibles Mall, Perry. Mon.–Sat. 10 a.m.–5 p.m.; Sun. 1–5 p.m. 351 Gen. Courtney Blvd. (US 41). 912-987-4001.

Rainbow's End, Perry. Crafts supplies, gifts, and antiques. Mon.–Sat. 10 a.m.–6 p.m. 1126 Macon Rd. 912-987-0994.

Rocky Wade Antiques, Buena Vista. Original wood carvings. Mon.–Sat. 6th Ave. on the square. 912-649-3485.

Royal Antique Mall & Flea Market, McRae. Antiques, collectibles, army surplus, arts, and crafts. More than 30 dealers. Mon.–Sat. 9:30 a.m.–6 p.m. US 441 south of McRae. 912-868-5229.

Turners, Marshallville. Antiques, collectibles, neons, and jukeboxes. 102 E. Main. 912-967-2112.

OUTDOORS

AN EXTRA TOUCH OF SOUTH GEORGIA: THE OKEFENOKEE SWAMP

Okefenokee (Land of the Trembling Earth) is a swampland of cypress, black gum, holly, and bay trees. On the west and north, miles of moss–draped cypress border lakes and boat runs. To the east are expanses of open watery marshes filled with aquatic plants.

Because of decaying vegetation, tannic acid has caused the shallow water to be widely known as black water, and the streams flow into the Suwanee and St. Marys Rivers. Along the watery lowland are nearly 70 pine-filled islands.

Once home to the Seminole, a Native American tribe, Georgia pioneers settled the region about 1850. They homesteaded on the swamp's borders and islands. They farmed and hunted until 1937, when the U.S. government declared the Okefenokee a National Wildlife Refuge. You may see alligators, otters, wild turkeys, hogs, waterfowl, and a variety of birds. For some unknown reason, no one has ever seen beavers in the swamp.

Twice, technology has threatened the area's natural beauty. First, in the 1890s, loggers failed to drain the swamp after floating cypress to the coast by way of the Suwanee Canal. Second, early in the 20th century, loggers created a railroad network to remove timber from deep within the swamp. In 1927, after they had taken more than 90 percent of the cypress of commercial value, they abandoned the area.

The government constructed an earthen dam, or sill, on the Suwanee River in 1960 to stabilize the Okefenokee's water levels. This keeps the swamp wet, which also protects the swampland from the threat of serious fires.

Fishing

Banks Lake. This 3,900–acre lake 22 miles northeast of Valdosta offers excellent fishing facilities. Call Okefenokee State Park at Waycross: 912-496-3331.

Grand Bay Wildlife Management Area. The area includes 5,000 acres, 10 miles north of Valdosta. Fishing, canoeing, birdwatching, hiking, camping at primitive campsites, and hunting (deer and small game). Weekends only. 912-423-2988.

Golf

American Legion, Albany. 912-432-6016.

Beaver Creek, Douglas. 912-384-8230.

Black Creek, Ellabell. 912-858-4653.

Blueberry Plantation, Alma. 912-632-2772.

Brickyard Plantation, Americus. 912-874-1234.

Bull Creek, Columbus. 706-561-1614.

Cedar Creek Golf and CC, Buena Vista. 912-649-3381.

Cherokee Rose CC, Hinesville. 912-876-5503.

Country Oaks, Thomasville. 912-225-4333.

Donalsonville CC, Donalsonville. 912-524-2955.

Douglas Community, Douglas. 912-384-7353.

Evans Heights, Claxton. 912-739-3003.

Folkston Golf and CC, Folkston. 912-496-7155.

Forest Lake, Tifton. 912-382-7626.

Fountain City, Columbus. 706-324-0583.

Foxfire, Vidalia. 912-538-8670.

Francis Lake, Lake Park. 912-559-7961.

Georgia Veterans, Cordele. State park. 912-276-2377.

Gordonia-Alatamaha, Reidsville. State park. 912-557-6445.

Green Valley, Jakin. 912-793-4481.

Hinson Hills, Douglas. 912-384-8984.

Houston Lake CC, Perry. 912-987-3243.

Industrial Park, Bainbridge. 912-246-8545.

Lakeview Golf and CC, Blackshear. 912-449-4411.

Little Ocmulgee, McRae. State park. 912-868-6651.

Mallard Point, Rochelle. 912-365-7810.

Maple Ridge, Columbus. 706-569-0966.

Northlake Golf and CC, Valdosta. 912-247-8613.

Pine Bluff CC, Eastman. 912-374-0991.

Pine Knoll CC, Sylvester. 912-776-3455.

Pointe South, Hephzibah. 706-592-2222.

Red Oak, Cusetta. 706-989-3312.

Stone Creek, Valdosta. 912-247-2527.

Sunsweet Hills, Tifton. 912-382-4244.

Turner Field, Albany. 912-430-5267.

Wanee Lake CC, Ashburn. 912-567-2727.

Wolf Creek, Americus. 912-928-4040.

Hunting

Quail, ducks, deer, and wild turkeys all inhabit Lowndes Co. and South Georgia. There is a season for each species, and you can hunt both private and commercial land. For information call Quail Creek

Shooting Preserve: 912-333-8611 or 794-2226; Indianola Hunting Preserve: 912-242-0903.

Pebble Hill Plantation, Thomasville. Southern shooting plantation. Tue.–Sat. 10 a.m.–5 p.m.; Sun. 1–5 p.m. US 319. 912-226-2344.

Tennis

Florence Marina, Omaha (near Lumpkin).

George T. Bagby Park, Ft. Gaines.

Gordonia Alatamaha, near Reidsville.

Little Ocmulgee Park and Lodge, near McRae.

Other Activities

Entrance to Okefenokee Swamp Park

Okefenokee Swamp Park, Waycross. Take a guided boat tour of the swamp. Enjoy the museum and wildlife exhibits, and wilderness walkway. No pets allowed inside park area. 9 a.m.–6:30 p.m. summer; 9 a.m.–5:30 p.m. the rest of the year. Open every day except Christmas. Admission charged. US 1, eight miles south of Waycross. 912-283-0583.

Providence Canyon

Providence Canyon State Conservation Park, Lumpkin. Sometimes called Georgia's Little Grand Canyon. The rare plum-leaf azalea grows here, but it blooms only July–September. Go to the Interpretive Center to get information and to arrange guided canyon tours. 7 a.m.–9 p.m. April 15–September 15; 7 a.m.–6 p.m. rest of year. Rt. 1, Box 158, Lumpkin, 31815. Seven miles west of Lumpkin on GA 39 C. 912-838-6202.

Radium Springs, Albany. You can swim (summers only!) in Georgia's largest natural spring waters. There's also an early 1900s Victorian lodge. 2511 Radium Springs Rd. 912-883-3871.

ENTERTAINMENT

Chehaw Wild Animal Park, Albany. Home to ostriches, elk, elephants, zebras, and other animals. Natural setting for animals on 193 acres. Petting zoo. Tue.–Sat. 9 a.m.–5 p.m. Admission charged. Off Hwy 19 north of town. 912-430-5275.

Massee Lane Gardens, Fort Valley. Walk through nine acres of camellias, explore a greenhouse, and stroll around a Japanese garden. Don't overlook the 15-minute slide presentation on the history of camellias and the American Camellia Society. Mon.–Sat. 9 a.m.–5 p.m.; Sun. 1–5 p.m. November–March. Mon.–Fri. 9 a.m.–4 p.m. off season. Admission charged. Off GA 49 below Fort Valley. 912-967-2358 or 967-2722.

Parrish Livery and Carriage Service, Thomasville. Carriage rides through historic district. 912-226-5910.

Springer Opera House, Columbus. A National Historic Landmark since 1975. The Springer Opera House today presents entertainment on two stages. 103 10th St. Information on production and tickets: 706-327-3688.

FESTIVALS

March

Dogwood Festival, Jesup. Antiques, crafts, and collectibles. 912-427-2080 or 427-7833.

Dulcimer Festival, Westville. Includes workshop. 912-838-6310.

April

Dogwood Festival, Leslie. 912-924-2646.

Dogwood Festival, Perry. First week in April. Arts, crafts, parade, and 5K run. 912-987-1234.

Hawkinsville Harness Festival, Hawkinsville. Trotters and pacers. 912-783-1717.

Mossy Creek Barnyard Arts and Crafts Festival, Perry. Third weekend. A showcase for nationally recognized artists and craft makers. Clogging, hayrides, and a petting zoo. 912-922-8265.

Rose Festival and Parade, Thomasville. Crafts, parade. 800-704-2350.

May

Andersonville Historic Fair, Andersonville. May and October. 912-924-2558.

Chehaw National Indian Festival, Albany. Native American celebration. 912-436-1625.

Hillside Bluegrass Festival, Cochran. May and September. Live entertainment. 912-934-6694.

Mayhaw Festival, Colquitt. One-day event celebrates the mayhaw berry, famous for the wonderful jelly it makes. Arts, crafts, games, contests, and a parade. Spring Creek Park. 912-758-2400.

Plains Country Days, Plains. Third weekend. This is Jimmy Carter country, and it's the town's major festival. (And you might

see the former president and first lady.)
Parade, street dance, hayrides, "homespun"
music, arts, and crafts. 912-824-7477.

June

Blueberry Festival, Alma. Blueberry products, arts, and crafts. 912-632-5859.

Gnat Days, Camilla. Second and third weeks. Boat cruises, professional tennis tournament, arts, and crafts. Especially visit the Gnat Market. 706-336-5255.

July

Fourth of July Festival, Columbus. July 4. A military pageant with skydiving paratroopers, gleaming bands, single-step parades in full battle dress, and fireworks. Fort Benning. 706-545-2238.

Watermelon Days Festival, Cordele. Runs a week to 10 days. 912-273-3526.

September

Hillside Bluegrass Festival, Cochran. May and September. Live entertainment. 912-934-6694.

Flatlanders Fall Frolic, Lakeland. 912-482-3100.

Labor Day County Fair of 1896, Tifton. At Georgia Agrirama. 912-386-3344.

Possum Hollow Arts and Crafts Fair and Country Music Show, Dexter. 912-875-3104.

October

Andersonville Historic Fair, Andersonville. May and October (first weekend). 912-924-2558.

Big Pig Jig, Vienna. Barbecue cooking championship, arts, and crafts. 912-268-8275.

Georgia National Fair, Perry. Fairgrounds and Agricenter. 800-987-3247; 912-988-6483.

Hahira Honeybee Festival, Hahira. Tribute to the honeybee. 912-794-3617.

Happy Acres Resort Arts and Crafts Festival, Screven. Antiques, arts, and crafts. Happy Acres Resort and RV Park. 912-586-6767.

Harvest Festival, Thomasville. 912-225-3920.

Indian Cultural Festival, Columbus. Native American celebration. 706-568-2049.

Kolomoki Festival, Blakely. Native American demonstrations. 912-723-3079 or 723-5296.

Mossy Creek Barnyard Arts and Crafts Festival, Perry. Third weekend. A showcase for nationally recognized artists and craft makers. Clogging, hayrides, and a petting zoo. 912-922-8265.

Mule Roundup, Guysie. Pioneer farm demonstrations and mule rodeo. 19 miles east of Douglas on GA 32. 912-632-5570.

Okefenokee Pogofest—A Swamp Celebration, Waycross. Exchange Club Fairgrounds. 912-285-4400.

Pelham Wildlife Festival, Pelham. Arts, wildflower exhibit, and street dance. 912-294-4924.

November

Fair of 1850, Westville. This 17-day festival profiles music, open-hearth cooking, cane grinding, syrup making, basket weaving, crafts, woodworking, and demonstrations of the only animal-powered cotton gin in Georgia. 912-838-6310.

Mistletoe Market, Albany. Albany Civic Center. 912-435-1897.

Swine Time Festival, Climax. Arts, crafts, and pork in many forms. Climax Community Club, P.O. Box 131, Climax, 31734.

December

Christmas on the Square, Blakely. Arts, crafts, parade, and car show. 912-723-3741.

Downtown Vidalia Christmas Festival, Vidalia. Includes parade. 912-538-8687.

CHAMBERS OF COMMERCE

(Italics indicate a county name.)

Adel-*Cook*	912-896-2281
Albany	912-434-8700
Alma-*Bacon*	912-632-5859
Americus-*Sumter*	912-924-2646
Ashburn-*Turner*	912-567-9696
Bainbridge-*Decatur*	912-246-4774
Baxley-*Appling*	912-367-7731
Blakely-*Early*	912-723-3741
Brantley	912-462-6282
Bryan	912-756-2676
Cairo-*Grady*	912-377-3663
Camilla	912-336-5255
Claxton-*Evans*	912-739-2281
Clinch	912-487-2360
Cochran-*Bleckley*	912-934-2965
Colquitt-*Miller*	912-758-2400
Columbus	706-327-1566
Cordele-*Crisp*	912-273-1668
Cuthbert-*Randolph*	912-732-2683
Dawson	912-995-2011
Donalsonville-*Seminole*	912-524-2588
Dooley	912-268-4554
Douglas-*Coffee*	912-384-1873
Eastman-*Dodge*	912-374-4723
Fitzgerald-*Ben Hill*	912-423-9357
Folkston-*Charlton*	912-496-2536
Fort Gaines	912-768-2934
Hawkinsville-*Pulaski*	912-783-1717
Hazlehurst-*Jeff Davis*	912-375-4543
Hinesville-*Liberty*	912-368-4445
Houston	912-953-5407
Lee	912-759-2422
Macon	912-472-2391
McIntosh	912-437-4192
Moultrie-*Colquitt*	912-985-2131
Nashville-*Berrien*	912-686-5123
Oglethorpe	912-472-6237

Oscilla-*Irwin*	912-468-9114	*Telfair*	912-868-6365
Pelham	912-294-4924	*Terrell*	912-995-2011
Perry Area	912-987-1234	Thomasville-*Thomas*	912-226-9600
Pierce	912-449-7044	Tifton-*Tift*	800-289-4293
Quitman-*Brooks*	912-263-4841	*Toombs*-Vidalia	912-537-4466
Soperton-*Treutlen*	912-529-6868	Valdosta-*Lowndes*	912-247-8100
Sylvester-*Worth*	912-776-7718	Waycross-*Ware*	912-283-3742
Tattnall, Greater	912-557-6323	*Wayne*	912-427-2028

**CHAPTER
FOURTEEN**

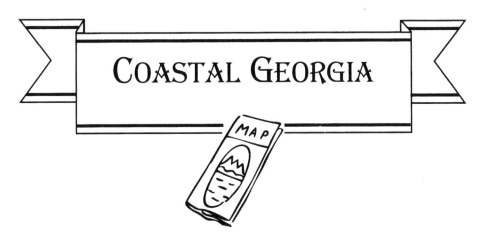

Cities of Coastal Georgia

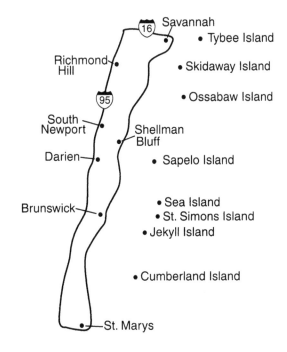

COASTAL GEORGIA AT A GLANCE				
LOCATION	**TO SEE/DO**	**EATING**	**SLEEPING**	**OTHER**
Brunswick	Mary Miller Doll Museum	Jinright's Seafood Royal Cafe	Brunswick Manor	
Cumberland Island			Greyfield Inn	National Seashore
Darien	Ft. King George Hofwyl-Broadfield Plant Tabby ruins	Archie's	Open Gates	
Jekyll Island	Mistletoe Cottage Museum Orientation Center	Grand Dining Room Jekyll Island Club	Jekyll Island Club	Summer Waves Water Park Airplane tours
Richmond Hill	Ft. McAllister			
St. Marys		Seagle's Restaurant	Goodbread House Historic Spencer House Inn Riverview Hotel	

St. Simons	Bloody Marsh
	Christ Church Frederica
	Ft. Frederica
	Hamilton Slave Cabins
	Lighthouse and Museum of
	    Coastal History
		Alfonza's Olde Plantation
		    Supper Club
		Allegro
		Allegro Cafe
		Blanche's Courtyard
		Chelsea
		Frederica House
		Mullet Bay
		St. Simons Club
			Epworth by the Sea
			King & Prince Beach Resort
			Little St. Simons Island
			Sea Palms Golf & Tennis
			    Resort
				Nature boat rides

Savannah	African-American Tours Beach Institute First African Baptist Church First Bryan Baptist Church Juliette G. Lowe G.S. Center King-Tisdell Cottage Old Ft. Jackson Savannah State College Ships of Sea Museum Telfair Mansion Museum	Elizabeth on 37th Johnny Harris Restaurant Mrs. Wilkes Boarding House Olde Pink House Williams Seafood	Ballastone Inn Bed & Breakfast Inn Eliza Thompson House Foley House Inn The Gastonian Lion's Head Inn Olde Harbour Inn	Antiques

COASTAL GEORGIA AT A GLANCE				
LOCATION	**TO SEE/DO**	**EATING**	**SLEEPING**	**OTHER**
Sea Island		The Cloister	The Cloister	
Shellman Bluff		Hunter's Cafe		
Skidaway Island	Wormsloe			
South Newport	Christ's Chapel			
Tybee Island	Ft. Pulaski Tybee Island Museum and Lighthouse			
Special Mention	Ft. Morris (Midway) Sapelo Island			

Think about 15 moss-draped, magnolia-dotted barrier islands of 165,600 acres, dividing about equally into dry land and marsh, changing continually in rhythm with the variations of water levels. Wind and tides reshape the shorelines and the land itself. You can visit these islands only by boat.

That's one part of Coastal Georgia. This coast covers about 100 miles between South Carolina and Florida and goes inland about 30 miles, of which only a small fraction is developed beachfront.

There is more. You can visit Savannah, a city of exceptional charm and history. It has become famous more recently for the bus bench Tom Hanks sat on in the film *Forrest Gump,* and for John Berendt's bestseller *Midnight in the Garden of Good and Evil.*

It's about 80 miles from Savannah to the

Golden Isles. Although you travel faster on I-95, you can enjoy a slower-paced drive through the many small towns if you take US 17. You'll see historic forts and fishing villages as well as old plantation sites.

Of special significance are the 15 Golden Isles. No one knows how they got that name. Some say it had to do with the Spaniards searching for gold. Others say that in 1717, an Englishman named Robert Montgomery wrote a pamphlet to promote settlement, and he coined the term. Still others say it's because of the tawny glow of the beach grass in the fall and winter light.

Some jokingly say it came from the fact that the gold owners lived there. A century ago, a group of northern millionaires hired experts to search the world to find the ideal vacationland for them. They chose the coastal area of Georgia—a 24-hour train ride from Wall Street. They came with names such as Vanderbilt, Rockefeller, Morgan, Pulitzer, Astor, Armour, Crane, Goodyear, Macy, Biddle, and Gould. For more than half a century those industry leaders who controlled a sixth of the world's wealth made one of the Golden Isles—Jekyll Island—their private paradise. Others, such as the Carnegies, the Wanamakers, and the R. J. Reynoldses, bought their own island. In the 1940s, after World War II, they began to abandon the Golden Isles. In 1947, the state of Georgia bought all of Jekyll, including the buildings, for $675,000.

Now anyone can visit the islands that once only the rich could enjoy. You'll find places like Jekyll and St. Simons developed and others reachable only by boat with a restricted number of people. Take a trip to the barrier islands (but you need to make reservations; see listings below). Cumberland Island, for instance, is an unspoiled land of dunes, bluffs, hardwood trees, freshwater lakes, and fertile marshes.

St. Catherine's Island was once the capital of an all–African-American republic. A

SPANISH MOSS

Along the coast you'll see the beautiful silver-green Spanish moss hanging from the live oaks. But it's not from Spain, and it's not moss. It's not a parasite, either. This odd plant is also known as vegetable horsehair or long moss, but Spanish moss is a much nicer name. Sometimes it grows as long as 25 feet with threadlike leaves up to three inches long.

Spanish moss is an epiphyte—a plant without roots. It lives off moisture in the atmosphere. Tiny scales on the moss's tendrils trap and absorb rain. Mineral-rich cells that wash from the host tree nourish the plant, which explains why you'll see the moss mostly on young, healthy trees.

Spanish Moss

Would it surprise you to learn that it's distantly related to the pineapple? Yep, although it bears no fruit, it occasionally produces small yellow flowers. A few enterprisers have used it for upholstery stuffing and packing material.

TABBY

When you're visiting Coastal Georgia, you'll probably hear mention of the "old tabby buildings." Tabby, which originated in the 13th century with the Moors of Africa, is a mixture of sand, lime, seashells, and water put into a foundation to harden. (Sometimes a stucco veneer went over the outside.) Probably one of the best-known tabby structures is the Tabby House at Epworth by the Sea on St. Simons Island. (Epworth, owned by the United Methodist Church, serves as a retreat and conference center. It is also open to the public for meals and lodging.)

The land where Epworth is located was once known as Gascoigne Bluff in honor of James Gascoigne, captain of General James Edward Oglethorpe's ship. In 1793, the land came into the possession of James Hamilton and became part of the Hamilton Plantation.

The Tabby House was the home of the Hamilton house servants. (See *Hamilton Island Slave Cabins* under *Where to Go and What to See* for viewing information.)

Another well-known tabby site is the ruins of the hospital where Ann Page King cared for her ill slaves. It is found at the Sea Island Golf Course (formerly Retreat Plantation). The hospital had two floors and a total of 10 rooms. Women and children stayed on the ground floor and men on the second. Attic rooms provided quarters for two nurses who took care of the patients.

The rooms were about 12 by 15 feet with a fireplace for heat and two windows for light and ventilation.

Tabby buildings need periodic attention to maintain their state of preservation against the elements.

decree in 1854 set the island aside as a haven for freed slaves. In 1864, Union General Sherman gave the former slaves "sole and exclusive management of affairs," subject only to Congress and military commanders. The head of the new state was Tunis Campbell, originally from New Jersey. At one time, they banned all Caucasians from the island.

You'll want to stop at the lighthouse on St. Simons Island and see Christ Church on Frederica Rd. Enjoy the huge live oaks draped by Spanish moss.

Most important, just let yourself unwind as you absorb the delights of Coastal Georgia.

WHERE TO GO AND WHAT TO SEE

Beach Institute, Savannah. Listed in the National Register District, it was established in 1865 by the American Missionary Association to educate newly freed slaves. Today it is a showcase for African-American arts. Acquired by the Savannah Institute of Art and Design in 1980, it has become the African-American Cultural Center. Mon.–Fri. 12–5 p.m.; weekends 1–4 p.m. 502 E. Harris St. 912-234-8000.

Bloody Marsh, St. Simons Island. The battle of Bloody Marsh, in 1742, pitted a small English force under Oglethorpe against Spaniards coming up from Florida. He defeated them in one of the decisive battles for control of this region. A monument on Demere Rd. marks the site.

Christ Church, Frederica, St. Simons Island. The first church on the present location was erected in 1820, and the congregation worshiped in it until its destruction during the Civil War. Under the leadership of Rev. Anson Green Phelps Dodge, Jr., it was rebuilt as a memorial to his first wife, Ellen. The church was consecrated in 1886.

The present church building is cruciform in design with trussed Gothic roof. Stained glass windows, given as memorials, commemorate incidents in the life of Christ and the early history of the church on St. Simons Island. Part of the Credence Table and an inset in the present altar are from the altar of the 1820 church. Rectors of Christ Church and the families of early settlers and of plantation days are buried in the Christ Church yard. This is the burial site for Georgia's first historian, Lucian Lamar Knight. The oldest tombstone discovered in the churchyard bears the date 1803. Services are still held in the church, and it's open to the public. 912-638-8683.

Christ Church Frederica

Christ's Chapel, South Newport. Labeled "the smallest church in Georgia," the building seats only 12 people. It was built as a place for rest and worship for travelers along scenic coastal route US 17. Daily 24 hours. Two miles off I-95.

First African Baptist Church and First Bryan Baptist Church, Savannah. These two churches occupy different buildings, but they share a common heritage. They are the continuous descendants of the oldest African-American Baptist congregation in

North America, which was founded in 1788 and divided by a doctrinal split in 1832. A majority of the congregation established the First African Baptist Church located at 23 Montgomery St. at Franklin Square. The others formed First Bryan Baptist Church at 575 W. Bryan St. The current structure for First African Baptist was built in 1859 and for First Bryan Church in 1873. Both churches lay legitimate claim to being the oldest African-American church. Churches are open daily 10 a.m.–2 p.m. Guided and self-guided tours. First Bryan Baptist Church: 912-233-6597. First African Baptist Church: 912-233-5586.

Fort Frederica, St. Simons Island. For enthusiasts of early American history, Fort Frederica is a place you need to visit. Frederica became a fortified town with the completion of the fort in 1736. It was the military headquarters on the frontier. There the settlers defended the land against the encroaching British forces.

Fort Frederica Cannons

Fort Frederica National Monument is an archaeological site preserved and maintained by the National Park Service. At the Visitors Center, you can go through the museum and view the informative, well-made film *This Is Frederica.* Tours, living history programs, and celebrations are offered periodically. A museum shop sells colonial gifts and publications on the history of the site. Park grounds are open daily 8 a.m.–5 p.m. with extended hours in summer. The Visitors Center opens daily at 9 a.m. Park is closed Christmas Day. Admission charged. National ParkPass holders are admitted without charge. All buildings are accessible to persons with disabilities.

Fort Frederica

Fort King George, Darien. Built in 1721, this was the first of a chain of forts erected to counteract the French expansion in America. Constructed 12 years before Oglethorpe founded Savannah, the fort is *the first English establishment in Georgia.* The fort features a museum, authentic blockhouse replica, reconstructed earthworks, and the fort itself. Open year-round. Tue.–Sat. 9 a.m.–5 p.m.; Sun. 2–5:30 p.m. Closed Mon. and holidays. Admission charged. 912-437-4770.

Fort McAllister, Richmond Hill. State historic park on the Ogeechee River. (This is actually in South Georgia, but we have included it here because of its connection with the coast.) Fort McAllister's fortifications once guarded Savannah from attack mounted from the water. In December 1864, the fall of Fort McAllister marked the end of General William T. Sherman's march to the sea. After Union naval forces bombarded the Confederates during the day, at night they repaired the sand ramparts. Sherman finally had to take the fort by fierce hand-to-hand combat.

Henry Ford acquired the property in the 1930s and immediately undertook massive restoration. Since 1958, the fort has belonged to the state, and it continues the work of restoration so that the fort is close to the condition of 1865. Many consider it the best-preserved earthwork fortification anywhere in the Confederacy. Tue.–Sat. 9 a.m.–5 p.m.; Sun. 2–5:30 p.m. Closed Mon. and holidays. Admission charged. 912-727-2339.

Fort Morris Historic Site, Midway. Fort Morris served as a Colonial defense against the British during the Revolutionary War. The Fort surrendered to the British on January 9, 1779, and was the last post in Coastal Georgia to fall. Visit earthwork fortifications, museum, and exhibits, and enjoy a walking tour. Hear the story of the "dead town" of Sudbury, once a prosperous seaport. Tue.–Sat. 9 a.m.–5 p.m.; Sun. 9:30 a.m.–5:30 p.m. Closed major holidays. Admission: $2; ages 6–18 $1. Seven miles east of I-95 on Fort Morris Road. 912-884-5999.

Fort Pulaski National Monument, Tybee Island. About half an hour's drive from Savannah, the fort is located on the salt marsh. It is named after a Revolutionary War hero, Count Casimir Pulaski, and was begun in 1829 to guard the entrance to the Savannah River.

In summer, Civil War demonstrations take place. It is surrounded by a moat that gives it a castlelike appearance. Bombardment by Federal troops in 1862 limited the food supply, and Confederate troops there faced disease, insects, and boredom. They surrendered to Union forces on April 11, 1862. The National Park Service maintains the monument. You'll see historical exhibits, weapons, and uniforms. Visitor Center is on Cockspur Island. Admission fluctuates during the year. 912-786-5787.

Hamilton Island Slave Cabins, St. Simons Island. You can see two of the few surviving slave cabin structures in the state, located at Epworth by the Sea. Open to the public. You can view the outside anytime, but inside open only on Wed. 10 a.m.–2 p.m.

Guided and self-guided tours available. 912-638-8688.

Hofwyl-Broadfield Plantation, Darien. This lovely plantation was owned by one family from 1806 to 1973. Especially enjoy the white frame house (built around 1850) that holds many original furnishings. Pause to view the slide presentation at the Visitors Center, then take a one-mile walking tour around the overgrown rice fields to the main house. Tue.–Sat. 9 a.m.–5 p.m.; Sun. 2–5:30 p.m. Admission charged. 912-264-9263.

Juliette Gordon Low Girl Scout National Center, Savannah. This English Regency-style mansion was the 1860 birthplace of Juliette Low, who founded the Girl Scouts of America. Mon.–Sat. 10 a.m.–4 p.m.; Sun. 12:30–4:30 p.m. Closed Wed. Admission charged. Bull St. and Oglethorpe Ave. 912-233-4501.

King-Tisdell Cottage, Savannah. This restored 1896 Victorian cottage—named for the owners, Eugene and Sarah King and Mrs. King's second husband, Robert Tisdell—is Savannah's center of African-American heritage. The house was moved from its old site on Ott St. when threatened by urban renewal. It now serves as a museum, with exhibit rooms displaying art objects, African-American historical documents, and typical coastal furniture. Costumed interpreters present African-American Heritage Trail Programs. Mon.–Fri. 10 a.m.–4:30 p.m.; weekends 1–4 p.m.

Admission charged. 514 E. Huntingdon St. 912-234-8000.

Mary Miller Doll Museum, Brunswick. An extensive collection of pre–Civil War dolls, dresses, and accessories. Mon.–Sat. 11 a.m.–5 p.m. Admission charged. 1523 Glynn Ave. 912-267-7569.

Mistletoe Cottage, Jekyll Island. The cottage displays the work of the late nationally renowned Jekyll sculptor, Rosario Fiore. Admission: free. Daily 2–4 p.m. 912-635-2119.

Museum of Coastal History, St. Simons Island. The museum offers you the chance to visit an authentic 1872 lighthouse and keeper's dwelling where changing exhibits on regional history are displayed. You'll see an 1890 brick oilhouse where you can purchase books, illustrations, and other lighthouse-related items. There's even an early-20th-century gazebo. In the Village at 101 12th St. Tue.–Sat. 10 a.m.–5 p.m.; Sun. 1:30–5 p.m. Closed Mon. and major holidays. Admission charged. 912-638-4666.

Museum Orientation Center, Jekyll Island. Here you can learn about Jekyll Island's history from the first known inhabitants to the present. Numerous artifacts are on display, and you can shop for gifts. Daily 9:30 a.m.–4 p.m. 912-635-4036.

Old Fort Jackson, Savannah. Oldest standing fort in Georgia. An earthen battery was constructed on the site in 1775 (Revolutionary War). The original fort, which was used in the war against England in 1812, got its beginning in 1808. It was also headquarters for the Confederate river defenses during the Civil War. Mon.–Sun. 9 a.m.–5 p.m. Admission charged. One Fort Jackson Rd. 912-232-3945.

St. Simons Lighthouse

St. Simons Lighthouse, featuring the *Museum of Coastal History*, St. Simons Island. The lighthouse was built in 1804. In 1862, during the Civil War, Confederate soldiers blew up the lighthouse to prevent Federal troops from using it. However, you can see the second lighthouse, constructed in 1872. *This is one of only five surviving light towers in Georgia.* Climb the 129 steps leading to the top. In the Village at 101 12th St. Tue.–Sat. 10 a.m.–5 p.m.; Sun. 1:30–5 p.m. Closed Mon. and major holidays. Admission charged. 912-638-4666.

Savannah African-American Tours. Available through King-Tisdell Foundation: 912-234-8000. Tours by BJ: 912-233-2616; 800-962-6595.

Museum at St. Simons Lighthouse

Savannah State College, Savannah. Founded in 1890, it was the first state school established in Georgia for training African-Americans. At the time of its founding, it was the only school of higher learning in the U.S. with an African-American president. He was also a former slave. It is now an integrated four-year college. Falligant Ave. and College St. 912-356-2186.

Ships of the Sea Museum, Savannah. Here are three floors filled with ornamental figureheads, scrimshaw artistry, a chandler's shop, and other artifacts. Daily 10 a.m.–5 p.m. Admission charged. 503 River St. (Riverfront Plaza). 912-232-1511.

Tabby Ruins, Darien. Reflecting former peaceful prosperity in Darien, the ruins are located on the scenic waterfront.

Erected between 1810 and 1830, these foundations are picturesque reminders of a time when Darien was a great commercial port. Until 1845, Darien was a world leader in cotton exports. During the Civil War, in 1863, Federal troops based on St. Simons Island looted and burned the city. The ruins are the vestiges of offices, warehouses, and wharves. The troops spared only five buildings.

Telfair Mansion and Museum, Savannah. English Regency-style mansion. On display are decorative pieces and English and American art and furnishings. Tue.–Sat. 10 a.m.–5 p.m.; Sun. 2–5 p.m. Admission charged except Sun. 121 Barnard St. 912-232-1177.

Tybee Island Museum and Lighthouse, Tybee Island. The museum is located inside a Spanish American War coastal artillery battery. The lighthouse was completed in 1867. Why not climb the 178 steps to the top? Hours of operation change. Admission charged. Museum: 912-786-4077. Lighthouse: 912-786-5801.

Wormsloe, Skidaway Island. State historic site. Tabby ruins of a colonial estate built by Noble Jones, one of the original settlers who arrived from England with General James Edward Oglethorpe in 1733. Wormsloe was in a strategic position to defend Georgia by guarding the inland waterway passage to Savannah from the south. Visitors Center; nature trail. Tue.–Sat. 9 a.m.–5 p.m.; Sun. 2–5:30 p.m. 7601 Skidaway Rd. 912-352-2548.

EATING

Recipes

Oyster Pie. Chicken isn't the only thing that goes great in a pie (such as chicken pot pie). Try this old recipe sometime.

Make a crust of 2 cups flour, 2 teaspoons baking powder, and 1/2 teaspoon salt sifted together in a bowl. Add 2 tablespoons shortening. Mix lightly with fingertips. Add enough cold milk to cause dough to hold together. Divide into two parts, and roll out on floured board. Line a large baking dish with one crust, sprinkle with flour. Put in about 12 oysters, sprinkle with salt and pepper, and add 2 cups boiled potatoes cut into small pieces. Add 12 more oysters, then 1 tablespoon butter and 3/4 cup milk. Add a dash of paprika, then cover the top with second crust. Make several slashes in top crust to let the steam escape. Brush top with milk, and bake in hot oven (about 425°) until nicely browned. Makes a large pie.

Scallops and Shrimp Southern-Style Casserole. In a bowl, combine 1 cup small scallops, an egg (slightly beaten), 2 cups cooked rice, and 1 cup boiled shrimp. In a skillet, brown 2 tablespoons of diced onion in a little oil. Add 1/3 cup tomato catsup, 1/2 teaspoon celery salt, and 1 teaspoon curry powder. Heat well, then stir into rice mixture. Bake in a shallow buttered dish in 350° oven about 30 minutes or until firm.

Hushpuppies. What is seafood without hushpuppies? Try this recipe. Mix 2 cups yellow cornmeal (stone ground is great if you can get it), 1 teaspoon salt, and 1 small onion chopped very fine. Pour about 4 cups *boiling* water into this mixture slowly but steadily, stirring as you pour. Keep adding more boiling water until it makes a soft dough. Drop batter by spoonfuls into hot oil in large skillet. Brown several minutes on each side. Drain on paper towels. Serve hot.

Coastal Cornbread. If you prefer cornbread instead of hushpuppies with your seafood, try this recipe.

Melt 1/2 stick of butter in 9-by-5-inch metal baking pan in 425° oven. Mix together 1 cup yellow cornmeal, 1 tablespoon flour, 2 teaspoons baking powder, and 1/8 teaspoon salt. Add 1 cup cold milk and 1 egg—mix together for just a minute. Pour into the hot pan (which has melted butter in it). Bake at 425° for 20 minutes.

Where to Eat

Alfonza's Olde Plantation Supper Club, St. Simons Island. Coastal atmosphere; local seafood. Dinner Mon.–Sat. Harrington Lane. 912-638-9883.

Allegro, St. Simons Island. Prestigious dining. Cuisine is elegant. Closed Mon. 912-638-7097.

Allegro Cafe, St. Simons Island. Casual dining, located upstairs in a shopping center. Dinner Tue.–Sun. 2465 Demere Rd. 912-638-6097.

Archie's, Darien. Southern-style food. Mon.–Sat. 7 a.m.–9 p.m. US 17. 912-437-4363.

Blanche's Courtyard, St. Simons Island. Fresh seafood and steaks. Named after Blanche LaRouge, a well-known woman who charmed the Louisiana coast in the 19th century. Rustic, sedate atmosphere. Daily 5:30–9:30 p.m. (seasonal). 440 Ocean Blvd. 912-638-3030.

Chelsea, St. Simons Island. Seafood. Check out early-bird specials (5:30–6:30). Dinner daily 5:30–closing (seasonal). 1226 Ocean Blvd. 912-638-2047.

The Cloister, Sea Island. Want something special? Here it is. You don't have to stay at the Cloister to dine, but remember it's formal dining with a six-course dinner priced at $50. Breakfast Mon.–Sat. 7–9:30 a.m.; Sun. 7–10 a.m.; Lunch (seasonal) Mon.–Sun. 12–1:30 p.m. Dinner Mon.–Sun. 7–9 p.m. Sea Island Dr. 912-638-5111.

Elizabeth's on 37th, Savannah. Luxury dining. Housed in an Edwardian mansion south of Savannah's historic district. Seafood dinners and southern desserts. Dinner Mon.–Sat. No smoking. 105 E. 37th St. 912-236-5547.

*Frederica House,** St. Simons Island. Casual and rustic. Dinner daily 5:30–9:30 p.m. 3611 Frederica Rd. 912-638-6789.

*Grand Dining Room,*** Jekyll Island. Luxury dining. Coastal and southern cuisine. Breakfast, lunch, and dinner daily. Jekyll Island Club, 371 Riverview Dr. 912-635-2600.

*Hunter's Cafe,** Shellman Bluff. Tue.–Sun. 6:30 a.m.–2 p.m. and 5–9:30 p.m. Follow the signs off US 17. 912-832-5848.

*Jekyll Island Club,*** Jekyll Island. Historic, vintage elegance that offers 8- to 12-course dinners. 371 Riverview Dr. 912-635-2600.

*Jinright's Seafood House,** Brunswick. Inexpensive, basic seafood dinners. Lunch and dinner daily. 2815 Glynn Ave. (US 17). 912-267-1590.

*Johnny Harris Restaurant,** Savannah. Oldest restaurant in Savannah. Formerly a roadside barbecue stand, today it's one of the city's largest full-service restaurants. Specializing in barbecue and ribs. Mon.–Thu. 11:30 a.m.–10:30 p.m.; Fri.–Sat. open until 12:30 a.m. Closed Sun. 1651 E. Victory. 912-354-7810.

*Mrs. Wilkes Boarding House,** Savannah. This is not only southern cooking, but one of the best-but-unadvertised eating spots.

No reservations accepted, so arrive early. No credit cards. Mon.–Fri. 8 a.m.–9 a.m. and 11:30 a.m.–3 p.m., 107 W. Jones St. 912-232-5997.

*Mullet Bay,** St. Simons Island. Casual and youthful. Daily 11:30 a.m. on. 512 Ocean Blvd. St. Simons Pier. 912-634-9977.

*Olde Pink House,*** Savannah. Georgian mansion built in 1771. Walls turned pink when soft native brick bled through the original white plaster. Seafood. Daily 6–10:30 p.m. 23 Abercorn St. 912-232-4286.

*Royal Cafe,** Brunswick. Small cafe in old hotel. Breakfast Mon.–Fri. 7:30–10 a.m. Lunch Mon.–Fri. 11:30 a.m.–2 p.m. Brunch Sun. 11 a.m.–2 p.m. 1618 Newcastle St. 912-262-1402.

*St. Simons Island Club,** St. Simons Island. Elegant and affordable. Lunch Mon.–Sat. 11:30 a.m.–4 p.m. Dinner Tue.–Sun. 6:30–9:30 p.m. Brunch Sun. 11 a.m.–2:30 p.m. Reservations recommended for dinner. 100 Kings Way. 912-638-5132.

*Seagle's Restaurant and Lounge,** St. Marys. Located in the Riverview Hotel, the restaurant offers the finest seafood dining in the area, especially Seagle's rock shrimp. Open every day, also packs picnic lunches. 105 Osborne St. 912-882-3242.

*Williams Seafood,** Savannah. First-class seafood in casual atmosphere. 8010 Tybee Rd. 912-892-2219.

Ballastone Inn and Townhouse, Savannah. This restored Victorian mansion of 1838 is in Savannah's historic district. It has 22 guest rooms with private baths. Antiques; fireplaces. Complimentary continental breakfast. 14 E. Oglethorpe Ave. 912-236-1484; 800-822-4553.

Bed & Breakfast Inn, Savannah. Built around 1853, it is furnished in a traditional style with antique and reproduction pieces. 117 W. Gordon St., Chatham Square. 912-238-0518.

Brunswick Manor, Brunswick. A historic B&B inn in a large Victorian home in the historic area, surrounded by moss-laden oaks. Furnished with antiques. 825 Egmont St. 912-265-6889.

The Cloister, Sea Island. Even if you don't stay at the Cloister, it's worth visiting this handsome Spanish-style inn bounded by the Atlantic Ocean on one side and the Marshes of Glynn on the other. Opened 1928, it remains the oldest, best-known, and probably fanciest retreat spot in Georgia. 800-732-4752.

Eliza Thompson House, Savannah. Built in 1847. Historic inn, cozy and gracious. 5 W. Jones. 912-236-3620; 800-348-9378.

Epworth by the Sea, St. Simons Island. Economical and pleasant. Built on the original site of the baronial Hamilton Plantation on Gascoigne Bluff and named after the Wesley birthplace in England. The South Georgia Conference of the United Methodist Church operates Epworth, but it is open to all. The motels, family apartments, and 21 youth cabins can accommodate up to 1,000 persons. Specially equipped rooms for persons with disabilities available. Cafeteria-style meals. No alcohol or pets permitted. No smoking in facilities. Follow St. Simons Causeway to Sea Island Rd., left at light, first left at Hamilton Rd., then right on Arthur J. Moore Dr. 912-232-2869; 800-322-6603.

Foley House Inn, Savannah. This 19th-century Victorian townhouse is filled with antiques, including lovely Persian rugs. Private baths, some with oversized Jacuzzi tubs. Breakfast served. Evening reception in parlor. 14 W. Hull St., Chippewa Square. 912-232-6622.

Gastonian, Savannah. An 1868 historic inn furnished with English antiques. 220 E. Gaston St. 912-232-2869; 800-322-6603.

Goodbread House, St. Marys. This 1875 restored Victorian home is in a quaint fishing village. 209 Osborne St. 912-882-7490.

Greyfield Inn, Cumberland Island. This is a favorite of many tourists who value the inn for its atmosphere. The inn was originally built by Thomas Carnegie as a residence for his daughter. No air-conditioning or heat and only one of the nine rooms has a private bath. 912-261-6408.

Historic Spencer House Inn, St. Marys. This 1872 inn with 14 rooms is one block from St. Marys River and Cumberland Island Ferry. Rooms furnished with antiques. Osborne at Bryant St. 912-882-1872.

Jekyll Island Club Hotel, Jekyll Island. See turn-of-the-century elegance in this 136-room hotel. 912-635-2600.

King and Prince Beach Resort, St. Simons Island. A vintage hotel with 155 rooms; an all-around resort and condominium operation. On the beach. 800-342-0212.

Lion's Head Inn, Savannah. Elegant 19th-century inn with six guest rooms with private baths. 120 E. Gaston St. 912-232-4580.

Little St. Simons Island, St. Simons Island. Little St. Simons Island is a privately owned barrier island. There is room for only 24 guests, and three meals are provided. You can go horseback riding, canoeing, boating, fishing, and hiking. P.O. Box 1078, St. Simons Island, GA 31522. 912-638-7472.

Olde Harbour Inn, Savannah. This 1892 inn offers 24 riverview suites. 508 E. Factors Walk. 912-234-4100; 800-553-6533.

Open Gates, Darien. Vintage 1876 residence. 912-437-6985.

Riverview Hotel, St. Marys. Built in 1916, the Riverview Hotel rests on the banks of the St. Marys River, near the ferry to Cumberland Island. Many visitors like the sitting room and veranda, complete with rocking chairs and a swing. There are 18 guest rooms with private baths. 105 Osborne St. 912-882-3242.

Sea Palms Golf and Tennis Resort, St. Simons Island. One- to three-bedroom villas. Emphasis is on sports; a fine golf course. 912-638-3351.

SHOPPING

Wherever you go along the coast, you'll find many opportunities to stop and shop for everything from clothing to gifts to souvenirs.

If you enjoy outlet stores, stop at the Magnolia Bluff Factory Shops off I-95 in Darien. Another frequently mentioned spot is G. J. Ford Cafe and Bookshop on Sea Island and St. Simons where you can shop and stop in the cafe for fresh desserts, baked goods, and sandwiches. 912-634-6168.

Junk House, Savannah. Country oak, re-production oak and mahogany, and antiques. Mon.–Sat. 10 a.m–6 p.m.; Sun. 1–6 p.m. 5950 Ogeechee Rd. 912-927-2354.

Memory Lane Antiques and Mall, Savannah. Golden pine furniture and German antiques, such as goat wagons, dough bowls, and sleds. Also antique and collectible furniture, glassware, and pottery. Mon.–Sat. 10 a.m.–5 p.m.; Sun. 11 a.m.–4 p.m. 230 W. Bay St. 912-232-0975 or 232-6010.

Piddlers, Brunswick. Closed Sun. and Wed. afternoon. 1505 M. L. King Blvd. 912-265-0890.

Waters Ave. Antiques Mall, Savannah. See 20 dealers under one roof. Estate items, antiques, collectibles, used furniture, and glassware. Mon.–Sat. 10:30 a.m.–5:30 p.m. 3405 Waters Ave. at 50th St. 912-351-9313.

OUTDOORS

Ansley-Hodges Memorial Marsh Project, Darien. This is a 21,000-acre Altamaha Wildlife Management Area located on the Atlantic Flyway. You can see wading birds, furbearers, and other wildlife. Observation tower provides an excellent vantage point for bird-watching and photography.

Cumberland Island National Seashore. This barrier island features 22 miles of beautiful beaches, sand dunes, wild horses, birds, sea turtles, and other wildlife. You can camp, hike, and enjoy nature, beaches, and the historic areas. Ferry departs across from Riverview Hotel. Mon.–Fri. 10 a.m.–4 p.m. Reservations needed: 912-882-4335.

St. Simons Island

Jekyll Island. Explore 20 miles of paved trails. You can bring your bike or rent one at the Mini Golf Course, hotels, airport, or Jekyll Harbor Marina or Campground. Mini Golf Course. N. Beachview Dr. 912-635-2648.

Water activities include fishing trips, sightseeing cruises, and boat dockage and fuel. Jekyll Historic Marina, N. Riverview Dr.: 912-635-2891. Also, boat launching, dockage, tours, and ship's store. Jekyll Harbor Marina: 912-635-3137.

Massengale Beach, St. Simons Island. Free showers, rest rooms, picnic tables, and snack bar.

Nature Boat Rides. You can take a ride through the tidal creeks between St. Simons

Island and Sea Island. Or perhaps you'd like a closer look at the beautiful birds of the marsh. On the ride you'll hear informative and entertaining anecdotes about the wildlife. The *Marsh Hen* is a 24-foot pontoon boat with cushioned seats and partial shade and binoculars for each person. The pontoon boat with its shallow draft is ideal for going up to the cordgrass for close inspection. Boat operates all year. Ask for the Pontoon Boat: 912-638-9354 or 638-3611.

Oatland Island Education Center, Savannah. Nature education programs for all ages. Nature trail. Mon.–Fri. 8:30 a.m.–5 p.m. Admission: one can of pet food. 711 Sandtown Rd. 912-897-3773.

Sapelo Island. At the Sapelo Island National Estuarine Research Reserve you can experience almost every facet of a typical barrier island natural community from the diversified wildlife of the forested uplands to the vast expanses of Spartina salt marsh and the complex beach and dunes systems. Exhibits and displays at the Long Tabby Interpretive Center bring to life the natural and cultural history of Sapelo Island. You can take a tour of the African-American community of Hog Hammock, the University of Georgia Marine Institute, and the Coffin-Reynolds mansion.

Georgia's Department of Natural Resources (DNR) operates daily ferry service from Meridian (10 miles north of Darien on GA 99) to Sapelo Island. Other ferries operate for residents and scientists, but visitors must take prearranged tour at 8:30

or 9 a.m. departure. Arrange tours through McIntosh Co. Welcome Center, downtown Darien (US 17 at the bridge). 912-437-6684.

Summer Waves, Jekyll Island. Maybe you'd enjoy a million gallons of splashing-water fun at this 11-acre water park. Open Memorial Day–Labor Day and on select weekends in May–September. Sun.–Fri. 10 a.m.–6 p.m.; Sat. 10 a.m.–8 p.m. Riverview Dr. 912-635-2074.

Camping

Blythe Island. Regional park and campground. 912-261-3805.

Jekyll Island. Camping. 912-635-3021.

Golf

Bacon Park, Savannah. 912-354-2625.

Glynco, Brunswick. 912-264-9521.

Hampton Club, St. Simons Island. 912-634-0255.

Jekyll Island. Four golf courses: Indian Mound Golf Course; Oleander Golf Course; Pine Lakes Golf Course; and Oceanside Golf Course. These courses and a temperate climate make Jekyll Island ideal for golfers. Rates include unlimited all-day play, except during the peak spring season. Winter golf packages. Golf Pro Shop. Capt. Wylly Rd. 912-635-3464 or 635-2368.

Mary Calder, Union Camp. 912-238-7100.

Oak Grove Island, Brunswick. 912-262-9575.

Osprey Cove, St. Marys. PGA Tour Champion Mark McCumber designed this 6,800-yard, par 72 course. Open to the public. 800-352-5575.

Sea Island Club, St. Simons Island. 912-638-5118.

Sea Palms Golf and Tennis Resort, St. Simons Island. 912-638-3351.

Sheraton Savannah, Savannah. 912-897-1615.

Southbridge, Savannah. 912-651-5455.

St. Simons Island Club, St. Simons Island. 912-638-5130.

Tennis

Jekyll Island. Home to a 13-court complex. Fast-dry clay courts and lights for night play. Jekyll Island Tennis Center. Capt. Wylly Rd. 912-635-3154.

Other

Airplane Tours. Jekyll Island airport. 912-635-2500.

Tybee Island. These beaches are popular for swimming and sunbathing.

FESTIVALS

As you look through this list, you'll see a few of the festivals are in towns that technically belong in the section on South Georgia. However, because of the nature of the festivals, we've decided to put them with Coastal Georgia.

Ongoing

First Saturday, Savannah. February–December. 912-234-0295.

January

Emancipation Proclamation Celebration, Midway. Dorchester Academy. 912-884-2347.

March

Christ Church Tour of Homes, St. Simons Island. 912-638-8683.

Saint Patrick's Day, Savannah. March 17. 912-233-4804.

Spring Encampment and Reenactment, Fort King George, Darien. 912-437-4770.

April

Blessing of the Fleet, Darien. April or May (depends on tides). 912-437-4192.

Soberfest, St. Marys. 800-868-8687.

May

Arts on the River Weekend, Savannah. 912-651-6417.

Blessing of the Fleet, Darien. April or May (depends on tides). 912-437-4192.

Memorial Day Celebration: Confederate

Reenactment, Fort McAllister, Richmond Hill. 912-727-2339.

Stand Up for America Day, Port Wentworth. 800-218-3554; 912-748-8080.

June

Country by the Sea Music Festival, Jekyll Island. 800-841-6586; 912-635-3636.

Tunis Campbell Festival on the Waterfront, Darien. Fourth Sat. 912-437-3900.

July

Cannons Across the Marsh, Fort King George, Darien. July 4. 912-437-4770.

Fourth of July Barbeque and Craft Show, Fort McAllister, Richmond Hill. July 4. 912-727-2339.

Fourth of July Festival, St. Marys. July 4. Downtown/waterfront. 800-868-8687.

Fourth of July Fireworks, Savannah. July 4. Tybee Beach. 912-786-5444.

Fourth of July Fireworks Extravaganza, Jekyll Island. July 4. 800-841-6586; 912-635-3636.

July Fest Shark Tournament, Yellow Bluff Fishing Camp. Near Midway. 912-876-3457.

Sunshine Festival, St. Simons Island. Fourth of July weekend. 912-638-9400.

August

Beach Music Festival, Jekyll Island. Usually third Sat. 800-841-6586; 912-635-3636.

Georgia–Sea Island Festival, St. Simons Island. Third weekend. 912-265-9545 or 264-5373.

Sea Island Festival, St. Simons Island. Celebration of the folklore, crafts, games, and rituals of former slaves who settled on the island. 912-638-9014.

September

Catfish Festival, Kingsland. Labor Day weekend. Steaming catfish stew, spicy Cajun-style or southern-fried catfish with "all the trimmings," parade, beauty contest, Catfish 5K Fun Run, bicycle races, arts, crafts, big-name entertainment, catfishing tournament, and Catfish Classic Golf tournament. I-95 exit 2. Kingsland Tourism Authority. 800-433-0225; 912-729-5999.

Fort Morris Revolutionary War Encampment, Midway. Second Sat. 912-884-5999.

Savannah Jazz Festival, Savannah. 912-944-0456.

October

Golden Isles Arts Festival, St. Simons Island. Second weekend. 912-638-8770.

Rock Shrimp Festival, St. Marys. First Sat. 800-868-8687; 912-882-6200.

St. Simons by the Sea Art Festival, St. Simons Island. First weekend. 912-634-0404.

November

Fall Encampment and Reenactment, Fort King George, Darien. 912-437-4770.

December

Christmas Candelight Tour of Homes, St. Marys. Admission: $10 advance; $12 at door. 912-882-4000.

Christmas Tour of Homes, Savannah. 912-234-4088.

CHAMBERS OF COMMERCE

(Italics indicate a county name.)

Brunswick–Golden Isles	912-265-0620
Camden-Kings Bay	912-729-5840
Pooler	912-748-8080
St. Simons Island	912-638-9014
Savannah Area	912-944-0444

A Final Word

Now that you've come to the end of *A Touch of Georgia,* we hope you've enjoyed our state as much as we do. One of the great things about Georgia is that there's always something for you to see or do no matter what season you come or how often you visit.

As you touched Georgia, you may have discovered some out-of-the-way spots on your own and wonder why we didn't list them. There are two answers to that. First, there are just too many good things in Georgia. We estimate it would take 10 volumes to list them all. *And they keep changing every year.*

Second, we may not have listed places or events because we haven't discovered them. If you'd like to share suggestions for things to see and do in Georgia, drop us a line at

A Touch of Georgia
3990 Admiral Drive, Chamblee, GA 30341

We hope you're already looking forward to your next visit to Georgia and the opportunity to visit the spots you didn't get to see this time.

So until we get to welcome you back again

- y'all take care,
- keep Georgia on your mind, and
- start fixing to get ready for one more piece of pecan pie.

INDEX

www.ingramcontent.com/pod-product-compliance
Ingram Content Group UK Ltd.
Pitfield, Milton Keynes, MK11 3LW, UK
UKHW052243240325
456661UK00008B/90